The Modern Intellectual Tradition: From Descartes to Derrida

Lawrence Cahoone, Ph.D.

PUBLISHED BY:

THE GREAT COURSES
Corporate Headquarters
4840 Westfields Boulevard, Suite 500
Chantilly, Virginia 20151-2299
Phone: 1-800-832-2412
Fax: 703-378-3819
www.thegreatcourses.com

Copyright © The Teaching Company, 2010

Printed in the United States of America

This book is in copyright. All rights reserved.

Without limiting the rights under copyright reserved above,
no part of this publication may be reproduced, stored in
or introduced into a retrieval system, or transmitted,
in any form, or by any means
(electronic, mechanical, photocopying, recording, or otherwise),
without the prior written permission of
The Teaching Company.

Lawrence Cahoone, Ph.D.
Professor of Philosophy
College of the Holy Cross

Professor Lawrence Cahoone was born in 1954 and grew up in a small town outside Providence, Rhode Island. He received his B.A. from Clark University, majoring in Psychology and Philosophy, then received his Ph.D. in Philosophy from Stony Brook University. He lived in Brooklyn, New York, for many years and, after graduate school, taught at several New York–area colleges. He accepted a position at Boston University, where he taught from 1987 to 2000 and received the Undergraduate Philosophy Association Teaching Award in 1991 and 1994. He joined the faculty at the College of the Holy Cross in 2000.

Professor Cahoone has taught more than 50 different course subjects, in many areas of philosophy. He is the author of *Cultural Revolutions: Reason versus Culture in Philosophy, Politics, and Jihad*; *Civil Society: The Conservative Meaning of Liberal Politics*; *The Ends of Philosophy: Pragmatism, Foundationalism, and Postmodernism*; and *The Dilemma of Modernity: Philosophy, Culture, and Anti-Culture*. He is the editor of *From Modernism to Postmodernism: An Anthology*. He is currently working on *The Orders of Nature*, a systematic naturalist metaphysics. His philosophical background is primarily in recent European, American, and social and political philosophy, with interests as well in postmodernism and the relation of metaphysics to the natural sciences.

Professor Cahoone is married to the philosopher Elizabeth Baeten of Green Bay, Wisconsin. They currently live with their two children, Isabel Rose and Harrison, in southeastern Massachusetts. Both children are artistic and musical; he and his wife do not know how that happened. ∎

Table of Contents

INTRODUCTION

Professor Biography i
Course Scope 1

LECTURE GUIDES

LECTURE 19
Rise of 20th-Century Philosophy—Phenomenology 4

LECTURE 20
Physics, Positivism, and Early Wittgenstein 16

LECTURE 21
Emergence and Whitehead 27

LECTURE 22
Dewey's American Naturalism 40

LECTURE 23
Heidegger's *Being and Time* 52

LECTURE 24
Existentialism and the Frankfurt School 64

LECTURE 25
Heidegger's Turn against Humanism 76

LECTURE 26
Culture, Hermeneutics, and Structuralism 89

LECTURE 27
Wittgenstein's Turn to Ordinary Language 102

LECTURE 28
Quine and the End of Positivism 114

Table of Contents

LECTURE 29
New Philosophies of Science 126

LECTURE 30
Derrida's Deconstruction of Philosophy 138

LECTURE 31
The Challenge of Postmodernism 150

LECTURE 32
Rorty and the End of Philosophy 163

LECTURE 33
Rediscovering the Premodern 175

LECTURE 34
Pragmatic Realism—Reforming the Modern 187

LECTURE 35
The Reemergence of Emergence 199

LECTURE 36
Philosophy's Death Greatly Exaggerated 211

SUPPLEMENTAL MATERIAL

Timeline 223
Glossary 226
Biographical Notes 237
Bibliography 249

The Modern Intellectual Tradition: From Descartes to Derrida

Scope:

Experience tells me my desk is solid, but physics says it is mostly empty space. How can both be right? Is the scientific view of the world compatible with human experience—or more difficult, with free will, moral responsibility, and religion? What is the mind's place in a physical world? Just what is the ultimate nature of reality, and what are the limitations of our knowledge of it?

In this course, we explore modern and contemporary Western philosophy of reality (metaphysics) and knowledge (epistemology), from the 17th century through the 20th century, spanning movements such as empiricism, rationalism, idealism, philosophy of language, logical positivism, existentialism, pragmatism, phenomenology, and postmodernism. In the process, we examine the thought of René Descartes, John Locke, Baruch Spinoza, David Hume, Immanuel Kant, Georg Wilhelm Friedrich Hegel, Charles Sanders Peirce, Friedrich Nietzsche, Gottlob Frege, Sigmund Freud, Max Weber, William James, Alfred North Whitehead, Ludwig Wittgenstein, Martin Heidegger, John Dewey, Willard Van Orman Quine, Thomas S. Kuhn, Richard Rorty, and Jacques Derrida, among others.

Philosophy and society affect each other. The contributions of philosophers have an impact on a historical period, but it is also true that historical changes drive philosophers to create novel theories. Modern Western philosophy is certainly no exception. Its development was encouraged by great social changes: the discovery of the Americas, the decline of feudal aristocratic institutions, the growth of a commercial middle class, the fragmentation of Christianity by the Protestant Reformation, the growth of the nation-state, the scientific revolution, and waves of industrial and technological change. Modernity is, as one of our philosophers has it, an era of permanent change. Such has been mirrored in the philosophies of the period.

Modern philosophy rests on the development of ancient and medieval philosophy. That is, the work of the ancient Greek philosophers, especially Plato and Aristotle, had been passed down through the Roman Empire and, in some cases through the Arabic world, before being taken up by medieval Christian scholars. Many of the problems that concerned the medievals were the same as those of ancient philosophers, namely, trying to understand nature, human being, the moral life, the nature of beauty, and what a just society should be. But in other respects, philosophy in the Middle Ages was quite different. It was the business of priests, one of the few literate sectors of society, some of whom belonged to holy orders and taught in the great medieval universities. They communicated across national boundaries with a universal scholarly language, Latin, the gift of the defunct Roman Empire. And the medievals of course had a concern foreign to the ancients: What is the nature of the monotheistic Judeo-Christian God, and how does God relate to all else?

Aristotle (384–322 B.C.E.) laid the groundwork for later thinkers.

Modern philosophy, beginning in the 16th and 17th centuries, marked a major departure from medieval thought. Certainly the many social and religious changes of the time helped to fragment the long-stable medieval worldview, but the greatest blow came with the scientific revolution and scientific speculations of early modern philosophers. These philosophers tended to be freelance intellectuals, often supported by aristocratic or royal patrons. Throughout the 17th-century Age of Reason, scientific change forced philosophers to reconceive the world and how we know it. Science ripped the wiring from the dominant medieval view of the universe, and rethinking was needed to integrate the new science into a philosophy that could understand it and its relation to ethics and religion. In the 18th-century Enlightenment, these lofty notions begin to have real-world impact; the modern view that science, political freedom, and education together yield social progress came of age. But along with such progress came a new philosophical skepticism. Then the great political revolutions of the late 18th century began to affect the political world with new ideas. In the 19th century, the Industrial Revolution remade societies themselves, and there arose great historical philosophical systems that tried to explain to modern people just how different they were from ages past. Modern thought became self-conscious about being modern. At the same time, a host of dissenters sprang up.

In the 20th century, Western philosophy became much more complicated. On the one hand, as in all disciplines, philosophers became more specialized in particular subfields. Logic and the physical sciences underwent a series of revolutions. Those who continued to follow scientific changes had a much more complex set of theories to deal with. Other philosophers abandoned the concern for science altogether. Philosophy fragmented as different schools of thought sought new foundations for knowledge in different places. Then in the second half of the century, the whole attempt to seek the foundations of knowledge, a project that had dominated philosophy from the 17th century, began to be abandoned; with it, attempts at comprehensive or systematic philosophies became discredited. Some claimed that philosophy itself was at an end. But by the start of the new millennium, it was clear that reports of philosophy's death had been greatly exaggerated. We pursue this complicated story from the beginning of the 17th century to the end of the 20th century. ∎

Rise of 20th-Century Philosophy—Phenomenology
Lecture 19

> When Husserl looks back at Locke, Berkeley, and Hume, what he sees is an attempt to describe experience, but that has too many presuppositions behind it. ... Husserl wants not to impose subsequent mathematical, scientific, or naturalistic concepts on the fields of evidence, the actual experience we have; he doesn't want to parse them into individual ideas or perceptions. Instead, he wants to describe the flowing life of consciousness as it occurs.

Like Gottlob Frege, **Edmund Husserl** believed that logic and mathematics require a theory of meanings or concepts that is not based in empirical experience, that is, experience caused by natural interactions. Husserl's aim was to create a nonempiricist, nonnaturalist ideal clarification of the meanings that compose experience—experience understood not as what happens to a human being in nature but as a pure field of evidence.

Husserl seemed to liberate the investigation of lived experience from empiricism, psychology, and natural science.

Husserl's analysis of experience was holistic, not atomistic like that of the early empiricists. He defined the new science of **phenomenology** as an ideal, nonempirical science that introspectively clarifies the essential features of types and objects of experiences. As such, all science, all philosophy, and even mathematics depend on phenomenology, because all inquiry depends on evidence presented to consciousness. The impact for **continental philosophy** was enormous: Husserl seemed to liberate the investigation of lived experience from empiricism, psychology, and natural science. ■

Name to Know

Husserl, Edmund (1859–1938): This German philosopher of arithmetic and logic took a major turn to become the foremost philosopher of experience in the early 20th century. He invented the science of phenomenology as a nonnaturalistic, nonpsychological analysis of the meanings that arise in pure consciousness.

Important Terms

continental philosophy: Philosophies from mainland Europe in the past two centuries, stemming from figures such as Georg Wilhelm Friedrich Hegel, Edmund Husserl, Martin Heidegger, Hans-Georg Gadamer, Jean-Paul Sartre, Theodor Adorno, Maurice Merleau-Ponty, Jacques Derrida, and others, typically nonnaturalistic and hermeneutic in orientation.

phenomenology: This term was used by Georg Wilhelm Friedrich Hegel for his account of the dialectical progression of human experience, by Charles Sanders Peirce for the study of the most general features of experience, but most famously by Edmund Husserl for his philosophical method of studying experience that brackets or ignores all questions of natural existence.

Suggested Reading

Husserl, *Cartesian Meditations*.
———, *The Crisis of the European Sciences*.
———, *Ideas Pertaining to a Pure Phenomenology*, vol. 1.
Kohák, *Idea and Experience*.

Questions to Consider

1. What is the difference between phenomenological and psychological introspection?

2. What is the relation between phenomenology and the sciences?

Rise of 20th-Century Philosophy—Phenomenology
Lecture 19—Transcript

Edmund Husserl began his career as a philosopher of logic and mathematics, like Frege, but his own flight away from the psychologism of Mill took a very different path. His path was heavily influenced by the work of Franz Brentano, who defined mental acts as intrinsically intentional, meaning that each such act contains its object, an intentional object. All that means is, an act of perception means that my mental act of perception contains within itself a perceptual object; it contains an object within itself. That's all intentionality means: that a mental act is always about something, an object that it contains. At any rate, Husserl set out, much like Frege, to try to create an objective science of mental acts and objects, primarily concerned—like Frege, at least at the beginning—with applying this to logic and mathematics. Today we'll follow Husserl from his early work in the philosophy of mathematics; through his creation of phenomenology (his own science) in the *Logical Investigations* and later in his book *Ideas*; and finally to later refinements in his book the *Cartesian Meditations* and his final work, *The Crisis of the European Sciences and Transcendental Phenomenology*.

Husserl's earliest book was an 1891 production called *The Philosophy of Arithmetic*. But Frege himself criticized it as psychologistic—in other words, said it was too close to Mill—and this, along with his own self-criticism, launched Husserl in a quite new direction. Like Frege, he realized that meanings or concepts could not be psychological, naturalistic creations. Why? Because if they did, that would mean our notions of logic and mathematics are a posteriori, drawn from experience, maybe even drawn from natural instincts. If all that's true, then they can't be universally and necessarily true; so they can't be naturalistic or psychologistic. However, unlike Frege, he pursued a transcendental notion of meaning—just as Kant had transcendental categories of the mind—that arise in consciousness but now not considered psychologically or naturalistically, rather simply as sheer presentations to consciousness.

Starting in 1900, with his book the *Logical Investigations*, Husserl wrote a series of books attempting to define what he considered a new science, and he called this new science phenomenology. I should say in passing, the

German term that's being translated here as "science" is *Wissenschaft*, and to the Germans, "science" really means more or less what we in English would mean by "inquiry." In other words, philosophy is a science, physics is a science, history is a science—they're all sciences. What Husserl hoped was, he believed that he as a philosopher had found a key to a new way of doing philosophy, and this new way was to be a nonempiricist, nonnaturalist ideal clarification of the meanings that compose experience or consciousness, understood not as what happens to a human being in nature but as a pure field of evidence.

It was nonnaturalistic in that it considered intentional acts and objects independent of empirical psychology, the biology of the organism, or the naturally perceived environment. Husserl, in fact, invoked a kind of slogan; his call was "to the things themselves." We must return to the directly perceived things themselves; forget about representational theories of perception. Remember, all the way since Descartes and Locke, we have had to say one way or the other that, as Locke put it, I have ideas in my mind, and then the big question is do those ideas correctly represent objects outside the mind? Husserl is part of a general reaction against representationalist epistemologies in the early 20th century. For Husserl, experience itself, not knowledge or representation of experience or experience understood as a representation of something else, is what we want to describe.

Husserl wants to describe sheer experience—whatever is experienced by consciousness without any presuppositions, without any metaphysical additions, without the intrusion of science, without the intrusion of Aristotle's substance metaphysics. From Husserl's point of view, if we were to go back to Descartes—and Husserl says this about Descartes—Descartes begins, as we saw several lectures ago, with the consciousness of the individual perceiver. But then what does he do? Before he actually describes much about the experience, the actual data that comes up in this consciousness, he starts introducing God, and introducing Aristotle's notion of substance, and then eventually putting consciousness inside, putting experience inside a larger circle of material objects composing nature. Husserl thinks that's all a mistake. Why? It's not that he believes there is no such thing as nature; it's that he believes we must begin with experience, and that means beginning with the description of whatever is experienced—a careful, scientific description of experience that doesn't presuppose anything about the existence of the physical world.

Husserl's approach was also holistic, and not atomistic, as was that of the early empiricists. When Husserl looks back at Locke, Berkeley, and Hume, what he sees is an attempt to describe experience, but that has too many presuppositions behind it. For example, why in the world should we say that all the contents of my experience are ideas, whether they're simple ideas or complex ideas? Why should they be impressions or ideas, as Hume said? All this is an atomistic description of experience. Husserl wants not to impose subsequent mathematical, scientific, or naturalistic concepts on the fields of evidence, the actual experience we have; he doesn't want to parse them into individual ideas or perceptions. Instead, he wants to describe the flowing life of consciousness as it occurs.

Husserl had a method to do this, and it began with a concept that he called, using a Greek word, *epochē*, or bracketing. This is what the *epochē* means: Husserl advises the working phenomenologist—and that's how he conceived of phenomenologists, as workers, researchers in the field of experience—what the phenomenologist must do is bracket the natural standpoint. The natural standpoint is the belief in our head that all our experience, our intentional acts and objects, are caused by natural things in the human body. In other words, normally when I experience the world, I assume that my experience is taking place inside a physical world described by science that's somehow causing my experiences. That whole notion of the natural standpoint, that experience is inside and is causally related to a natural world, is to be suspended or bracketed. He's being a little more abstemious than Descartes. He's not saying that the natural standpoint is false; he's not even saying that we should doubt its truth, as in Descartes; he's simply asking us to put it out of play. We make no judgment about it; we make no judgment about the causation of our experiences, about whether our experiences represent extramental objects or the role of consciousness in nature. We're just not going to talk about that while we're doing our phenomenology.

There are some people who objected and said, wait a second, isn't this just psychological, personal introspection? Husserl had an answer to that: The second part of his method is what he called the eidetic reduction; "eidetic" comes from the Greek word *eidos*, which is actually the word translated as "form" or "Idea" (with a capital "I") when you read Plato. What he means is the eidetic reduction is the attempt to discover the *eidos*, or essence, of each type of intentional act or object. The phenomenologist brackets everything idiosyncratic or unique to him- or herself and tries to describe the essence or form of each kind of intentional act with its specific type of intentional objects. Literally speaking, if I'm a phenomenologist, I perform the *epochē*—that is, I'm simply going to stop thinking about, put out of practice, the thesis of the natural standpoint—and I'm going to perform the eidetic reduction.

What does that mean? Let's say I fix my attention on my perception of material objects; so at this moment, I'm perceiving a series of material objects in this room. I'm not making any decision about whether material objects exist outside my mind or anything; I'm not concerned about such things; I'm just saying I perceive objects that are opaque to light, that are solid, that resist my touch; I experience them. Once I look at these experiences, I try to describe any universal and necessary features of those experiences. And one Husserl says—he comes up with—is that in every visual perceptual intention of a three-dimensional object, part of the object must always be hidden, that is, the back. There's always something about every intentional object that's not presented in a single intentional act of perception.

Husserl's real aim, his most basic aim, was to be this kind of eidetic phenomenological scientist—literally, to produce a scientific, systematic study of the essences of things, where "things" means whatever appears in consciousness, whatever appears as the most fundamental evidence in conscious life. The phenomenologist, then, is an ideal, nonempirical scientist; this is precisely the idea that you have to understand if you understand Husserl. Historically, it looked like if you studied experience, you were an empiricist; and the empiricists presupposed the existence of nature; and the empiricists historically—from Locke, Berkeley, Hume, and all the rest—presuppose that, "I'm going to look at experience, but that means I analyze the ideas in my mind and I relate them to what's the likely causes of things in the external world." Husserl doesn't want to do that; he wants to perform an ideal study, more like a mathematician or a geometer, someone who contemplates what a triangle is and figures out its essential features with the mind. But he wants to bring that kind of ideal thought experiment to whatever appears in consciousness; so he wants a nonnatural, nonempiricist, ideal analysis of experience. In this, he thinks he has something new that no one's had before.

Why should it matter to have this new kind of science, this nonnaturalistic—scientific in a broader sense—but not a natural science, not a psychologistic analysis of intentional acts and experience? What does the phenomenologist do? The phenomenologist carefully distinguishes all sorts of types of intentional acts, such as perception or memory or imagination. That's what Husserl did and what other phenomenologists did after him; they tried to say, what's the structure of memory? What's the structure of the experience of the word "ought"? What's the structure of the experience of beauty? They tried to describe their corresponding types of intentional objects. But it is such objects, Husserl insisted, on which all other knowledge and sciences depend for their evidence; after all, all sciences, all philosophy, and all mathematics depend on his phenomenology. How can he say that? His point is this: I, the phenomenologist, my business is describing the flow of human experience. And it's important to recognize not just the snapshots of experience, but the temporal flow—one of the most important works of Husserl was his description of *The Phenomenology of Internal Time-Consciousness*, which I'll get to in a moment. But the phenomenologist is going to describe his or her experience and look at the ideal types of experience. When a physicist is in a lab and is going to make inferences from data, what is the data? The data is the physicist's experience in the lab; that is, the physicist sees the meter turn this way: That, too, is an experience that the phenomenologist would investigate. The mathematician sitting in his or her study contemplating shapes and forms in the mind: That, too, is a type of conscious experience that the phenomenologist can study. In other words, what turns out to be the data or evidence for all other kinds of inquiry, the phenomenologist will study in its pristine, pure, original form. Phenomenology will become the foundation of all other disciplines, and that means experience is more philosophically fundamental than natural science. Natural science gets its evidence from the conscious experience of scientists, which the phenomenologist studies.

Let's return briefly to the notion of the internal time consciousness. In that book, which he published in 1905, *The Phenomenology of Internal Time-Consciousness*, Husserl shows in a way very reminiscent of Bergson how the present cannot be conceived as a point on a line; Bergson had already denied this. What Husserl shows in his description is that what I experience as the present must contain an experiential retention of past moments and must contain an experiential protention, or anticipation of the future. The experience of time shows that it is impossible to divide time up into successive, independent, simple instants. Time is much more complicated when we actually look at how it's experienced. The implication here, again, is that scientific time—clock time, the objective time by which our society determines what time it is, if you're late, what time everybody should get to work in the morning—this is a construction out of something more fundamental, the phenomenological, directly experienced sense of time.

While the fundamental aim of phenomenology is phenomenological research, Husserl did not neglect to form a broader theory of the source of structure of flowing intentional acts. Here we're going a step further: Husserl drew broader philosophical conclusions about experience, not about research into the modes and forms of experience, but the philosophical context into which you would put the description of experience. Husserl came to the view—and he expressed this first in 1913 in the first volume of his book *Ideas*—that my experience must be constituted by what he called the transcendental ego, a pole (not a physical pole) that constitutes ongoing experience. He introduced a transcendental reduction to lead to the source of that experience, the transcendental ego.

Here we seem to be getting into an idealist metaphysics, the idea that the mind is constituting reality. Husserl wanted to avoid this; he wanted to avoid an idealist kind of metaphysics; he wanted to avoid all metaphysics. He said he had no interest in metaphysics. However, he had to describe the ongoing constitution of experience—how it's being woven into a flowing, integrated whole. He has to find some agency to do that, or at least he feels he must. Denying the thesis, or bracketing the thesis, of the natural attitude means he cannot rely on something outside experience to do it. He can't say, my experience flows and is coordinated by the fact that I have a nervous system; there are objects in the world impacting my nervous system. He also can't use Berkeley's or Leibniz's option, which is to say God is coordinating experience. Instead he says there must be, as part of my consciousness, a transcendental ego. He never denies that nature impacts the experience of consciousness, but he's bound to say that the meanings of experience were the responsibility of consciousness itself.

In other words, and this is a rather subtle point, he wants to remain agnostic on the question of whether or not there's something outside consciousness that's affecting my experience. "That may well be, but it's none of my business; I'm just a phenomenologist." Nevertheless, he has to say, if something outside consciousness is affecting my consciousness, once it's in consciousness, its status, its meaning, its quality is determined by the transcendental ego itself. In other words, you can't make a translation from saying here's a character of an object independent of consciousness (here's a feature of nature, in other words), now let's explain what's going on inside consciousness by looking at the nature of this object outside. You can't do that, because the nature or the status inside consciousness is determined by consciousness itself.

Thus in his book the *Cartesian Meditations*, Husserl must say that, "The being of the pure ego, and his *cogitations* [or thoughts, we might say] ... is antecedent to the natural being of the world. ... [The latter] continually presupposes the realm of transcendental being." In other words, anything I have to say about the natural world—and he's not saying there's no such thing as the natural world, he doesn't want to get into that question—he's simply saying we phenomenologists don't need to concern ourselves with it, because it is the case that whenever a human being says something or refers to something, that presupposes consciousness and their own transcendental ego, and the transcendental ego explains and shows how those things we experience and refer to are constituted within my pure ego. For this, he actually introduces yet another *epochē*, this one that brackets all other subjectivities—this he does in the book the *Cartesian Meditations*—in which it constitutes an inner monadic-like sphere of, primarily, consciousness distinct from the consciousness of others. All this set of reductions are simply ways of trying to get to what he thinks of as the most basic, inner, determinative, causal sphere of my consciousness, which determines everything else in experience.

It's in his last work, *The Crisis of the European Sciences and Transcendental Phenomenology*, which went unfinished, that Husserl began to write in a somewhat different way, and this is possibly a response to Heidegger. Heidegger learned much from Husserl's phenomenology but then changed phenomenology and applied it in a different way. It was also in part a response to the growing European crisis: In the 1920s, the German economy, as we know, was in a total shambles, and this fed the rising conflicts between, on the one hand, Communists, and on the other hand, the growing Nazi Party; eventually this would lead to the triumph of Nazism in Germany. There was this great sense of crisis in the air. In this last book, Husserl widened his scope from beyond the phenomenologist's careful concern with meaning and ideas. Husserl emphasized that science and technology, far from being opposed to phenomenology, were actually built upon the primary experience that phenomenology could uncover, but like most contemporary civilization, technology willfully covered over and forgot the human experiential reality that lay beneath them.

What he was claiming is that we in the modern world, because of our technological improvements, because of the complexity of our bureaucratic society, because of our belief that science, an ever-growing and ever-more complicated set of natural sciences, is the ultimate truth about the world; putting all these things together, we are estranged from or foreign from our own experience, our own primary experience of the world. We are still having that experience; indeed, the sciences, the bureaucracy, the new technologies must, like everything else, ultimately arise from human experience, which phenomenology investigates. However, these layers, as he called, of sedimentations of these different cultural activities were such that we less and less are able to recognize our own ordinary experience as living human beings in the flow of time. In other words, we are leaving behind a kind of authentic, basic, immediate life experience in favor of mass culture, science, and technology; all these things are kind of blocking our recognition of our own experience, which is, after all, our very existence.

What was the impact of Husserl's work? For continental philosophers, it was very great. Husserl seemed to liberate the investigation of lived experience from empiricism and naturalism, as well as natural science. French and German graduate students flocked to Husserlian phenomenology. They flocked to Husserl to see that a philosopher—it seemed new to them in their generation—who actually wanted to describe immediate experience and yet claim that this is not reducible to psychology nor to natural science nor to anything else. Phenomenology seemed a method tailor-made to describing basic experience; and of course, this is a time, in the 1920s and '30s, of crisis when many people wanted a new method to try to describe some experiences.

In what may be an apocryphal story, but I've read it in several places, supposedly the young French philosopher Jean-Paul Sartre (who we'll see soon) asked his friend Raymond Aron (who later became a great theoretical sociologist), what is this new phenomenology business that the Germans are all talking about? Supposedly, Aron pointed to Sartre's drink—whether the drink was an Alsatian beer or a Pernod has been lost to history—and Aron's summary of phenomenology was to say, phenomenology is the kind of philosophy so you can describe the experience of that drink and say you're doing philosophy. Supposedly, Sartre was an instant convert.

The example is mundane, but it was that phenomenological concern that led the cry "to the things themselves"; and remember, here "things themselves" mean the concrete experience away from the abstractions of the Hegelian system, away from the abstractions of mathematics and natural science into the actual process of lived experience. This is what Husserl's phenomenology seemed to offer: a nonpsychological, nonempirical way to put consciousness first. In fact, for many people for the next 50 years, Husserl's phenomenology seemed the foremost humanistic alternative to a philosophy based in natural science. You might say, as the 20th century developed, more and more intellectuals tended to divide into what C. P. Snow came to call the two cultures: the scientific, technical work of some intellectuals; the humanistic intellectuals on the other side; undoubtedly the social sciences struggling in the middle, not knowing what side to jump to. But from many points of view, phenomenology for many European philosophers became the method that would justify keeping the human sciences—history, maybe psychology, but certainly the study of literature—separate from and distinct from the natural sciences. That is to say, it became crucial to those philosophers who did not want to accept new science—physics, chemistry, and biology—on the last word on reality.

But nevertheless, we have to say, Husserl's followers started changing his phenomenology almost immediately (as soon as it was out of his mouth, or out of his pen, you might say). What was about to happen was the French and even German students who had been affected by Husserl would very quickly reject the remnant idealism of his position, namely the whole concept of the transcendental ego. Heidegger was the most famous of these. He began his work with Husserl's phenomenology explicitly, crediting Husserl, saying, I'm going to do phenomenology, but essentially ejects anything that looks like the transcendental ego and also imbibes a dose of existentialist thinkers, which were totally unlike Husserl: Nietzsche and Kierkegaard. On the one hand, Husserl; on the other hand, Nietzsche and Kierkegaard lead to Heidegger.

It was then as existential phenomenology that phenomenology became dominant in France and Germany; and it was this movement of existential phenomenology—Husserl's phenomenology plus existentialism—that was led by Heidegger, and by Sartre, Maurice Merleau-Ponty, Karl Jaspers, and figures of this type. It was these alterations, more than Husserl, which pushed continental philosophy further from English-language philosophy. That is, the early Husserl is in the same ball game, is playing soccer along with, Frege. But once we get to existential phenomenology in the work of Heidegger, Sartre, and Husserl, they are playing a game that's nothing like the game being played in analytic philosophy and not much like the game being played in pragmatism. Nevertheless, it was Husserl's work that gave the original impetus and center of gravity that later continental philosophers would, however much they altered his work, nevertheless always return to.

Physics, Positivism, and Early Wittgenstein
Lecture 20

> The banishing of the ether and the substitution of relativistic formula for Newton's laws seem to imply ... that science does not try to know the ultimate underlying entities that cause observable phenomena but merely create mathematical models for predicting observable phenomena.

From 1900 to 1930, the greatest revolutions in physics since the 17th century had a manifold effect on philosophy. Special relativity, then general relativity, then quantum mechanics, along with Hubble's discovery of the universe's expansion, completely remade the physical view of the world. This scientific revolution banished absolute space and time, the ether, and strict determinism from physics. The universe could no longer be pictured simply, and the invariances among natural events were now highly mathematical. The impact on philosophy was complex; the most famous and most influential response was positivism.

The new science fueled logical empiricism, or positivism, which argues that science mathematically coordinates and predicts sense data, rather than seeking underlying metaphysical realities. The goal of philosophy is then to create a logically clear language that will clarify the task of science. Such positivism was promoted by the Vienna Circle in the 1920s, which was organized by Moritz Schlick and included **Otto Neurath**, **Rudolf Carnap**, and Kurt Gödel. Separately, the young **Ludwig Wittgenstein** concluded that the only strictly true method of philosophy would be to rehearse the findings of science and then show that any further philosophical questions that arose were due to misunderstandings of language. ∎

Names to Know

Carnap, Rudolf (1891–1970): A Viennese philosopher of logic and science and one of the moving forces behind the logical positivism of the Vienna Circle. His principle of tolerance and incipient pragmatism remained modern as positivism came under attack.

Neurath, Otto (1882–1945): One of the Vienna Circle positivists. He is famous for his metaphor that in epistemology and logic we are like seamen trying to fix a ship we are sailing in, since we can only use the knowledge we have while we work on the same.

Wittgenstein, Ludwig (1889–1951): This Austrian was perhaps the most influential philosopher of the 20th century. His early work in logic led to the *Tractatus Logico-Philosophicus*, which influenced the Vienna Circle. After leaving philosophy for many years, he returned to Cambridge to formulate a new philosophy of meaning as used in his *Philosophical Investigations*.

Suggested Reading

Carnap, *The Logical Syntax of Language.*

Wittgenstein, *Tractatus-Logico Philosophicus.*

Questions to Consider

1. What is the logical status of the arguments used to establish the logical picture of the world?

2. Can the verification criterion of meaning hold for all linguistic meaning?

Physics, Positivism, and Early Wittgenstein
Lecture 20—Transcript

From 1900–1930, the greatest revolutions in physics since the 17th century had a manifold effect on philosophy: some thinkers came to take philosophy now to be the handmaiden of science; a few try to form their own scientific metaphysics; and many decide that the new science has become too abstract for philosophy to combine with human experience, and they turn against any attempt to incorporate science into philosophy. The most famous and most influential response is the first, which we call positivism. The logical positivists all embraced the first book of a young genius named Ludwig Wittgenstein. After briefly reviewing some of the new science, we will examine positivism and Wittgenstein's early classic, his *Tractatus Logico-Philosophicus*.

Special relativity, general relativity, and quantum mechanics—the three great discoveries of the early 20th century—not only change the scientific view of the world, but essentially make a metaphysical picture of the world difficult to achieve. The special theory of relativity shows that there is no "ether" for light to propagate through—as it was believed necessary before that, that for any kind of electromagnetic radiation to propagate, it had to have a medium; but that seemed not to be true—furthermore, relativity showed that space and time are interdependent, they're part of one phenomenon called space-time, and space-time measurements are relative to the movement of reference frames. There is no simultaneity at a distance anymore: Measurements of lengths of space and time are objective; they're not dependent on our subjective experience, but they're relative to the relations and relative velocities of what we measure and what we measure with.

General relativity expands these notions of special relativity and shows that space itself is altered by the bodies in it. This means that Leibniz was at least partly right in his argument with Newton; he wasn't completely right because he thought (Leibniz thought) that space-time was internal to substances, whereas Einstein's field equations in general relativity have vacuum solutions, meaning that there is space-time for Einstein's theory of general relativity even where there is no matter or substance at all. Leibniz wasn't all correct. The invariance of space-time measurements appear only in highly abstract mathematical formulae. But then there's quantum mechanics: Quantum mechanics shows that the small components of matter do not behave like scaled-down versions of macroscopic material objects; they exhibit wave and particle features depending on our interaction with them. They do not have trajectories at all, and as individuals they are indeterministic. What we have now is on the one hand from special and general relativity; you have what you might call a very weird picture of the universe. On the other hand, from quantum mechanics, it seems likely that one can't even picture what's happening at the microphysical level.

The banishing of the ether and the substitution of relativistic formula for Newton's laws seem to imply something else as well: that science does not try to know the ultimate underlying entities that cause observable phenomena but merely create mathematical models for predicting observable phenomena. Let me say a bit more about that: The way Einstein was interpreted by scientists was one thing, but the way Einstein was interpreted by philosophers was a little different; that is, philosophers of science were particularly concerned with the way he came to his conclusions, and it certainly appeared that what Einstein had done was to look at the observations and to change the picture of the physical reality to match the observations. In other words, experimental data showed that measured phenomena—for example, the velocity of an object in its time measurements would change as the velocity approaches the speed of light—didn't make sense to anyone in terms of their picture of the real world, but the observation showed that it was true; the observation showed that there was no ether, so he banished the ether. The general picture that philosophers of science took from Einstein was that we should forget about trying to model or picture things themselves, and focus instead on explaining and predicting observations.

This meant that in a mathematical model—and all scientists, especially in physics, are employing mathematical models—the terms in the model do not need to refer to existences, they only have meaning in the sense of being placeholders that translate observations into predictions. In other words, the presence of a particular variable or a particular concept of an entity in a physical law needn't imply that the entity really exists as something independent of the law; it merely has to make the equation work out in the end. This was one way of interpreting Einstein's achievement.

This particular way of interpreting it was, in fact, the view of logical empiricism, or logical positivism. This movement was created by members of what was called the Vienna Circle: Moritz Schlick, Otto Neurath, perhaps most importantly Rudolf Carnap, and several others. They had been influenced by the earlier philosopher of science, Ernst Mach, and by what they took to be, as I said, the methodological implications of Einstein's theory of relativity. Certainly the positivists disagreed with each other; they were each different philosophers with their own views. But they agreed more or less on the following, self-consciously revolutionary program, and it was revolutionary. For the positivists, all positive—and the term "positivism" and the adjective "positive" simply go back to Auguste Comte's 19th-century work, it simply means empirical, dealing with empirical data—or empirical data, all knowledge of them, hence all knowledge of facts, come from sense experience narrowly construed, without theoretical additions. This is clearly a kind of empiricism. These statements of observations are supposed to be expressed in atomic statements, or "protocol sentences," of the most primitive data we have.

Let me give you an example: We might in everyday life say—and even a scientist might say—when we ask, "What do I observe here?" I observe the lectern. But that's not quite good enough for the positivist, because "lectern," after all, is a term of everyday language. Suppose we brought in someone here who had never seen a lectern and we ask, "What are you observing?" They cannot say, "We see a lectern." But what you and the person who has never seen a lectern before can agree on is you both see the color brown, you see an object this high, you feel something solid, you feel something with a certain texture. The protocol sentences—the sentences in the theory that actually state just what's observed—would not say, "I observe," or "a lectern was observed at a certain moment in time," but rather, "A brown patch covering a rectangular object with high density was observed." Calling it a "lectern" is not a primitive statement of the sheer data we're receiving.

The theories of science exist to explain and predict the occurrence of such observations. The entities posited by the theories, as I've said, need not exist in themselves; they may only serve to facilitate predictions. The philosopher's job is to produce a system of logic that can be used to construct such theories and justify their inferences. This is, in effect, an ideal, logical language, and it's precisely what Russell and Whitehead had tried to formulate. What's happening is the positivists are trying to take advantage of the great logical revolution that started with Frege and was brought to a fairly high level by Russell and Whitehead; to take this new logic and use it now in science or to clarify science, particularly physics and what physics is achieved. All scientific claims should, in principle, prove to be reducible to claims about the most basic science, hence physics; in this sense, science itself should be unified. Perhaps we can't do it yet; perhaps right now we're unable to see how biological claims can be reduced to chemical claims, which can be reduced to physical claims. But in principle, we should be able to do that; so the positivists were also physical reductionists by and large.

Continuing our discussion of positivism, statements have meaning only in two ways, as I hope is clear by now: They have meaning as logical statements, which reveal logical structure; and as verifiable empirical claims about observations. In fact, verifiability—famously for the positivists—is the criterion of meaning, not merely of truth. Statements incapable of test or verification are simply meaningless. This is an enormous thing to say, because what the positivists took from this was simply that ethics, aesthetics, political philosophy, and metaphysics are meaningless uses of words. In a sense, you might say they're going back to Hume's old dictum: If you can't show that it's true logically or mathematically—in other words, through relations of ideas—and you can't show that it's true as matters of fact, which is now being interpreted as true in terms of the protocol sentences that summarize actually observed data, if it's not true by those criteria then there's nothing to be said at all; and it's not something we can claim to be rationally true, although the positivists are going one better and saying it's not even meaningful at all.

Carnap (one of the positivists) did, however, entertain what he called a "principle of tolerance," and eventually accepted a bit of pragmatism; that is, he admitted that there is no one ontological language that is determined by sense data, but several. What does that mean? It means that in principle, if you were to gather up all the statements of observation we can about whatever is happening in the world and whatever scientists are experimenting on, it's by no means clear that there's only one theory of reality, one ontology, that would explain all those; there could, in fact, be several different types of ontologies, several different theories of reality. For example, on the one hand, an ontology of mere phenomena in Hume's sense, just of sense data themselves; or on the other hand, an ontology of physical objects or events. They might hold equally well. So Carnap accepted that it might be the case that the data themselves in the form of protocol sentences did not singularly determine one ultimate metaphysically theory.

Last, before we move on in this discussion, I want to emphasize that one of the most crucial distinctions for the positivists remains the distinction between observation statements and theory statements. This is another example of a very old program in the history of philosophy—I've mentioned in earlier lectures—namely that even Aristotle thought that there must be some level of experience that essentially can't be doubted; it's indubitably true in the sense that it's simply the shared data that we get from our senses. Then we may make errors when we interpret that. When you are driving on a long road and in the distance you see something by the side of the road, and you think you're seeing a person; you get closer and you realize it's a sign. The mistake was not that you actually saw a person instead of a sign, the mistake was that based on a very limited amount of data that you actually were receiving, and that was being caused by the object in the world that you were looking toward, you leapt to interpret that as something; it's the interpretation that was wrong. In the same sense, positivism absolutely requires that we can separate statements of sense data—the facts, ma'am; just the facts—from any theoretical interpretation of it. We then try to pick the best, most reliable, most predictive theoretical interpretation, but we have to keep the two separate.

While the positivists were just starting up and gaining ground in Vienna, an odd thing happened. A young man from a wealthy Viennese family, born in 1889, had gone to Manchester, England, to study aeronautical engineering. But he found himself caught up in conceptual problems about the mathematics he was learning. He eventually read Russell's 1903 book, *The [Principles] of Mathematics*, along with Frege's book *The Foundations of Arithmetic*, and he became so obsessed with the questions of mathematical logic that he dropped his interest in aeronautics and engineering, and he decided to go to Cambridge to study logic with Russell in 1911. A year later, Russell said, this 23-year-old knew so much logic that Russell had nothing left to teach him. That was Ludwig Wittgenstein. In 1914, Wittgenstein enlisted in the Austrian army and saw action during the First World War. During his four years of service, he composed much of the only book that he would publish during his lifetime, his *Tractatus-Logico Philosophicus*.

I'll just say in general something that's useful, because we'll be coming back to Wittgenstein later in the course. Wittgenstein is one of those philosophers, same thing is true of Heidegger, of which we typically speak of his early work and his later work; because while everybody's work changes over the course of their lifetime—at least one hopes it hopes it does as they grow and mature—in Wittgenstein's and Heidegger's case, the later work is in some ways very different than the early work. In this lecture, we're looking at his early work, his first book, the *Tractatus*, and the picture it presents. One might say that the *Tractatus* is an attempt to clarify—and this is a rather abstract way of putting it, but it's probably the best way to put it—just what Frege's *Begriffsschrift* (remember his new logic, his new logical notation) does and what it does not accomplish; in effect, the meaning of the new logic that Frege developed; that's what Wittgenstein is after. While Wittgenstein's work ultimately differed from the work of the Vienna Circle and hence the positivists in some significant ways, the circle looked on this book as a crucial, kindred achievement; so it's perfectly appropriate to give our analysis of the *Tractatus* along with logical positivism.

What Wittgenstein did in the *Tractatus*—which, by the way, is a little book organized into, in effect, atomic statements; little statements that are numbered on the side—Wittgenstein analyzed all phenomena as states of affairs or facts; so everything we see in the world is a state of affairs. Language represents or "pictures" those facts, those states of affairs. So we have the states of affairs, and we have language. But then there's logic: Logic gives language the structure that makes this representation possible. The logical forms of propositions match the logical form of the world. Logic is then the form that is shared by both the language that we use to describe the world and the states of affairs that are the world, and that's what makes possible linguistic representation, or true representation. Some philosophers put it this way: How does language hook onto the world? The way language hooks onto the world, and hence has the possibility of being true, is that there's an underlying form shared by both—the world, the states of affairs, and our language—and that's the rules of language. The rules of logic reveal the scaffolding of language and hence of states of affairs.

Wittgenstein then made a bold statement: Logic is pure syntax, a structure necessary for meaning, but by itself is meaningless. As you know, when we speak in language, we not only say words that have meanings, but those words have to be organized in a specific patter or order or you get no meaning. Syntax is the pattern, the rules for structuring sentences. In the case of logic, Wittgenstein is saying logic is just pure syntax; it's a structure necessary for anything to be meaningful. But that means—and Wittgenstein is thinking like a real philosopher here—if logic is the structure that makes meaning possible, that structure itself is meaningless, as he said; *sinnlos*, has no meaning. Logical truths, tautologies—for example, "all bachelors are bachelors"—do not say anything; rather, what he says, they show or exhibit logical form. This is Wittgenstein's say/show distinction. The reason he's saying this is he has to give a way to distinguish: If logic is the structure held in common by language that means and states of affairs that are meant, then logic can't be like language; it has to be something else, and hence it can't mean. But it has to do something; and so he says logic displays or shows structure, but does not say it. "Saying" is something language does.

The statements of logic that portray the logical structure are therefore *sinnlos* or meaningless; however, they are to be distinguished from metaphysical and ethical statements. Remember, the positivists say that ethical and metaphysical statements, and aesthetic statements—statements about values, and about things that can't be observed—that these are meaningless. Wittgenstein here had another category of meaninglessness: Statements of ethics or metaphysics are not senseless, *sinnlos* in German, but rather they are nonsense, *unsinnig*; they don't say anything, nor do they exhibit any logical structure, they neither say nor show.

Wittgenstein did not, however, think that ethics or metaphysics, or religion, was unimportant nonsense. In fact, he thought it was doubtless more important than science or logic, but it was still outside the bounds of rationality. It is *das Mystische*; the mystical. Wittgenstein is a remarkable figure in his early life, also in his later life; but in this remarkable book, he concludes it talking about the mystical. As he concludes his book, he finally says, "Whatever can be said, can be said logically. Beyond that, one must be silent." For Wittgenstein's perspective, whatever can be said can be said clearly. He thinks he's displayed how it is that what we say can mean states of affairs because of the shared structure of logic; he's shown that logic, by itself, of course, doesn't say because it's not language, but it does show; and yet he said that there are all sorts of other things in the world that we try to talk about, but there is no rational meaning to what we're saying. But in that case, when we're talking about ethics, metaphysics, and religion, Wittgenstein literally says, "Those are the most important things, but they cannot be discussed rationally." He meant this quite seriously: Ethics and religion are far more important than logic, science, and philosophy of science, but there's nothing we can say about them; they're outside the realm of rational, meaningful speech.

In the succeeding 30 years, much important work was done by the positivists and their offspring. The fundamental features of positivism, we could say are the belief that science is the last word on fact; the empirical sciences, operating with a scientific method, are our best shot at understanding facts or states of affairs. Second, that all such facts ultimately reduce to the facts of physics; we may not be able to reduce them at this point in time, we may not know enough, but in principle they must be reducible to the most basic atomic facts, you might say, about physics; and that the observation language and the theoretical language of science must be kept strictly separate. The reason they must be kept separate is we want the data, the protocol statements that say what's been observed at what time, that's how we adjudicate between which theoretical statement is true or false. If the observation statements were mixed together with theory, they could not act as a fair judge of which theorctical statement is true; so these have to be separate. Lastly, what is the job of philosophy in all this? The job of conceptual clarification and the formulation of logic; metaphysics is pointless. From the point of view of the logical positivists, the proper aim of philosophy is to explain how science, mathematics, and logic work. These are the realms where we can talk about rational meaning and about fact, about truth about the world; and they're inspired to do this by the great achievements in physics, really the unparalleled achievements, from 1905–1930. Outside the realm of science, philosophy really has no other role.

But one part of the scheme failed early; and that is even during the heyday of logical positivism. If you remember from an earlier lecture, the logicist project—started by Frege and which Russell and Whitehead tried to fulfill in their *Principia Mathematica*—was to derive all mathematics from simple logical notions. This project faltered, as I mentioned before, on the shoals of the paradoxes of set theory that Russell himself had discovered. In 1931, the great genius Kurt Gödel eventually showed that it was impossible for any logical system rich enough to include arithmetic—and that's the kind of system that *Principia Mathematica* tried to portray—will not be able to prove all the statements made in it to be true or false, and not be able to prove that contradictions can never occur in the system. That's a big problem: If our logical system could generate, if our language can generate the worst possible thing, the extreme form of falsehood, a contradiction; if we can't prevent that, then the language has a problem in it.

Consequently, Gödel showed that the paradoxes of set theory that we talked about earlier with the barber of Seville in an earlier lecture were ineliminable. However useful advances in logic might be in serving to clarify philosophical arguments—and this should be mad clear, that usefulness is not in doubt; first and second order of logic remain for the rest of the 20th century ways by which many philosophers, analytic philosophers in particular, try to clarify arguments in order to then examine them. However, the attempt to form a complete logical language that would be self-enclosed and self-contained, that hope died in 1931 with Gödel. We cannot find a complete, ideal language.

As for Wittgenstein, on the last page of the *Tractatus*, he famously declared that the proper method in philosophy would be to say everything that "can be said," meaning, say all facts as determined by the natural sciences; and then, he said the best way to teach philosophy would be to simply sit in the seminar room and wait until somebody said something metaphysical, and show them that their statement was nonsensical. In other words, there is nothing else for philosophy to do. This is how radical 20th century philosophy is becoming. In his mind, Wittgenstein resolved the only problems philosophy could resolve and showed that it could do nothing else. True to his word, at the height of his celebrated youthful fame, he felt he had solved the problems of philosophy that could be solved, the rest are completely unsolvable, they are mystical; and so he quit the university and found work as a school teacher.

Emergence and Whitehead
Lecture 21

> Despite the growing influence of positivism, and its distaste for metaphysics ... there was a tradition of speculative naturalistic metaphysics, largely inspired by responses to Darwin, starting in the late 19th century that climaxed in the 1920s.

Ever since Charles Darwin, some philosophers, including Henri Bergson, William James, and John Dewey, had tried to formulate a global evolutionary account of nature that included not only the physical and chemical, but also life and mind. While positivism was to become the dominant philosophy of science, two openly metaphysical interpretations of science continued this older tradition in the 1920s. **British emergentism** arose in the work of **Samuel Alexander**, **Conwy Lloyd Morgan**, and **C. D. Broad**, along with the American **Roy Wood Sellars**. The emergentists argued that complex systems of simple components can, by dint of their organization, exhibit properties not possessed by, and hence not reducible to, the components. Thus mental properties, while dependent upon neurology, are not reducible to neurology; biological properties cannot be reduced to chemical properties, nor chemical to physical properties.

> **Whitehead created a metaphysics of the ultimate processes and entities of nature that took relativity and the quantum into account.**

At the same time, **Alfred North Whitehead**, a collaborator of Bertrand Russell, was the one 20th-century philosopher to attempt what the 17th-century philosophers had done: to create a metaphysical system that was consistent with physics and explained the place of mind, values, and God in such a universe. Whitehead created a metaphysics of the ultimate processes and entities of nature that took relativity and the quantum into account. He made the ultimate realities "actual occasions," events that undergo an internal process of development that integrates a multiplicity into a unity. Each occasion prehends all others, as with Gottfried Wilhelm Leibniz's monads. The entire world process is the evolution of unity out of multiplicity, which is the creative act of God. Thus Whitehead created the most famous **process philosophy.** ∎

Names to Know

Alexander, Samuel (1859–1938): An influential English philosopher, one of the British emergentists, and the author of *Space, Time, and Deity*.

Broad, C. D. (**Charlie Dunbar**; 1887–1971): A member of the British emergentists and the author of *Mind and Its Place in Nature*.

Morgan, Conwy Lloyd (1852–1936): This English psychologist was the moving force behind the British emergentists and the author of *Emergent Evolution*.

Sellars, Roy Wood (1880–1973): An American critical realist philosopher who also produced an evolutionary emergent metaphysics akin to that of the British emergentists. He is also father of the philosopher Wilfred Sellars.

Whitehead, Alfred North (1861–1947): A British mathematician by training, he collaborated with Bertrand Russell to compose the most important work of logic of the 20th century, *Principia Mathematica*, and went on to formulate a unique process metaphysics of reality that incorporated relativity and quantum theory.

Important Terms

British emergentism: A school of thought in the 1920s that proposed an alternative to mechanism and vitalism by which complex organization of components of one level (e.g., physical) yield novel, irreducible properties at a higher level (e.g., chemical). Its most prominent exponents were Samuel Alexander, Conwy Lloyd Morgan, and C. D. Broad.

process philosophy: Any philosophy that makes all reality and all forms or norms subject to a process of change. Most commonly applied to the work of Alfred North Whitehead but would also fit Henri Bergson and John Dewey, among others.

Suggested Reading

Blitz, *Emergent Evolution.*

Sherburne, *A Key to Whitehead's "Process and Reality."*

Whitehead, *Process and Reality.*

———, *Science and the Modern World.*

Questions to Consider

1. How can there be emergence if science's greatest successes seem to come from reductive explanation?

2. Do the simplest components of reality contain protomental properties, and if so, what is their effect?

Emergence and Whitehead
Lecture 21—Transcript

Despite the growing influence of positivism, and its distaste for metaphysics—which we've seen—there was a tradition of speculative naturalistic metaphysics, largely inspired by responses to Darwin, starting in the late 19th century that climaxed in the 1920s. Several of the American pragmatists, especially Peirce, James, Mead, and Dewey, were part of that discussion. In this lecture, we'll examine some of the other discussants, particularly Henri Bergson, a group called the British emergentists, and then Russell's teacher and collaborator, Alfred North Whitehead. In the following lecture, we'll turn to a different kind of naturalism in the thought of John Dewey.

Henri Bergson, winner of the 1927 Nobel Prize for Literature, was in many ways the first and most influential of these post-Darwinian naturalist philosophers who tried to extend the notion of evolution to all of nature. Bergson's first and most famous work, dating from 1889, denied that time can be analyzed as points on a line; the smallest component of time is, for Bergson, a duration, a finite span of time revealed in experience, rather than the abstract, mathematical notion of time, which, it so happens more or less dominates philosophical thought about nature really from the time of Aristotle and right through the modern period. Bergson is most famous for changing this notion of time; and he went on to posit what he called an élan vital, a vital impetus that drives the evolution of biological forms. But it was just this vitalism—meaning the notion that if biology can't be reduce to physics and chemistry, some held the notion that biology or living forms must have their own special life force, something not chemical or physical at all—it was this notion of vitalism, the idea of a specifically biological force, that later natural scientists most objected to in Bergson.

Minimally, naturalism claims that everything is natural or part of nature, hence nothing is supernatural. By this definition, materialists and physicalists—who believe that everything is material or physical, respectively—would, naturally, be naturalists. But there's some reason to reserve the term "naturalism" to mean something a little narrower; in particular, nonreductive naturalists, those naturalists who are not reductive materialists or reductive physicalists; people who believe everything is natural, but refuse to accept that the natural can be reduced to the physical or material. So while the term "naturalism" is fair game for physicalists who think everything is nature and nature is all physical, I will use it in the rest of this course more for pluralistic thinkers who take the physical as an inexhaustive account of nature; in other words, nature has more in it than just the physical.

The word "reduction"—which is very important in the philosophy of science in the 20th century—here can mean two different kinds of philosophical positions: ontological or explanatory; that is, the claim that a complex system is nothing but an aggregation of its simpler components. That's ontological reduction: reducing a whole to its parts. But explanatory reduction is a little different: That's the claim that a complex system can be explained by the theory governing its components alone. These two things can go together, but it's possible to assert one, not the other. Many contemporary philosophers, for example—here at the beginning of the 20th century—accept the first but not the second; that is, I am in fact nothing but a collection of subatomic physical particles—that's ontological reduction of me to my fundamental parts—but (these philosophers usually hold) we'll never be able to substitute a purely physical explanation of me for the biological and psychological accounts of me due to their tremendously greater complexity. The sciences that we have, other than physics, we'll always have, because we could never in practice give a physical explanation using physics of everything in a living thing. Nevertheless, it must be the case (many philosophers think) that the parts of me are nothing but quarks and leptons (leptons being a class of fundamental particle that includes, for example, electrons). From an ontological reductionist point of view, I'm nothing but a complicated collection of quarks and electrons, but we'll never be able to produce an explanation of me and my behavior by thinking of me that way.

In the 1920s, interest in nonreductionist naturalism peaked. Gestalt psychology had arisen, along with various notions of "holism"; all of these were becoming rather popular. But most of all, 1920s brought a school of emergence, or emergent thought, represented by Samuel Alexander, C. Lloyd Morgan, and C. D. Broad, among others. They sought a way between two different views: on the one hand, mechanism, or the reduction of biology to physics and chemistry, the notion that someday we'll know enough that biology and biological phenomena will just be reduced to physics and chemistry; and on the other hand vitalism (that was Bergson's view), the view that there is a unique "life force" over and above the physical and chemical components of an organism, which made it living, and which, as you remember, Bergson had championed.

What the emergentists sought to do, to go between these two views they wanted to avoid, was to say that the entities of the more complex sciences—like biology and even psychology—were, in fact, composed of nothing more than the entities of the less complex; for example, biological organisms composed by chemical substances, and chemical substances by physical substances. That sounds a bit like the reductionists. However, they asserted that the complex relations and processes holding among those components could generate "novel" properties at the higher level, properties that couldn't be reduced; and those higher entities and properties could actually "downwardly cause"—that is to say, have a causal influence—on what's happening at lower levels. Note that this view—the view of the emergentists—flies directly in the face of positivist reductionism. The emergentists claim must be that some properties and performances at each natural level—for example, the psychological, the biological, etc.—are irreducible to the lower, and hence irreducible to physics.

The reason they gave was complexity of organization, not a special force like Bergson's élan vital. Let's try to imagine what this means: Imagine for a moment three geometrical figures on a sheet of paper, each of the three made up of the same number of little components. Imagine two triangles: one made of nine asterisks, call that A; another triangle made nine little plus signs in the same of a triangle, call that B; and then one circle made of nine asterisks, call that C. If I ask you, "What is A?" you will rightly say, "It's a triangle." Likewise, B is another triangle, and C is a circle. But notice: A the triangle and C the circle have exactly the same components, nine little asterisks; and A and B have no components in common, one is an asterisk and one is little plus signs, yet are both triangles. The whole figures are determined not only by components but by the way the components are organized, and nowhere among the components are little triangles or little circles. The point here, the emergentist would just say, is simply this: The circularity of the circle and the triangularity of the two triangles are not properties of the parts; the organization of these little components (plus signs and asterisks), because complex organization has been imposed on it, there's a new property that's come into, so to speak, the world of plus signs and asterisks, namely the property of being a triangle or the property of being a circle.

The emergentists, then, understood nature as composed of a hierarchy of levels at which novel, irreducible properties and entities arose; the physical, the chemical, the biological, and the psychological, usually those four. Each higher level depends on the lower—it wouldn't exist without the lower—but it can't be reduced to it or explained by it; and higher levels can cause changes in lower levels. This is the way they try to apply the notion of evolution to all of nature.

At the same time as the emergentists were putting their theory together, Alfred North Whitehead, who we met before, was coming into his most mature period of philosophy. Whitehead was by early inclination and training a mathematician, eventually at Cambridge University in England; remember he was one of Russell's first teachers at Cambridge, which led to their collaboration on that logicist classic *Principia Mathematica*. Whitehead's interests tended more toward the philosophy and the significance of mathematics, however, rather than actually solving mathematical puzzles. He also constructed a theory of general relativity alternate to Einstein's, whose empirical predictions were no worse than Einstein's for a couple of decades. As a philosopher, Whitehead wrote on many topics including education; but today, we're interested in his metaphysics. He wrote a series of works on the concept of nature in the first two decades of the 20th century, but after moving to Harvard in 1924, he produced the most comprehensive, and perhaps most difficult, naturalistic metaphysical scheme of the 20th century in the 1926 book *Process and Reality*. He admits, interestingly, to having been influenced by both Bergson and William James.

Whitehead is famously called a "process philosopher"; in fact, his name is almost synonymous with the term—if you tell a philosopher, "I study process philosophy," he or she would say, "Oh, you study Whitehead"—this isn't quite fair, because arguably we could include others under the label "process philosophers": Hegel, several of the Americanist philosophers like Dewey, and certainly Bergson. For all of these, including Whitehead, the ontological focus is on processes of which entities are phases, rather than on substances or entities whose interactions must then be explained. Nevertheless, today Whitehead is pretty much the most famous process philosopher.

Whitehead believed that if 20th century physics is right, then we have to reorient our metaphysics around the idea that things, substances, corpuscles (atoms), are not the most fundamental or invariant or decisive elements of reality. The "things" are a consequence of a more fundamental and comprehensive "process"; that is, the correct initial response to the question, "What is real?" is a verb, not a noun. It's helpful to begin this with his early view. Whitehead began in his early metaphysical work by positing what we would call an event-ontology, which happens to have been in accordance with Minkowski's account of special relativity. What this means is reality is atomic or simple events, not atomic substances; reality is events or happenings. Further, each event or happening has a nonzero duration. He took this notion from Bergson: We can't assume that time can be analyzed as durationless, infinitesimal point-presents. Space-time properties of these events and their relations he then conceived as part of what he called an extensive continuum whose measures are relative—he's trying to build in special relativity here—and external to the events. Space-time relations are a shifting framework determined by events. The events are the fundamental reality; space-time is a set of relations among them.

Whitehead then argued that the very act of perception selects out a kind of "slab," he said, of this space-time continuum; that is to say, the act of perception fixes this space-time flux into an order of objective reality. Fixed space-time locations for events are the artifact or act of perception; they're dependent on somebody doing the perceiving. The percipient act of a minded creature fixes out one of indefinitely many space-time slabs of reality. This sounds bizarre perhaps, but all he's trying to do is work out the metaphysical implications of the principle of Einstein's special relativity in particular, but also later general relativity.

Objects Whitehead takes to be enduring entities. Inside his event ontology, Whitehead claims that objects either enter into or are built up out of events. This view of "object" rests on two things: First, objects have to be properties of events or collections of events, for both relativistic and quantum reasons. Second, "objects," like "human body" or "red" (that's an object, it's a property, hence an object) or "tree" (that is also an object, a set of properties) are universal categories we impose on events through our percipient slabs; this notion is rather difficult, it will make a little more sense as we turn to his later work. For it was in the 1920s that he put together his mature metaphysical book in the famously difficult *Process and Reality*. Here he tries to not only special and general relativity and some awareness of quantum theory—although Whitehead did not employ the completed quantum mechanical theory of the late 1920s—but as well life and mind, because Whitehead believed you can't have a complete picture of reality or the cosmos unless you include an account of life and mind.

His mature work goes like this: All reals in process and reality can be called actual occasions or atomic events. Either the event language or the language of atomic entities will do, but as we'll see, if these are entities they're intrinsically dynamic and endure over vanishingly small amounts of time. Each one of these actual occasions is actually a discrete, atomic process undergoing a creative development, which all reality is undergoing, and in this process, the process of creative development is the process of integrating many effects, causal interactions, or features into one. For each actual occasion, all its relations to other actual occasions are "prehended" by it; so an individual actual occasion prehends, in a certain sense perceives, all that is going on with other actual occasions in their relation to it. Again following Bergson, Whitehead takes creativity to be a fundamental principle. Reality just is a creative process in which unities are formed out of components; there's no further explanation for that, that's part of the nature of reality.

You might, thinking back to earlier in the course, recognize there is a bit of a Leibnizian element here; and you certainly would be right if you thought that. Following Leibniz, each actual occasion is related to all others, and its relations are integral to what it is, part of its essential nature. Each occasion develops from the relations among others, incorporating and integrating them in a process that he calls "concrescence"; each actual occasion becomes a systematic whole, until, at full integration, the occasion actually "dies." That's the metaphor he uses, but what he means is ceases to change, ceases to become. Like Leibniz, actual occasions are therefore "proto-mental"; that is, Whitehead is actually claiming that the only way to explain the presence of life and mind in nature is to claim that there is rudimentary life and mind in the most fundamental particles or events that constitute reality. These actual occasions possess a rudimentary dynamic representation of the outside world, and hence a form of minded life. Indeed, Whitehead's name for his scheme in *Process and Reality* is the philosophy of "organism," implying that there's a kind of life to everything. This is a form of panpsychism, or the view that mind is somehow in everything.

Whitehead does not try to exemplify actual occasions in any more traditional or easily accessible terms. What I mean by that is he doesn't give us examples of actual occasions. However, it becomes quite clear that it has to be the case that actual occasions, or at least some of them, are as small as the smallest existing particles in subatomic physics, and as brief in duration as the shortest lived particles. That's very, very small, and that's very, very brief. Everything else in the universe, and every complex thing—you, me, the lectern, anything you can name—is a "society" of actual occasions, each of them prehending their unified organization into a larger whole. Space-time is then the extensive continuum of relations among actual occasions; again, here he's following Leibniz, but now Einstein as well.

But there's a second ontological category in Whitehead beside actual occasions. All properties, he claims, are eternal objects. To pause for a moment, he's literally responding to the old problem in philosophy on what is the status of universals. That is, when we use the word "horse," we can point to individual horses. Does the word "horse" just mean the individual horses, or does the word "horse" mean something else, an essence, a nature, a general set of properties that are instantiated in individual horses? If that's true, what's the existential status of that universal, that "horseness"? Does "horseness" exist, would it exist if there weren't any horses? If you say, "No, of course not, if you destroy all the horses, 'horseness' wouldn't be there"; how could we still talk about it and know that all the horses were gone? This is an old problem in philosophy. What Whitehead is saying is all properties are eternal objects that ingress into the concrescence of an actual occasion. What he's really doing is recapturing the doctrine of Platonic realism for properties, but here he's calling them objects. Whitehead is accepting that everything we know about actual occasions is a universal—a universal property, an eternal object—that comes to characterize it in its development.

In a sense, you could think a bit like a snowball rolling down a hill that gets bigger. Except the metaphor isn't that great, because he doesn't mean that the actual occasion is getting bigger, he means that as it develops, more is incorporated into it; it has more properties, more relations to other things, up to the point where it dies or ceases to change. When it develops, evolves, creatively increases in the complexity of its nature and its relation to other things, that means these eternal objects or properties become instantiated in it; this is a language that's not that far off from Plato, although it's being applied to these effervescent events called actual occasions. The totality of actual occasions is developing toward greater integration; that is, everything is in process toward oneness for Whitehead.

Like the great 17th century metaphysicians, Whitehead did not neglect theology. He had a very interesting notion of God; and, in fact, it happens that this is perhaps one of the best-known parts of Whitehead, since Whitehead was not taken seriously by many scientists or metaphysicians, but he was taken more seriously by more theologians and philosophers or religion. What's his notion of God? God, for Whitehead, is a unique actual occasion—God has to be an actual occasion, there's nothing else for God to be—but God, in Whitehead's description, has a tripartite nature. The first aspect of God, you might say, is the consequent nature of God. Under this aspect, God prehends all actual occasions; that means all are preserved in his memory. Everything that happens to an actual occasion and every actual occasion is somehow preserved in the prehension of God; god prehends them all. The second aspect of God's nature is the primordial nature of God. In this aspect or feature, God prehends all eternal objects, hence maintains them all as possibilities until they get actualized in actual atomic occasions.

Then, as in everything in Whitehead there has to be something third and there has to be a unity, the third feature of God is God as superject; this is as opposed to being God as subject. As superject, God creatively unifies both the eternal objects and the actual occasions. God is identified with the creative process of achieving unity, which governs the activities of all things. This has several implications: On the one hand, this is more or less a pantheist or pantheistic notion of God, which we've talked about earlier in the series; that is, God is integrated with the world, God is not identical to the world but God is part of the world. At the same time, God is undergoing a process; God is not holding mind and matter together as for Descartes, Spinoza, Locke, and Berkeley—remember in the 17th century how common it was for God to be thought of as solving the problem of how mind and body get together; that's no longer a problem for Whitehead, so God doesn't fulfill that function—rather, God provides the temporal functions of preserving past actualities, embodying possibilities for the future, and provides the ontological basis for possibilities and actualities to interpenetrate, or for one to be prehended by and joined into the other. The whole process of the universe is a consequence of the nature of God; God is not personal in the traditional Judaic, Christian, or Islamic senses, but God nevertheless is certainly worthy of love, and God, in a way, is a kind of love because God is this unifying force, this integrating force. It also means, though—as was made clear by another philosopher Charles Hartshorne, who commented on Whitehead—that this means God changes. In Whitehead, God changes over time. God must undergo processes just like the world does.

What has Whitehead accomplished if he's right? What he's tried to do is to integrate a relativistic view of space-time from Einstein's special and general theories of relativity with a recognition of the quantum or discrete nature of reality that we get from the quantum theory—you could say the two greatest physical discoveries of the 20th century—and third, he's trying to integrate both with the existence of life, mind, and even God; so to provide a full cosmology, as he liked to call it, or a full naturalistic system.

Whitehead, Bergson, and the British emergentists, and we could include the naturalists among the Americanist philosophers—Dewey, Peirce, Mead, etc.—were all but forgotten after the 1920s and '30s. Why was this? For a few reasons: First of all, quantum mechanics in the late 1920s seemed to reduce chemistry to physics; that's what many thought, because quantum mechanics explained the electronic structure of atoms. If that were true, then one of the things the British emergentists used to argue for their emergentism would disappear, namely chemistry; chemistry would seem to be reducible to physics, that's what many thought. Second, of course, the rise of positivism; positivism became the dominant philosophy of science, and it promoted physicalist reductionism. Finally, you could say, yet another great victory for the reductionist program was Watson's and Crick's discovery of the structure of DNA in 1953, because this, again, seemed to promote the possibility that biology might just be reducible to chemistry after all.

Nevertheless, Whitehead remains the only major 20th century thinker who tried to do with relativity and quantum theory what the great 17th century metaphysicians tried to do for Galilean and Newtonian physics—Descartes, Spinoza, Locke, and Leibniz—that is, to create a metaphysics adequate to their work that also was adequate to life, mind, and meaning. As we'll see, some of the factors that led to Whitehead and the emergentists being ignored in the middle of the 20th century started to disappear or modify in the late 20th century; and in this later time we'll see, further down the road in the course, that there's a bit of resurgence of the notion of emergence and, to some extent, of Whitehead. In our next lecture, as I mentioned before, we'll look at another form of this mostly-neglected naturalism in the work of John Dewey.

Dewey's American Naturalism
Lecture 22

> What Dewey sought more than anything else was a humanistic naturalism ... to be a naturalist in such a way that the unique properties of the human mind, ethics, politics, aesthetics, ... could be incorporated within his naturalism rather than declared irrational and impossible to account for, as with the positivists.

John Dewey was the most famous American philosopher of the early and mid-20th century. He was influenced early by Georg Wilhelm Friedrich Hegel, but like Karl Marx, he stood Hegel on his head, using Hegel's dialectic inside a Darwinian **naturalism**. Like Alfred North Whitehead and Henri Bergson, Dewey was a process philosopher. Beginning with psychology and the philosophy of education, he became systematic, applying his dynamic naturalism to virtually every area of philosophy, from science to logic to politics to aesthetics.

Dewey was also the most prominent philosopher of democracy, arguing that science and democracy are akin. He was famously associated with the American progressive movement. Like William James, Dewey was a genuinely public philosopher, lecturing and taking positions on the public issues of the day. For Dewey, philosophy does not seek the fixed foundations of knowledge or morality; it articulates the methods by which humans change their ideas and actions over time, toward greater integration of experience. ■

> Dewey was also the most prominent philosopher of democracy, arguing that science and democracy are akin.

Name to Know

Dewey, John (1859–1952): The most prominent of the Americanist philosophers, Dewey made major contributions to philosophy, psychology, and education. He was politically active and associated with progressivism.

Important Term

naturalism: Strictly, the view that everything is natural or part of nature, so nothing is supernatural. As such, physicalism and materialism would be versions of naturalism, but the term has often been used more narrowly for views that do not equate the natural with the physical or material.

Suggested Reading

Dewey, *Art as Experience.*

———, *Experience and Nature.*

———, *Reconstruction in Philosophy.*

Questions to Consider

1. How do aesthetic values arise out of ordinary human experience?

2. What is the aim of philosophical reflection?

Dewey's American Naturalism
Lecture 22—Transcript

John Dewey was the most famous philosopher in America through the mid-20th century. He was certainly the most famous of the classical Americanist or pragmatist philosophers. Dewey was a systematic thinker and a public philosopher, taking positions on political issues of the day, involved in experimental education and psychology, and he wrote on everything from logic to aesthetics; he was truly a systematic philosopher. Born in Vermont, Dewey graduated from the University of Vermont, and then received his Ph.D. from Johns Hopkins where he studied with Peirce. After going to teach at the University of Michigan, where he would teach philosophy and psychology, his early interest in Hegelian philosophy was replaced by an attraction to new research in psychology involving G. Stanley Hall of Clark University and the fellow pragmatist William James. He moved to the University of Chicago where he became involved in educational reform. Eventually, Dewey went to Columbia University, where he became the central figure of what would later be known as the school of Columbia naturalism.

What Dewey sought more than anything else was a humanistic naturalism, by which I mean he sought to be a naturalist in such a way that the unique properties of the human mind, ethics, politics, aesthetics, etc. could be incorporated within his naturalism rather than declared irrational and impossible to account for, as with the positivists. Second, Dewey was above all concerned with the philosophical importance of democracy, which is something quite special. That is to say, from Dewey's perspective, it's not really the case that he was a political philosopher interested in giving a conception of democracy; rather it was that he thought the existence of democracy allows us to see things philosophically that couldn't be seen in earlier, pre-democratic political regimes.

While it's usually said of Marx that he "stood Hegel on his head"—meaning that Marx took Hegel's dialectical method and instead of having that method as in Hegel founded in idealism, Marx flipped it around so that his dialectical method was founded on materialism—that quip could equally be made of John Dewey, who began as a Hegelian but whose conversion to Darwinism forced him to reconceive the Hegelian dialectic in naturalistic terms. In other words, once again, he's going to take the evolutionary dialectical perspective that's in Hegel, but regard it as something taking place in nature; a naturalistic Hegelianism, if you will.

One of the earliest indications of this new view of his was an essay that he wrote on "The Reflex Arc Concept in Psychology"; and this is just a little essay, but it's a very good indicator of the kind of thing Dewey was to do for the rest of his career. Psychological learning theory had posited a one-way relation between stimulus and response that could be set up by what was called operant conditioning; for example, Pavlov's dogs salivating whenever they hear a dinner bell after having been trained to expect food, which they associated with a dinner bell in the past. But Dewey pointed out that this so-called reflex "arc" from stimulus, which causes a response, is actually a circuit, or a circle, for perception itself is an act of the organism for which preparation must be made. In other words, it's not the case that the stimulus or the phase in which a stimulus is accepted by the organism is a kind of passive state from which things begin; the state of receptiveness itself is an act of the organism, and that must be a response to something else. Depending on the nature of the stimulus, the organism must be in an attentive, properly oriented state, which itself will be the fruit of a preceding action for the stimulus to register and then create the action that itself sets up the conditions for the next stimulus reception; so while stimulus x precedes response y, x is preceded by a response w, and so on, and so on. You notice here the characteristic pragmatist concern to see everything, including the perception of a stimulus, in the context of activity; the organism is always active.

Dewey was here, as elsewhere in his thought, applying both the Hegelian notion of reality as a process of development and the pragmatic notion of meaning as located in the context of social action. You could, if you want, even say there's a bit of a Kantian element here that is being expressed in pragmatic terms. For Kant, the mind actively structures the perception; for Dewey and the pragmatists, the organism's activity sets up the possibility of the perception in the first. Place. But typically for Dewey, as we'll see in the rest of his thought, like a good Hegelian, Dewey never met a dualism he liked. If you oppose stimulus in response to him, he's going to say they're not totally separate; they're simply two phases of an ongoing process.

Whenever another philosopher sees a dualism of divergent processes, Dewey will always see two phases of a single process. He applied this way of thought to all fields; thus Dewey can legitimately be called, like Bergson and Whitehead, a process philosopher.

Dewey was an unalloyed modernist, a critic of pre-modern thought. From his point of view, Dewey would say classical, Greek, medieval thought made contemplation the point of philosophy. The highest human activity, for Aristotle most of the time and for many of the medieval other than the worship of God, but beyond that the highest human activity is simple contemplation, simple knowing, the recognition of reality and especially the recognition of the most invariant, highest, universal features of reality. The reason, Dewey speculated, was actually quite practical: namely, that for the ancients, action was a debased category because it was linked to the activity of slaves. In other words, Dewey is saying that ancient Greek philosophers valued contemplation so highly and devalued action so greatly because of the social structure in which they exist; this is an almost Marxist point, you might say. But since modern science began with Bacon and Galileo, we've recognized that it is in action or work, the need to reconstruct the world through action, which philosophical problems arise and knowledge advances. The value of action and work has been recognized in the egalitarianism of modern democracy.

But what Dewey wanted to point out was that intellectual problems, too, arise in action, when our habits or rules for behavior confront obstacles. That is to say, at any moment in time, we're engaged in a series of activities, like any organism. Rule-governed activities: Do we refer to habits? A habit is not a bad thing in Dewey, as it is for some romanticists; a habit is simply a regular or rule-governed set of actions, a practice you might say. We're commonly engaged in practices; it's only when those practices break down against anomalous difficulties—that is, when something goes wrong in a practice—that we then raise questions; those questions lead to inquiry, and certain kinds of inquiry are philosophical inquiry. So philosophical inquiry itself, he thinks, gets generated out of social action. Again, one could say this is a bit of a Marxist side to Dewey; that is, the refusal to separate the work of head and hand. But we should mention in passing that Dewey was no Marxist; when asked if he were a Marxist, his response was that he had struggled for many years to free himself from one religion and had no intention of taking on another.

Dewey's merger of thought and practice was best modeled by modern science in its experimental attitude. Knowledge is the fruit of an active response to problems. Philosophy itself grows out of stresses in community life, and its goal is the reconstruction of the conditions of community life toward greatest possible inclusiveness of evidence, of voices, of experiments, just as the scientific community must listen to every theory, every possible solution in seeking its next advance. Science, I should say, is active—and this is crucial to Dewey's perspective—science isn't merely wandering through the woods and writing down observations; modern science has discovered the need for experiment. What happens in experiment? Kant himself had once said that the modern experimental approach to nature doesn't involve simply passively waiting for nature to speak to us, but involves, so to speak, grasping nature by the throat and forcing it to answer our questions yes or no. In other words, we have a hypothesis; we force nature into a very narrow set of experimental conditions, and then we see whether nature gives us a yes or not to our hypothesis. That's a very active, structured process; and what Dewey is claiming is that modern science recognizes the need for an active pursuit of knowledge, that knowing arises in the form of the way we grasp the world after our practices or habits run into trouble, and furthermore science requires that we have open inquiry that includes as many opinions as possible. What's happening is Dewey, like Mill before him, is taking the view that a modern free society—free individualism and egalitarianism—go together with science; there's something common to both of them.

For Dewey, the search for knowledge actually serves human action. This is an important thing, and again, it's very non-Greek. Aristotle had said in the first line of the *Metaphysics*, "All men by nature desire to know." Dewey doesn't say this is wrong, but he says our search for knowledge is, in fact, in service of our need to act and achieve an equilibrium with the world. But, it's important to recognize, this action that leads to truth through inquiry isn't action governed by a simple aim; it's the discovery of heretofore unknown considerations that expand and include more and more of the world and of ourselves. Philosophy, then, for Dewey, actually must be conceived as an attempt to reconstruct the world, including the human world, so as to bring out and exploit finer and previously neglected connections leading to the progressive intelligibility of the world. This may sound like a set of pleasantries, but it's quite a serious criticism of classical, medieval, and even early modern conceptions of philosophy. Philosophy is and has value as part of an ongoing active reconstruction of the conditions of life by human communities. That's what it is, that's what it serves, and it's that in respect to which it has value.

Dewey's metaphysics was, as I mentioned, a "humanist naturalism"; or as we would say today, a naturalism that does not believe complex levels of natural operation can be reduced to their simplest physical components. This means Dewey implicitly accepted something like an emergentist theory: that more complex components act in processes that exhibit properties that aren't exhibited by the parts themselves; so there are novel properties and entities that emerge at higher levels of analysis, there are biological properties and biological entities that are constructed of chemical and physical entities but they are not themselves chemical or physical entities. Physical systems operate at sufficiently complex level; when they do that, novel and irreducible properties are manifested.

For Dewey, mind—while certainly dependent on the complex neural systems, and certainly developed by natural selection—emerges from social communication as the means of adjustment among social organisms. Let's stop here for a moment. This is characteristic of many in the American tradition, characteristic of George Herbert Mead and associates of Dewey's, but Dewey perhaps expressed it most directly and completely: Mind is not a thing; mind is not a mental substance; mind is a type of activity, a means of adjustment, which emerges from social communication among social organisms. Thought is simply reflexive or internalized communication. My thoughts are the communication between, you might say, the different perspectives that I can adopt in social life, and they converse among each other in my mind. For Dewey, social communication is the source of a mind, and not the other way around.

Dewey also had a theory of value in nature; this is another respect in which he's very unlike the positivists or other physicalists. Natural events function in two respects for Dewey: Any natural event can serve as means and or as an end. If it serves as a means, that status of serving as a means signifies that the natural event or property or object leads to other changes, is part of a process; but as an end, a thing is the culmination of a process or change. Anything we could name in nature could willy-nilly serve as a means in one respect, an end in another respect, etc. Human intelligence, for example in science, focuses on the means, the how of the processes by which culminations are achieved; whereas our aesthetic and moral sense perceive and value the ends themselves, we focus on certain events or states of affairs as ends and use those as ends to judge the process, the steps in the process, that lead up to them. The value perspective, there's a long question in philosophy, it's been around a long time, what's the role of values in nature?—what Dewey is claiming is that values are indeed in nature; they are part of our experience of nature, they are part of nature. A value is the status of a natural event as the culmination of a process, as supposed to the means by which the process leads to that culmination.

Like John Stuart Mill before him, as I mentioned, and like Jürgen Habermas—a German philosopher we'll see later in the course—after him, Dewey believed that modern science and political democracy were continuous. This doesn't mean they're identical, but they're on the same page; they're connected to each other, and it's no accident that it is in the context of modern science or societies that developed modern science that we get the modern republican revolutions, democracy, and individualism. Democracy is the widest inclusion of opinions in interaction; and as I've said before, modern science has figured out that it has to do the same. Indeed, a bit like Aristotle, and the political philosopher Hannah Arendt—who we'll also mention later in the course—Dewey makes democracy the only true form of politics. For Dewey, all other types of regimes that are nondemocratic are not other types of political regimes, they are nonpolitical regimes; that is, politics, for Dewey, is the discourse among citizens about their communal life. That is politics. There is certainly power that isn't political, there are certainly institutions and forms of power that impose themselves on the citizenry, but they aren't political forms of power; that power is political which derives from the discourse, social communication, among citizens about their common needs and problems. Again, an authoritarian regime: It's an authoritarian regime, but it's not an authoritarian political regime; in fact, it's the negation of politics.

Dewey's most powerful criticisms of contemporary society were both political and, interestingly enough, aesthetic. They were political in that Dewey felt we have not yet at as a society—and he's speaking above all of 20th century America, but also of related developed societies—mobilized the intelligence of all social members to contribute to the solution of community problems. Dewey was criticized greatly for this by some other 20th century philosophical movements, especially European, or continental, philosophy. The reason was, Dewey seemed to think—and he said this several times—that the biggest problem in social and political philosophy, and social and political institutions in the 20th century, is that we have failed to apply scientific methods to social and political problems. From the point of view of most European philosophers that sounds like a recipe for disaster. Heidegger and others would say, "Listen, social problems are already overrun by science and technology; we don't need more of that, we need less."

But Dewey meant something quite specific. He didn't mean, like Bentham once thought, that we could actually have a mathematical procedure to determine what social policy will lead to the greatest good for the greatest number, and so resolve ethical and political problems with mathematics or science. That's not at all what Dewey meant; what he meant was that in the sciences we have our best model—in the community of scientific enquirers we have our best model—of an open, ongoing inquiry in which people are free to voice their opinions and the group tries out those opinions, and then as a group affirms the ones that work best; that is, they affirm the theory that works best. Dewey thinks that communal problem solving in which all members have a roughly equal right to make a contribution to the solution, to him that is the method of democracy and we need to use that method more and more prominently in our political and social arrangements. In terms of real-world politics, Dewey aligned himself clearly with early 20th century American progressivism, which sought to use state power to restrain corporate behavior and support public institutions, especially in the areas of health and education. Progressivism in the early 20th century, which was represented in part by Teddy Roosevelt, played somewhat the role in the politics of that time that roughly speaking the liberal wing of the Democratic Party has played in American politics since the Second World War.

I said before that one of his set of objections to our society is based on aesthetics. His aesthetic objection is that we tend to engineer of solutions to commercial problems that ignore what he called the consummatory values or ends that endow our activities with meaning. Dewey's criticism of the modern Western aesthetic tradition—and he has an important book called *Art as Experience* on aesthetics—was its self-reduction to what he called the "museum-concept" of aesthetics. In other words, what we have tended to do in modern aesthetics is try to separate the aesthetic from the non-aesthetic, separate art from everything else, idolize art, place it in the museum. This is the museum concept of art: What is art? It's what's over there in that museum; that's where you have aesthetic experiences, or in the theater, or in the concert hall. These are special places and spots where aesthetics is supposed to be enjoyed. But what that also means is the implication that these are the locations to which aesthetics is supposed to be restricted, like a zoo.

Dewey thought the point is rather to recognize the aesthetic dimension of everyday life and enhance it. In particular, he saw commercial America's indifference to aesthetic value as a major failing. For example, our tendency to say the factory must be efficient, and in the name of efficiency we're going to remove anything that might have aesthetic value." Or, the building, the style of architecture is supposed to be efficient above all, and for that reason we're not going to pay attention to aesthetics; aesthetics are to be paid attention to in another part of life. It's this separating out of parts of life and saying one is to be devoted purely to x and another purely to y, this is the kind of dualism that Dewey always opposed. He thought this was a really serious problem: that, especially for the life of the working classes, essentially that life was organized in such a way that aesthetic values were stripped out of most working class experience.

This may seem a strange concern for a naturalist, but Dewey held the aesthetic in very high regard. Experience, for Dewey, has an incorrigibly aesthetic dimension that lies in those consummatory values, those ends of processes, which we take on as goals for ourselves. His own ultimate value, as a moral philosopher, was this—we move into the realm of morality— growth. Dewey espoused the ultimate value of growth. What does that mean? He reviewed moral rules, theories of the virtues, and goals—Dewey reviews the whole history of moral theory, he's entirely familiar with it—and he indeed accepts that there are many different ways of trying to figure out where morality lies in human life: We have theories of the moral virtues that go back to Aristotle, which say that the centerpiece of the moral life is to cultivate certain dispositions or character traits that are good; those are called the virtues. We have utilitarians who say, following John Stuart Mill and Jeremy Bentham, that our goal is to maximize certain results in society like pleasure or happiness. Then we have what are called deontological theories, or theories of moral duty, like from Kant that say there are certain rules of duty, like "thou shalt not lie," which can be proved to be morally obligatory, and it doesn't matter what the results are.

Dewey doesn't want to adopt any of these famous alternatives; again, he wants to transcend oppositions and dualisms. From his point of view, moral rules, virtues, and utilitarian goals are salutary only when they expand the range of the desirable and the valuable, just as science expands the range of truth, or what knowledge, and democracy expands the range of fellow citizens whose opinions matter. What Dewey is saying is: In morality, there is no end point or goal; no ultimate criterion or rule we're trying to reach or embody. The rules of Kant's moral theory, or Bentham's, or Aristotle's are all limited goods, but none of them are adequate for all situations. There is no ultimate moral rule or goal; there is no fixed point to shoot for or judge from; all there is, is growth. There is improvement, but there is no perfect end to the improvement to shoot for. This view was seen by some as relativist; it seemed to imply that Dewey could accept any moral principle if it lead to growth. The view of many was moral philosophy needs to posit an ultimate end or goal, but Dewey refused to do so; he thought that his was part and parcel of his belief in process and evolution. After all, Dewey knew very well, Darwinian evolution—which was part of his inspiration—shows us how things have changed and how there's improvement; but not for a second Darwinian evolution say what the goal or end of that improvement is; there is no such thing, there is no goal of evolution. From Dewey's perspective, what we try to do in human existence and human society is to enlarge and integrate social perspectives; to improve and deal with our problems. But this view of Dewey's was thought by some to be so disturbing, that actually a fellow named Paul Crosser published a book called *The Nihilism of John Dewey*. Dewey, the sober Vermonter, never struck anybody except for

Crosser as a nihilist; but it's important to remember that Dewey, who was now seen as a rather middle of the road figure, when he wrote was actually a rather radical philosopher.

Dewey forged a philosophy that both described the natural world of which humans are a part and explicated the norms of human life as processes. You see, typically in the history of philosophy what we often do, we describe a set of phenomena in process, and then we posit certain norms—like goodness, beauty, or truth—and we take the norm as external to the process and use the norm to criticize or evaluate what goes on in the process. But in Dewey's naturalism, there can't be a distinction; values or norms are imminent in the processes of the world. Beauty, goodness, and truth are all phases of our process of growth, which has no goal or rule outside itself; and that, from his perspective, is what a naturalistic theory has to say.

Heidegger's *Being and Time*
Lecture 23

> The result of Heidegger's analysis ... was shattering. What Heidegger produced was a new kind of phenomenology of appearances as they present themselves in experience.

Martin Heidegger's *Being and Time* (1927) is one of the most influential books of 20th-century philosophy. In it, he aimed to determine the meaning of being itself through the method of Edmund Husserl's phenomenology. His approach was to begin by determining the meaning of that being for whom being is a question: human being, or in his terms, *Dasein*, translated as "being-there." He worked out an analysis of what is it like to be a human being, a finite creature, thrown into and vulnerable to the world, fundamentally anxious in the face of its inevitable guilt and death.

Heidegger created the basis for modern existentialism.

This philosophy was a rejection of Aristotelian substance, Cartesian mental substance, and Kantian and Husserlian transcendentalism. Heidegger put Husserl together with Søren Kierkegaard and Friedrich Nietzsche to forge a new kind of phenomenology that sought the meaning of human existence. In so doing, Heidegger created the basis for modern existentialism: All later existentialists trace their work to *Being and Time*. In his later work, Heidegger took a different direction, but throughout his career he was unfailingly provocative and the most influential continental philosopher of the century. ■

Heidedgger's Existential Analytic of *Dasein* in *Being and Time*

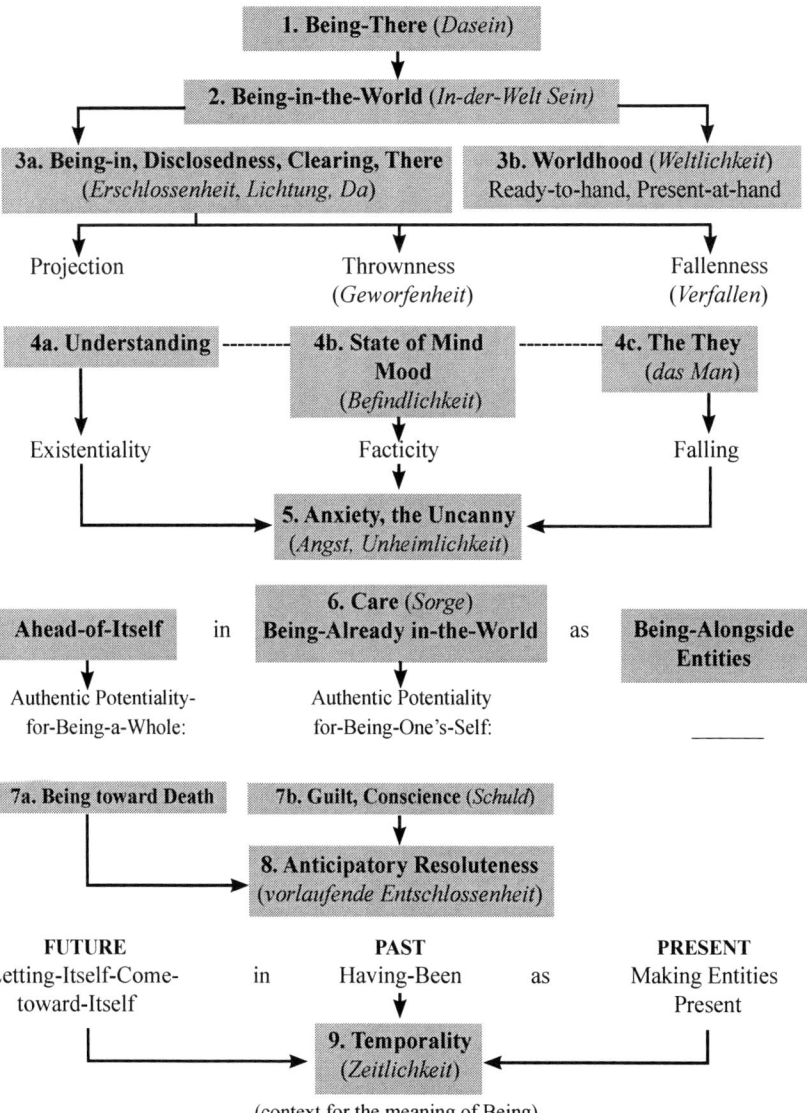

Name to Know

Heidegger, Martin (1889–1976): One of the most influential philosophers of the 20th century, he combined the work of Edmund Husserl's phenomenology with that of Friedrich Nietzsche and Søren Kierkegaard to formulate existential phenomenology. Later, after joining the Nazi Party in 1933 and supporting national socialism throughout the war, he promoted a quasi-mystical philosophy of attentiveness to being.

Suggested Reading

Heidegger, *Being and Time.*

Questions to Consider

1. What is the difference between being and beings?

2. What is anticipatory resoluteness?

Heidegger's *Being and Time*
Lecture 23—Transcript

Heidegger's *Being and Time* is one of the two most influential books of 20th century Western philosophy. Its method is explicitly that of Husserl's phenomenology, which we covered in an earlier lecture, but now Heidegger is going to apply that method to perhaps the biggest philosophical question of all, the question of ontology; that is, what is the meaning of being or existence itself? We will explore the argument of *Being and Time*, from his notions of *Dasein* and *Dasein*'s existential angst or anxiety; being in the world; through being toward death, guilt, and finally temporality. All those are crucial terms in Heidegger's analysis, as we'll see.

Martin Heidegger was born Roman Catholic in humble circumstances, but eventually attended the University of Freiburg where he studied with Husserl. After a spiritual crisis and a conversion to Lutheranism, he completed his graduate work in philosophy, being influenced as well by Aristotle, Kierkegaard, and Brentano, an important late 19th century philosopher. He became a professor of philosophy at Marburg, and his early promise seemed to indicate that he would be the natural heir to Husserl as leader of Husserl's phenomenological movement.

The most fundamental distinction for Heidegger in *Being and Time* is the distinction between, in German, *Sein* (which means "being") and *Seiende* ("beings or things"). Let's pause for a moment and see what that means. What he means is simply this: I'm an entity, you're an entity, and the lectern is an entity; things, beings are entities. All these entities exist. What Heidegger is interested in is not their character as entities, but what it means for them to exist; in a sense, he's looking at existence as an activity: Being, or existence, is something these entities have and do. Heidegger is not interested in entities, except insofar as he wants to go deeper and understand their mode of being or mode of existence, their *Sein* in German.

To do this, Heidegger reformulates Husserl's methodological language in a quite remarkable way. If you think back to Husserl and remember his talk about the transcendental Ego and his roughly Cartesian way of thinking about human experience, all that disappears in Heidegger: talk of the transcendental ego, the natural attitude, even consciousness itself (I'm talking about the language of consciousness, the word "consciousness" is thrown out by Heidegger). Phenomenology is now defined from the point of view of the phenomena. In other words, the way Heidegger uses Husserl's phenomenology to try to, just as Husserl wanted to, understand our primordial basic experience, uninfluenced by science, history, or popular culture, just look at the things themselves as they emerge in experience. Heidegger now describes this project as literally letting what shows itself show itself in the way that it shows itself; which is simply another way of saying we're going to describe what other people call "experience" as the appearances that come before us, and we're going to have no other presuppositions about them, we're going to describe that basic level of experience or evidence.

Heidegger says, in the book *Being and Time*, that while he above all wants to understand the meaning of being per se; and, in fact, that question (what's the meaning of being or *Sein*) is the dominant question of his entire philosophical career. But, he says, you can't just jump into that question; we have to interrogate one kind of entity, and ask about its mode of existence as a way into the question: What is the meaning of existence or being in general? Which entity should we pick? He thinks it's obvious: We ought to interrogate that entity that itself has an understanding of being as our mode of access to being. In other words, instead of asking ourselves what's the mode of being of a rock, a dog, or a plant, we're going to ask what's that specific mode of being of that one entity we know that asks questions about being (in other words, human beings).

Heidegger was very clear that this is just the starting point of his inquiry; in other words, what he says he's going to do is, "I'm really interested in the meaning of being. I'm using the analysis of human beings, of human existence, just as a ladder that I could later kick away." Nevertheless, that further part of his book was never completed or published; in other words, there never was a part of *Being and Time*, or a *Being and Time II* where he moved from talking about *Dasein*'s being to talking about the meaning of all being. We'll see in a later lecture the character of Heidegger's later philosophy; but nevertheless, it can be said that even many of the ideas of his later philosophy were here implicit in *Being and Time*.

The result of Heidegger's analysis—and you haven't seen it yet, but I'll tell you in advance—was shattering. What Heidegger produced was a new kind of phenomenology of appearances as they present themselves in experience, but it's no longer Aristotelian, or Cartesian, or Kantian, or Husserlian. He does not describe us as an ego, a mental substance, a mind inside a physical world; that way of describing things is banished. The human modes of existence, or way of being as he'll present it, are different from that of physical objects or other animals. We aren't just a different thing; we have a different way of existing. The human existence that he's going to describe is the existence of a bodily, active agent, open to, vulnerable to, literally defined in relation to the world; a being that is finite both in time (which means a being that dies) and is finite in its moral capacities (meaning in many ways it is inadequate). In effect, Heidegger produced a wholly new picture of the human subject, an analysis devoid of Aristotelian substances, Cartesian minds, Kantian transcendental activity, and Husserl's transcendental ego; so this is genuinely new.

What we're going to try to do in this lecture is describe Heidegger's analysis of the human mode of being. To do this, before we proceed, let me just give you a brief picture of the whole. Essentially, what Heidegger is going to do is start out with a basic characterization of what he thinks the human mode of being, or of existence, is. He's then going to proceed to analyze this in several steps: He's going to get essentially halfway done; there's one big state that he will complete. When he does that, which is his description of what he calls our "average everyday way of being," the way humans are every day, he comes to the end of that and says, "Wait, there's more, we now have to analyze not just how we are every day, but how we might be if we were authentic or true to ourselves," and that's the second half of being in time; we will go through both. One more part of that is in each of these two stages of analysis, *Dasein*'s existence is going to have a tripartite structure; there are going to be in each case three aspects of *Dasein*'s being, and by the end of our analysis we'll see that those three aspects have something to do with time, with the past, present and future.

Let's begin: Heidegger labels human being as *Dasein*; this word just means "existence" in German, but etymologically—and Heidegger loves etymologies—you can analyze the world into *Da Sein*, "there being," or as it's usually translated, "being-there." This means, for Heidegger, that *Dasein*—which is just his name for us; we are *Dasein*—is a being that's thrown into and open to the world; in other words, *Dasein* is not Descartes' *cogito ergo sum* shut up inside a mind where we have to ask, "How does the mind know the world outside of it?" We aren't like that, we are *Dasein*; that is, beings thrown into the world. Heidegger then says the structure of the existence of *Dasein*—this is the most basic characterization he gives now—is what he calls being-in-the-world. This means a couple of things: First, the world is actually a part of *Dasein*'s existential structure. Unlike Aristotle's *animale rationale* (rational animal), or Descartes' mental substance, *Dasein* is in the world by definition. This he calls the worldhood that we constantly project as we move through our experience.

The core phenomenon of being-in-the-world, in addition to worldhood, is being in, or literally "inness"; this sounds rather strange, but what Heidegger likes to do is take the simplest words he can and find tremendous meaning in them. According to Heidegger, only *Dasein* is in the world, in the sense of being open to it and by its presence, disclosing it. Essentially that means having experiences. Let's stop for a minute: The lectern for Heidegger is within the world, that's just his term for it. I am in the world; in other words, the way I am in the world is a fundamentally different mode of existence than the way the lectern is in the world. Why? Using a different language, you would say, because I experience the world; the lectern doesn't experience anything.

Heidegger goes on to call *Dasein*, in *Dasein*'s inness, the *Lichtung*, which in German means both "light" and "a clearing in the woods." Think of a clearing in the woods. There's a place where it's dark outside and in the clearing it's light, meaning things are revealed, you can see things; you can see the grass, you can see the bushes, you can see rabbits and deer running around. I, *Dasein*, am like a clearing in the woods. Without human beings, there would be just the woods; but when I enter a room or any environment, I bring with me this capacity to experience, which means things get revealed around me. *Dasein* does that to things. In effect, Heidegger is reinterpreting the word "consciousness" and the word "experience" through this notion of the clearing where things are revealed.

Dasein finds in being-in-the-world, as I said before, a tripartite structure. First we're going to look at *Dasein*'s average, everyday being in the world and see how it's characterized in three different ways by this tripartite structure. The first part of this structure is called existentiality. Existentiality, for Heidegger, is the projection of possibilities of disclosing things, and that simply means for him understanding; *Dasein* understands things. For Heidegger, it makes no sense to ask the philosophical question, "Does *Dasein* understand anything? Maybe we're wrong about everything?" For Heidegger, this is just absurd: Human beings always understand things; that's how we experience. We may also misunderstand some things; we carry around with us and project around us a network of meanings in which the objects of experience are revealed and that shows how they are related. *Dasein*, as it lives, is constantly projecting out from itself contexts of possibilities in which experience is revealed to it.

Let's pause for a second to note: Understanding is, for Heidegger, constantly connected with the idea of possibility. When I understand what a chair is, it's not because when I walk into a room and I see an object with a brown seat, metal legs, etc., that from sense data I then make an inference that it's a chair, and what can I do with chairs? Chairs, by definition, I can sit on. When I see or experience the chair, because I'm already familiar with it, I understand the chair in terms of what can be done with it; in other words, its possibilities of use, and possibilities have to do with the future. In other words, understanding is oriented toward the context of possibilities pointing towards possible actions and possible experiences that can be had with an object in the future.

The second existential characteristic of, or part of the structure of, *Dasein*'s existence is facticity, or the fact that we are thrown into the world open and vulnerable to it. That's a rather abstract term; but what Heidegger gets out of this is that *Dasein* is always already characterized by a state of mind or mood. That is to say, my facticity means that I am just in some state or another, some contingent state, at every moment. I am carrying the weight of the just past. You see, mood or state of mind has something to do with the past; something that's happened has put me in a mood, and I carry that mood into my next moment of experience.

The third crucial feature of *Dasein*'s everyday existence is what he calls falling. Falling is the inauthentic identification of *Dasein* with things within in the world. *Dasein*, for reasons that will become clear, typically understands itself through present objects and subjects—that is, other people—in the world. In falling, we submerge ourselves into what Heidegger called *das Man*. Heidegger was always taking everyday German terms and twisting them into a new usage. *Man* in German just means one, as if we're going to say in English, "One shouldn't do that." To say "*das Man*," is to speak of "the One" with a capital "O." It's very similar to what we say in English when we say, "You know what they say"; and that's why the translators of Heidegger have rendered *das Man* as "the they-self." In other words, in our average everyday understanding, or misunderstanding, of being, I identify with both the present entities that surround me in the day—especially the ones I'm after, the objects of desire, money, for example—on the one hand present objects; on the other hand, I am overwhelmed by, and identify myself with, whatever the public culture thinks, whatever they think, whatever the newspapers say. There is here in Heidegger a very basic critique of modern mass culture. Most of us live according to the "they," rather than according to our own, authentic phenomena of existence.

Indeed, *Dasein* flees into the they-self and absorption in things or entities. Why? Because—and now we're going to get Heideggerian existentialism—*Dasein* wants to avoid angst or anxiety. Anxiety isn't a bad thing for Heidegger; anxiety is the proper response to the finite, open-ended nature of human existence. It's only when we begin to feel anxiety—and here we don't have to try to define anxiety too carefully except to say it's not the fear of a specific event, but an open-ended sense of fear or dread about existing as a human being—that fear is a good for Heidegger, because it's only when we feel it that we're beginning to recognize the truth about human existence. The truth of anxiety, and what lies behind it, is *Sorge* in German, or care; and this now brings us to the end of the first half of the book, *Being and Time*. I said there were two stages in the analysis of *Dasein*; we're now at the end of the first one.

What Heidegger claims is that the fundamental truth about everyday human being is that we are care. *Dasein* existentially cares; it cannot not care, its being is an issue for itself. To care is to be anxious; so the preliminary analysis of the everyday existence of *Dasein* is that *Dasein* is care. Heidegger then defines "care"; he gives it again a tripartite structure to reflect the tripartite structure of the analysis that we mentioned earlier: In care, *Dasein* is ahead of itself—in always-being already in the world—as being alongside entities. You'll notice that those three modes: "Ahead of itself" links to understanding and possibility, hence the future; "always-being already in the world" links to the past and mood (state of mind, facticity); and "being alongside entities" connects with the present, which is where the they and the entities surrounding me are. This is the mode of *Dasein*'s existence. The structure of *Dasein*'s existence is tracking those three components: understanding or existentiality, mood and facticity, and finally falling into identification with entities and the they-self in the present.

Such is everyday *Dasein*; and indeed, for Heidegger, everyday *Dasein* is the most fundamental. This is how we are most of the time, in these three modes; combining these three modes. We're typically, as fallen, inauthentic; we're caring most about buying objects, about whatever is on the news, about whatever they around us say, failing to recognize the truth of our existence. Heidegger realizes at the end of part one of *Being and Time* he has to go further to understand what *Dasein* would be if it completed itself; in other words, if it were authentic, in the sense of being truly its own. For authentic *Dasein*, understanding or being ahead of itself, and facticity or always already-being in the world are reconceived in the second half of *Being and Time* in two ways; and there are two crucial aspects to this authentic *Dasein*.

Let's go back to the notion of the ahead of itself, projective, understanding; understanding the possibilities of future: As ahead of itself and projecting its understanding into the future, if we take that understanding of my future as far as it can go, where does it lead? My death; *Dasein* is the only being that knows it's going to die. *Dasein*'s potentiality for being a whole can only mean what Heidegger calls "being toward death." To live toward death doesn't mean go out and try to die, or try to hasten the time or minimize the time between now and then; to live toward death is what's required for an authentic *Dasein*, the recognition that my being is always moving towards its finite end. For Heidegger, who was an atheist at this point and who does not believe in any sense in survival of any part of *Dasein* beyond the grave, my death is my complete ending. So the first part of authentic *Dasein* is living with its being toward death.

As always already having been in the world—remember that's the past related, mood related component of the tripartite structure—*Dasein* has the potentiality of being guilty. What does that mean? Guilt for Heidegger—the German is *Schuld*—means recognizing what I am not. *Dasein* recognizes, if it's authentic, all that it's not, has not ever been, and will not ever be. This is an awareness of a kind of existential guilt in Heidegger. In Heidegger, guilt is, if you will, a good thing; but it means not just guilt in the narrow sense of "did I lie to my wife" or "did I yell at my children," "what particular acts have I done," although that's part of it. It's an awareness of my finitude; just like awareness of my oncoming death is awareness of my finitude in time, awareness of guilt is an awareness of how I am literally, in his German, that I am "full of knots," I am filled with absences and lacks what I haven't been and what I won't be. When *Dasein* incorporates these two recognitions into its self, to use Heidegger's language, it begins to listen to its *Existenz* (meaning its actual mode of being) calling it; it ceases to fall into the they of everydayness, and instead achieves what Heidegger calls "anticipatory resoluteness" (anticipation has to do with death, resoluteness has to do with guilt in the past). Anticipatory resoluteness is a resolute acceptance of my guilt in the anticipation of my death. *Dasein* now is hearing the call of its own authentic existence; it is no longer falling.

It's clear at this point that the structure of being underlies *Dasein*'s existential series of structures; what most underlies it is temporality. Heidegger—I've told you this from the beginning—in the actual book *Being and Time*, it's only towards the end that we suddenly realize, aha, what's been unifying the whole analysis of *Being and Time* from beginning through anticipatory resoluteness is, in fact, the three modes of time: past, present, and future. Now, Heidegger tells us, *Dasein*'s existential structure, the deepest meaning of what my mode of existence is, is, as he says, "Letting-itself come toward itself in having-been as making entities present"; or, to put it more simply, time is one's authentic self coming towards oneself as already always having been there. That is, one recognizes it's always been there, in the act of making entities present or recognizing the presence of entities. In conclusion, *Dasein*'s existence is based in a time structure.

To summarize, we have essentially probed the archaeology of the structure of the existence of human being from (and let's go through some of the stages): from the naming of human being as *Dasein*; to the basic fundamental characterization of *Dasein*'s mode of being as being in the world; to the two structures of world and, on the other hand, being-in or disclosedness or the clearing; then the tripartite structure of understanding, state of mind, and the they; anxiety about these conditions was the clue to then reveal care as the fundamental structure of everyday *Dasein*; but then we being-towards-death and being-guilty as revealing to us the need for anticipatory resoluteness; all of which shows us that what it means to be human above all is to be temporal, to be a finite entity in time. This implies the possibility that time is the context in which being itself must be interpreted; remember we went through all this in order to interpret *Dasein*, but then so we could interpret the meaning of being. Does this mean time is the meaning of being? Heidegger never fulfilled this project, although he came closest in a later essay called "On Time and Being."

Let's step back for a moment and look what we've gotten from Heidegger: Heidegger's impact was enormous. A generation of young German and French students were taken not so much by the search for the meaning of being—in other words, the big, long-term ontological project was not so much what moved most readers of *Being and Time*—but rather Heidegger's existentialism, and this is the beginning of 20th century existentialism in Heidegger's *Being and Time*. For Heidegger gives us a nonscientific account of human being, influenced by his unique readings of the Greeks, Nietzsche, and Kierkegaard. As with Wittgenstein, students were overwhelmed by the power of Heidegger's concentration and depth of thought in his classes; but in Heidegger's case, finitude, death, and resolute action were the lessons to be learned. This way of understanding human existence in terms of finitude without God, without an unending future, but simply recognizing one's limited time as a kind of template or a kind of scaffolding on which one must hang one's own resolute acts, realizing at all times one's limitations and one's guilt; that conception became the core of 20th century existentialism, and it all comes from Heidegger's *Being and Time*.

Existentialism and the Frankfurt School
Lecture 24

> Alienation was the natural theme of European thinkers during the greatest crisis of the 20th century. ... The great theme of this time was the notion that human beings, the human self, is somehow alienated from its surroundings, overwhelmed by modern technologies, overwhelmed by social pressures, by mass culture, and it seemed to many that this was, of course, the worst of times; and that was not an unreasoning judgment.

Just before and during World War II, European philosophers lived the apocalypse, and their philosophies reflected that fact. Their thought, oddly enough, was dominated by prewar German ideas, particularly phenomenology, existentialism, psychoanalysis, and Marxism. The common current of these four systems was that the individual human subject is alienated from and by the social, cultural world, which forces the subject to abandon its own inner, authentic truth.

Two strains in particular were influential: French existentialism learned from Martin Heidegger but also brought Sigmund Freud and Karl Marx into play. The most famous philosophers in this school were **Jean-Paul Sartre**, **Maurice Merleau-Ponty**, **Albert Camus**, and **Simone de Beauvoir**. Another group of continental philosophers developed a unique strain of social criticism, a combination of elements based in Georg Wilhelm Friedrich Hegel, in Marx, and also in Freud. This school of thought was German neo-Marxism. It was seen most famously in the work of the Frankfurt School thinkers **Theodor Adorno** and **Max Horkheimer**—and much later, in

French existentialist Albert Camus.

the work of **Herbert Marcuse**, who strongly influenced the American new left in the 1960s. Each of these new strains came to bleak conclusions about the human prospect, as befitted their era. ■

Names to Know

Adorno, Theodor (1903–1969): One of the prominent thinkers of the neo-Marxist Frankfurt Institute for Social Research, which combined the thought of Karl Marx, Georg Wilhelm Friedrich Hegel, and Sigmund Freud. Adorno is the author of *Negative Dialectics* and, with Max Horkheimer, *Dialectic of Enlightenment*.

Camus, Albert (1913–1960): The French existentialist author of *The Stranger*, *The Rebel*, and *The Plague*. After being rejected by the French postwar intellectual establishment because of his political moderation, he received a deserved rehabilitation as a major moral writer in the late 20th century.

de Beauvoir, Simone (1908–1986): One of the group of French existentialists, she was the author of *The Ethics of Ambiguity*. She also contributed one of the major works of midcentury feminism, *The Second Sex*.

Horkheimer, Max (1895–1973): A member of the Frankfurt Institute before the Second World War, this philosopher was the author of *A Critique of Instrumental Reason* and a collaborator with Theodor Adorno on *Dialectic of Enlightenment*.

Marcuse, Herbert (1898–1979): An associate of the Frankfurt Institute of Social Research, he became most famous later in his career as the theorist of the American new left in the 1960s, through his combination of neo-Marxist and Freudian social analysis.

Merleau-Ponty, Maurice (1908–1961): One of the circle of Second World War existentialists, Merleau-Ponty was perhaps the superior phenomenologist of the group, his works (in particular, *The Phenomenology of Perception*) having remained compelling far longer than those of Jean-Paul Sartre and others.

Sartre, Jean-Paul (1905–1980): The French philosopher who adapted Martin Heidegger's *Being and Time* into French existentialism. A member of the French resistance and a voluminous writer of essays, books, and plays, Sartre was perhaps the most famous philosopher in the world in the two decades after the Second World War.

Suggested Reading

Adorno and Horkheimer, *Dialectic of Enlightenment.*
Barrett, *Irrational Man.*
Marcuse, *One-Dimensional Man.*
Sartre, "Existentialism as a Humanism."

Questions to Consider

1. What ethics can be drawn from existentialism, other than a commitment to be fully conscious rather than in bad faith?

2. How can it be that enlightenment is simultaneously the only source of a free society and, by itself, leads inevitably to totalitarianism?

Existentialism and the Frankfurt School
Lecture 24—Transcript

Before the Second World War, young French philosophers traveled to Germany to hear Heidegger and become converts to phenomenology and to Heidegger's existential analytic of *Dasein*. They then began to develop their own "existential phenomenology," adding psychoanalytic concepts to their stew; at about the same time, German political philosophers in Frankfurt, Germany, who were also incorporated psychoanalysis into their neo-Marxist views. We will examine these two schools of thought, which became prominent during the worst crisis of the modern West. We will also see Heidegger's reaction. In a sense, the topic of today's lecture is, "What did you do during the war, Daddy?" asked of three European philosophical movements. What we are not doing is a general survey of all the different stances and responses to the greatest crisis of the 20th century that different philosophers took or could have taken; we're just looking at three in particular whose philosophies, you might say, of crisis ripened in the greatest crisis of the modern West.

First the existentialists: Unlike Heidegger, they brought Freud and Marx into play. Heidegger, of course, is the beginning of modern 20th century existentialists, but the French who learned from him added some new elements; as I said, Freud and Marx. They also become world famous as literary writers in addition to being philosophers. I'm speaking of, above all, Jean-Paul Sartre, but as well, Albert Camus, Simone de Beauvoir, and Maurice Merleau-Ponty. Once the war came, the French existentialists that I've just mentioned were all active in the French resistance, and war experiences fueled their sense of existentialism. French existentialism, as Sartre defined it, makes existence logically and temporally prior to essence, at least in the case of human beings; this is a pretty dry definition, but it has direct meaning that we can understand.

If you went back to Aristotle or Aquinas, both would agree that for humans, our essence—and when you hear that word, you could just substitute "definition" or "our nature"— or definition is logically and temporally prior to our existence. Philosophers distinguish logical and temporal priority. Something is temporally prior to something else if it comes before; Monday is temporally prior to Tuesday. Logical priority, though, is just as important, in some cases more important. A is logically prior to B if the concept of B depends on the concept of A. For example, the concept of pitching is logically dependent on the concept of baseball; so the concept of baseball is logically prior to the concept of pitching. I can't explain pitching to you unless I explain baseball first. At any rate, for Aquinas and Aristotle, they both would have held that humans have a nature independent of and before they actually exist in the world. From Aquinas's point of view, simply, God dictates that nature; we're built as God wishes us to be, so God gives us an essence. From Aristotle's point of view, it's not a God that's necessary, it's simply that human beings all have a certain nature, we're born according to that nature or plan and then we exist. But existentialism claims that we're thrown into existence without an essence or definition, either from God or from nature. What does that mean? In effect, we're free to make and define ourselves in action.

Sartre was by far the most famous of the French existentialists. His metaphysical views, formulated in his most complicated philosophical work named *Being and Nothingness*, were actually remarkably Cartesian. In that book—we won't go into it in great depth—what Sartre tried to say was think of being as matter; in other words, think of all being as stuff, things. Consciousness is utterly unlike everything in the universe; consciousness is, therefore, a kind of "non-being." One way to think of this is, think of consciousness as no thing, not a thing; for Sartre, consciousness is a pure intentionality. He actually used the metaphor it's a "wind blowing toward objects." This sounds utterly negative, but it's that negativity that gives consciousness a freedom unique in reality. That is, for Sartre—and this is one of Sartre's most famous doctrines—we human beings are absolutely free; nothing can determine our mental attitudes or our consciousness, except our mental attitudes or our consciousness. We are free and we get no guidance from anything outside our selves; that is to say, if we're authentic we get no guidance from outside ourselves. Of course, most human beings try to get guidance from everything; but from Sartre's point of view, neither God, nor nature—God doesn't exist for Sartre in the first place; nature exists but is totally irrelevant to what human beings are, because we are, again, consciousness, which is totally unlike anything in nature, and human society.

None of these things can tell us how to live, we must simply choose; we're utterly free.

But such freedom is terrifying, and humans commonly flee from the anxiety and dread it causes. Here's the notion of angst, which we saw in Heidegger. Where do we normally flee? We flee into what Sartre called "bad faith." "Bad faith" can be very simply defined: it's lying to one's self. In bad faith, I lie to myself about one existence. Usually this is done by identifying my self or my consciousness with something fixed and material, something that has no free choices and is filled with excuses to escape responsibility. To pause for a moment: The flip side of the notion of freedom, if we're absolutely free, then we're also absolutely responsible; I can never give an excuse, I can never say, "Well, I had to do it because of what my parents taught me; the culture I lived in, the world, something conspired to make me live my life in a way I would not have. If you chose to do it, you're responsible for it, in Sartre's perspective.

Sartre also parlayed Hegel's master-slave dialectic—which we saw in an earlier lecture—into a modern theory of the power games in human relations, sexual in particular. In fact, Sartre remains one of the few philosophers— at least until the last decade or two; one of the few, let's say, classical or famous philosophers— to write insightfully about sex, even if sometimes from a jaundiced point of view. While existentialism may seem apolitical, the French version considered it a philosophy of engagement; for the choices of the self are revealed only in action. Action reveals the self; and in their context, radical choice was always thrust in their faces. To ignore the Nazi presence during the Nazi occupation of France, or to collaborate, or to fight; but in the case of fighting, to risk not only one's own death but the reprisals to others. That is why Sartre wrote, "We were never as free as during the German occupation." What he meant was that during the German occupation, when you stepped out of your apartment door and onto the street and saw a German soldier with a rifle, you could not ignore that you had an absolute choice as to whether to knuckle under or to fight.

One of Sartre's most famous plays, called *The Flies*, is an adaptation of the Greek tale of Orestes; Orestes is the ancient Greek who must decide whether to avenge his father's murder. This play was produced during the Nazi occupation. Sartre later said that he had written *The Flies* because he couldn't write the play he really wanted to write; meaning he couldn't produce under the Nazi occupation the play he really wanted to write. What he really wanted to write would have been the story of a young man of the French resistance who must decide whether to assassinate a German official, knowing full well that in reprisal the Germans would kill many French citizens. If you think about that for a moment, for Sartre, the choice of whether or not—this is part and parcel of Sartre's existentialism—to participate in the resistance, or refuse or to collaborate, Sartre doesn't presume that there's an obviously right answer to this question. For him, it's a deep existential choice, and God, nature, society, and philosophy, the history of human reason, none of these things can tell us what the right thing to do is. The way Sartre would put it is: Even if someone gives you a great philosophical explanation of what you should do, you still have to decide whether to agree with it or not; so you never get away from free choice. In the case of the young man who must decide whether or not to fight with the resistance or do nothing, but where fighting risks great reprisals, that young man, to fight in the resistance, must say to himself, "I am choosing to fight in the resistance even though 40 schoolchildren may be shot." Sartre wishes to push our face up against the consequences of our actions and leave us dangling there to make the choice on our own.

Of the existentialist group, Camus was the moderate liberal, and eventually rejected by the far more left-leaning Sartre and Merleau-Ponty. He was nevertheless arguably the superior literary figure of the group, his works including things like *The Myth of Sisyphus*, *The Plague*, and *The Rebel*. But there were others as well, especially Simone de Beauvoir. Simone de Beauvoir is best remembered as one of the most prominent feminist authors of the mid-20th century; she's the author of *The Second Sex*. She was close to Sartre and also wrote one of the most interesting, perhaps the best book, written by any of the major existentialists on ethics, her book called *The Ethics of Ambiguity*.

Then there was Merleau-Ponty: Merleau-Ponty remains perhaps the most interesting philosopher of the group; and what I mean is, particularly as a phenomenologist; remember that Sartre, de Beauvoir, Merleau-Ponty acknowledge that they are using Husserlian phenomenology then modified by Heidegger. They all think they're phenomenologists. Merleau-Ponty is the one who went on to make the most interesting modifications to phenomenology; in fact, one could argue—to refer to an earlier lecture—that just as the German idealist philosopher Schelling pressed the categories and ideas of German idealism so far that he almost became a naturalist, Merleau-Ponty virtually did the same thing: pressed the perspective of phenomenology so far that it almost became a kind of naturalism. In particular, he did that in his book *The Phenomenology of Perception*, another book *The Primacy of Perception*, and finally *The Visible and the Invisible*.

At the same time as the existentialism was growing and becoming this powerful movement, partly through the crisis of the war, at the same time and a little before in Frankfurt, Germany, there had been a school of neo-Marxist social critics—this is now before Hitler came to power in 1933—and this school of social critics developed their own unique strain of social criticism, a very famous kind of stew or combination of elements based on the one hand in Hegel, on the other hand in Marx, and then also in Freud. This, again, is a little strange, because you could argue that Freud and Marxism really shouldn't have much to do with each other. This school of thought claimed they did have much to do with each other. The most famous of these were Theodor Adorno, Max Horkheimer, and later, Herbert Marcuse, who actually became an American philosophy professor long after the Second World War and was a crucial figure in the American "new left" of the 1960s.

What the Frankfurt School theorists did was integrate psychoanalysis and Hegel with their neo- or Western Marxism. When we say "Western Marxism," we mean a Marxism that tries to avoid Leninist party authoritarianism and seeks to be compatible with Western democracy. In other words, somebody trying to be a Marxist but avoid the Gulag, avoid the slave-labor camps of Stalin, find a kind of Marxism that's compatible with Western democracy and individualism; not compatible with capitalism, but with democracy and individualism. That's what the people called Western Marxists were trying to do, and the Frankfurt School was one of the most famous groups trying to do that.

After Hitler came to power, as you might imagine, they were forced to leave Germany in 1933. In exile, Adorno and Horkheimer begin composing a radical work called *Dialectic of Enlightenment*, a deeply pessimistic answer to what was to them the fundamental question: How in the world at the height of European civilization, at the moment in the 20th century where it looks like we have the most sophisticated kind of society, many democracies (at least in central and western Europe), a concern for individualism and individual rights; how could, exactly at this moment, European civilization turn into the most regressive barbarism that's ever been seen? What they mean is Fascism in general, which is all over Europe, but especially, of course, Nazism. The Frankfurt School is literally trying to say, "How could it be that at the height of European civilization, at the height of what seems the most rational civilization in history based on rational science, could we see this most irrational barbarism develop? The anti-Semitism, the Holocaust, the camps; how could this happen here, so to speak?

They tried to find a deep answer. They argued that since the time of Homer, all through Western civilization, the differentiation of the ego of the aristocracy from the body, women, slaves, and the rest of nature had been the way of Enlightenment. That is, progress, whatever good it brought, came at the price of separation of the rational ego of those in power from the emotion, from the body, and from others. Let's pause; this is a very abstract point, but let's see what this means. What they have in mind is this; and it comes partly from Hegel, partly from Marx, and now, you can see, partly from Freud: The notion is the self of the individual who seeks power—the members of the aristocracy; in the modern world, the members of the capitalist bourgeoisie—must differentiate itself from the lower classes; those in power must say, "I am not like them." How do they do that? They have to repress in themselves—they're using a Freudian concept—their own bodily impulses in those things that they have in common with the lower classes; and with the lower classes might also be included women, all other races, as well as lower economic classes. In other words, between he or whoever is in power and those who are to be controlled there has to be a differentiation of self-understanding; the ruler must think, "I alone am in control of myself; my ego or self or mind is in control of my body. That's not the case for those disgusting people lower down in the socioeconomic scale."

But modern scientific rationality since the 18th century—this Adorno and Horkheimer claim—has performed a critique of this rational ego or self, emptying it of concrete values, sentimental commitments, and religious metaphysics, leaving only a supremely powerful instrumentally rational center of power, whose sense of self flourishes in separating it from all others. In short, what they are claiming is—Adorno and Horkheimer are trying to say—that we are left with an ego that can do anything but believes in nothing. If we pause here for a moment, you might hear in this something interesting: These Marxists are producing a social criticism of the modern Western world that is almost a little conservative—that is, it starts to sound like some political conservatives—namely the claim that a problem with the modern West is that it has lost belief in substantial moral norms and such things. That is, indeed, what they're claiming; what they're saying is the modern world was based on reason or rationality—rational science, the belief that every person is rational therefore they can have democratic freedom—the belief in rationality has been central. What they're saying is, however, the more you base social order on reason alone, the more you discover that reason has nothing substantive to say morally. Their loathsome example of this is actually—and they use this in the book—the philosophical pornography of the Marquis de Sade. This sounds like a very bizarre example, but essentially what they argue is the more the modern scientific consciousness becomes sophisticated, the more it believes in nothing; and when it believes in nothing, it is led to use other human beings as objects for any kind of pleasure.

The unhappy conclusion to this (and it is very unhappy, if you take it seriously) is that the enlightened self—the whole notion of the Enlightenment, the 18th century; we've talked about before: the belief that we're entering a new age where if we get rid of superstition and, perhaps to some extent, tradition, aristocracy, and the slavery of the past, and if instead we're going to enter an era where the scientific rational search for truth is going to join with enlightened leadership, individual liberty, and equality; that whole Enlightenment notion, freedom and power coming together—what Adorno and Horkheimer warn is that in shedding the trappings of tradition and nature and religion, this enlightenment self turns into the Fascist self, capable of any act of subjugation of others. The implication—and they say this explicitly, actually—is that while social freedom, the modern notion of a free society (liberalism and democracy) is dependent on enlightened thought, enlightenment thought must inevitably destroy itself in a new kind of barbarism, and that was called Fascism in general and Nazism in particular.

This was a very unhappy conclusion, because what it tried to claim is—and this is why the title of Adorno and Horkheimer's text is *Dialectic of Enlightenment*; we've seen the word "dialectic" used in various places in the course, for example in Hegel; but really all it means here is the self-undermining or self-negating of enlightenment—there's something about the modern view of the world that emerged in the 18th century that is self-undermining; and they're saying this as fans of the Enlightenment. They're saying the Enlightenment that we, Adorno and Horkheimer, have believed in all our lives and tried to extend, it looks like there's something about it that is self-undermining and self-destructive. In other words, enlightened thought leads to Fascism; that's the conclusion.

Meanwhile, while on the one hand we saw the French existentialists responding to the great crisis of the middle of the 20th century without religion, without guidance from society, looking towards this pure existentialism of individual freedom, and on the other hand we've seen Adorno and Horkheimer of the Frankfurt School coming to the conclusion that enlightenment thought is self-undermining and self-destructive, the author of existential phenomenology and the person who actually started existential phenomenology made his own choices. In 1933, all German university officials were required to take a loyalty oath to the Nazi regime. Heidegger, who was the rector—or you might say the dean—of Freiburg University, agreed. Beyond this, Heidegger continued to speak out all during the prewar years from 1933 to 1939 in the most forceful terms in favor of Hitler and the crucial role Germany ought to play as the European leader confronted by the uncivilized powers of America and Russia. In other words, Heidegger was a Nazi; he chose to be a member of the Nazi Party.

Twenty or 30 years ago, many philosophers that I knew, and perhaps myself as well, thought that this just meant that Heidegger maybe was an absent-minded professor who made a kind of silly mistake, etc.; but much work has come to light in the last 20 years to show that this was not true. Heidegger was committed to National Socialism; he wrote speeches calling Hitler the destiny of the German people; he continued to pay a party subscription fee to the Nazi Party until 1945, until there was no party any longer. For some people, especially some philosophers—we are, after all, talking about someone everyone admits is one of the two or three greatest philosophers of the 20th century—that doesn't mean you have to agree that Heidegger is right, but it's very hard to say that he's not one of the most supremely important 20th century philosophers. But Heidegger, for the rest of his career, refused to admit that his association with the Nazi Party was an error; he refused to speak against the Holocaust. In fact, at one point—Heidegger spent the remaining decades of his life writing philosophy, also teaching it, but distancing himself from public conversation—he granted a magazine interview, and in that interview he was asked, "What about the Holocaust? What about the murder of all these Jews?" Heidegger's response was to say, "Well, you know, the Sudeten Germans suffered greatly, too"; he was referring to the fact that in western Czechoslovakia after the war ended, many of the local Czechs made refugees out of the Germans that had lived in Czechoslovakia before then.

What does this leave us with? Alienation was the natural theme of European thinkers during the greatest crisis of the 20th century. All of them—on the one hand the existentialists, on the other hand the Western Marxists, their notion of alienation partly taken from Marx, partly taken from Weber—the great theme of this time was the notion that human beings, the human self, is somehow alienated from its surroundings, overwhelmed by modern technologies, overwhelmed by social pressures, by mass culture, and it seemed to many that this was, of course, the worst of times; and that was not an unreasoning judgment. But all this attitude was to change at bit in the years to come; and as we'll see in the next few lectures, philosophy entered a new and still perhaps disturbing phases in the far less horrifying but still tense atmosphere of the Cold War.

Heidegger's Turn against Humanism
Lecture 25

In Heidegger's *Being and Time*, his true goal was the meaning of being itself; he only chose the analysis of *Dasein*'s way of existence as a mode of access to the larger question of the meaning of being. But in his later work—and this essentially means very shortly after *Being and Time*—he came to see his original starting point with *Dasein* as a humanist or anthropocentric mistake; this is to say, he came to reject what was most existentialist in his early work.

Martin Heidegger made clear that the existential analysis of *Dasein* in his monumental *Being and Time* was merely a mode of access to the more important question: What is the meaning of being? After *Being and Time*, his thought underwent a self-confessed turn in which, instead of conceiving *Dasein* as the clearing where phenomena are revealed, being reveals itself through *Dasein*: The active party is being.

> **It is being that has alternately concealed and revealed itself through different epochs of human history.**

During and after the war, Heidegger concluded that since Plato, through René Descartes and Immanuel Kant, Western philosophy has projected its concepts onto being, conceiving itself as the active power. Modern technology, which treats being as mere resources to be appropriated, is just the most complete expression of this ancient philosophic attitude. But this was always an illusion: It is being that has alternately concealed and revealed itself through different epochs of human history. Heidegger considered the United States and the Soviet Union the epitome of this domination of being, whose only hope lay in the Greco-German cultural heritage. ∎

Heidegger's "Question Concerning Technology"

In "The Question Concerning Technology," Martin Heidegger produced a theory in which technology enframes beings as "standing reserve." What he means by this is that technology treats being as stuff. At the same time, technology enframes beings that way, meaning the use of modern technological devices, along with the scientific theories that understand them, imposes a framework through which we understand the world. He is saying that in our age, there is this new threat to our understanding of being: Science and technology are themselves the completion of the task of metaphysics that began with Plato, which treated being through presence or the present, one mode of time, and projects onto this presence the idea, the concept, a creation of the philosophical imagination. In other words, being is then shrunk to what is present, and the present is made dependent on the mind's ideas.

How can we overcome this, our ignoring being as it reveals itself to us? This can only be overcome by returning to the notion of *aletheia*, of truth as unconcealment rather than as accurate representation or propositional truth. Only then can we safeguard the mysterious non-entitative disclosure of being. Being discloses itself; there is mystery in that. Our job is to think that without destroying it; and the philosophical tradition destroys it, or rather destroys the possibility of thinking about it in any deep way. But overcoming technology does not mean rejecting or destroying it; it means returning to the concealed truth that technology has covered over. That technology was itself a creative act; attending to the creative act of the invention of technology can be a way to understand what lies beneath the technology. Always the aim for Heidegger in his later period was to look back historically to the fork in the road; at some point in the fork in the road, human beings create something novel. That creation can teach us something, because being has disclosed something to us whenever we create something new. But quickly we get so concerned with the created thing, with the new technology, that we forget the being that lies under it. The technology fascinates us and lets our attention pass over without noticing its origin. What we need is not the absence of technology but sensitiveness to the truth, what he thinks of as the originary *aletheia*; what is originally being disclosed by the creation and use of the technology.

Suggested Reading

Heidegger, "On the Essence of Truth," "The Question Concerning Technology," and "Letter on Humanism," in *Martin Heidegger.*

Questions to Consider

1. Which is ontologically prior, truth or being?

2. How can a recognition of the origin of technology liberate us from treating being as enframed?

Heidegger's Turn against Humanism
Lecture 25—Transcript

In the last few lectures, we have outlined the initial movements of 20th century philosophy: on the one hand, the search for an ideal language and a foundation for science in analytic philosophy; and on the other hand, the search for the ultimate language of experience, the sources of meaning in the self in continental philosophy, what we might particularly call "philosophies of the subject." In the next three lectures—this one and the two after—we're going to chart the demise of those views: the beginning of the collapse, on the one hand, of foundationalism, the view that we can find the ultimate sources of human knowledge that can, in Descartes' old sense, give us certainly or great reliability in our knowledge of the world; and, on the other hand, simultaneously, the collapse of the philosophies of the subject, the view that the human subject, his or her experience, while perhaps alienated in the common social world, nevertheless is the true source of meaning. This demise, the joint demise, of the philosophies of the subject on the one hand and of foundationalism on the other will ultimately lead both continental and analytic philosophy into forms of what are called postmodernism, for which it will seem (for postmodernism it will seem) that all the metaphysical and epistemological aims of modern philosophy since the 17th century—that is, since the beginning of our course in Descartes—were bankrupt. We're going to start the discussion of this demise with a return to Heidegger.

In Heidegger's *Being and Time*, his true goal was the meaning of being itself; he only chose the analysis of *Dasein*'s way of existence as a mode of access to the larger question of the meaning of being. But in his later work—and this essentially means very shortly after *Being and Time*—he came to see his original starting point with *Dasein* as a humanist or anthropocentric mistake; this is to say, he came to reject what was most existentialist in his early work. In today's lecture, we will follow his "turn" through a number of crucial essays on the essence of truth, humanism, his new interest in technology, and his call, not unlike the early Wittgenstein's—if you remember from a few lectures ago—for an end to philosophy itself. At any rate, that's where he's going to end up.

More and more, Heidegger was drawn to Greek etymologies of currently used philosophical terms, because he came to see the entire Western tradition since the Greeks as a kind of error, a mistaken approach to being. I might say in passing here, this mistaken approach was connected to the notion of "fallenness" in *Being and Time*, because if you remember in *Being and Time*, our fallen everyday selves concerned with the they-self and things, that's the component of the structure of *Dasein*'s existence that deals with the present. For Heidegger, the focus on what he called "presence"—things here and now, in this moment, understood outside the context of time—is part and parcel of the mistake of Western philosophy throughout his history. His solution, though, is not to replace Western philosophy's mistaken concepts with a new set of concepts, but to think carefully what was being revealed in the very origin of the error at the beginning of Western philosophy; to return to the fork in the road, so to speak, where the wrong fork was taken, and meditate on that moment. His later work became an unremitting criticism of the whole genre of Western philosophy, a truly radical view.

Heidegger turned, as I've already said, more towards being; that is, he's trying to, as he'll say, think the meaning of being without thinking through or following *Dasein*. He continued to press his all important ontological difference, as he called it, between being and beings; that's what we started with in *Being and Time*, he still totally accepts that, he's looking for the meaning of being, not the meaning of beings. He recognized that being, as he understood it, could not be formulated and described in the propositional language of traditional philosophy, logic, and science. That's crucial: He's beginning to think so radically that he believes to try to talk about the meaning of being, you have to abandon the very logical form of the proposition and of discussion that most philosophical inquiries engage in. Indeed, being, in a certain sense he says, is equivalent to "nothing," in the sense of "no-thing," not being a thing, not being an entity at all. Crucial to this change—or as he himself called it, the *Kehre*, or "the turning" in German—in his thought was the concept of truth; and that's where we're going to start.

In *Being and Time*, Heidegger had defined truth not as correspondence— you remember one of the three most prominent philosophical or standard philosophical definitions of truth; one of them is correspondence, the other being coherence and the pragmatic notion of truth—as it's traditionally thought of, but through the ancient Greek word for truth, *aletheia*, which means "disclosure" or "unconcealment." At one level, all that really means is, nothing really fancy: Instead of thinking about truth as a characteristic of propositions, beliefs, or ideas in our heads, what we mean by "truth" most fundamentally is just that things are revealed to us. In *Being and Time*, remember, he had called man "the clearing," *Lichtung* in German, meaning both "light" and "a clearing in the woods." Man, or *Dasein* (human being), is, in effect, the place where being reveals itself; that's his way of saying what other philosophers would mean by saying, "We experience the world." Now he says—because he wants to avoid the discussion of *Dasein* and being in time—the way he is going to describe the human being as disclosure, he's now going to say being is responsible for the disclosure and for concealment; that is to say, truth is when being reveals itself; falsehood or error is when being conceals itself.

He wrote an essay in 1943, "On the Essence of Truth," and appended to it in 1949 a note that made this clear. Heidegger wrote, "The essence of truth is the truth of essence." If we could pause for a moment, Heidegger's late philosophy is famously difficult, and I don't mean to imply that it in any way can be understood simply. But there is a bit of a code here, which, if you understand it, you can understand these terms. When Heidegger says, "The essence of truth is the truth of essence," he simply means that the essence or being of truth, what truth really is, is the unconcealment of being; it's being's self-disclosure. Again, he's merely turning around, so to speak, what we might say is the subject and the predicate; it's not that I reveal the world by my presence, it's that being reveals itself through me. Being, he then says, is a kind of "sheltering that lightens," that in its nature shows or conceals itself. He says this remains unthought in philosophy; in other words, philosophy, by nature, since Plato, has been unable to see this. Philosophy cannot get beyond—Western philosophy since Plato—cannot get beyond the *Lichtung* or the light that *Dasein* brings to see that what is lightened or revealed is made so by being itself in its various epochs of history. In other words, we are turning the tables on the idealism that began with Kant and was continued in a different way by Husserl.

Heidegger presses his critique far enough to regard his own *Being and Time* as an outworn continuation of that tradition; in other words, *Being and Time* was wrong, he thinks, in a deep way. All of these works, from Plato through his own *Being and Time*, shared a humanism. What does this mean? For Heidegger it means, the philosophical tradition in the West has conceived being through human being or *Dasein*, or some feature of *Dasein* like experience, or ideas, or understanding, or concepts. One could think here of Descartes' notion of the mental substance, or of Kant's synthetic a priori, claiming that being or the world is always understood through some piece of ourselves, some piece of our mind, the synthetic a priori. Heidegger now tries to portray what appears—whatever appears, that's phenomena, reality for us—as the work of being's self-disclosure; all former philosophical thought is now seen by Heidegger as human-centered and anthropocentric, and that's a bad thing.In a series of lectures on Nietzsche, Heidegger remarkably holds that Nietzsche's will to power—Nietzsche's notion that we saw in an earlier lecture that, in effect, nature itself can be seen as sheer power; an idea he partly gets from Schopenhauer—is actually the fulfillment of the metaphysics of ideas begun by Plato. This seems very strange; Nietzsche and Plato. Nietzsche certainly didn't think he was continuing anything that Plato had said. But what Heidegger is saying is the heart of Western thought's approach to being is power; the attempt has always been to understand being through and in terms of something about us, to put humanity in the center, not being, and thereby gain a kind of conceptual control of being. Humanism is now a very bad thing in Heidegger's thought.

The Platonic form, Plato's notions of forms, the ideas, like Kant's Copernican revolution—which says that experience or reality or objectivity must conform to my concepts rather than the other way around—in each case, just as in the natural tradition and Aristotelian substances and modern science and technology, in all these aspects of the Western tradition, being is made subject to human creations; in other words, we think of being as something over which we have control, as something that's strained through, some feature of our understanding. For this reason, Heidegger thinks, this is an expression of what Nietzsche would call "our will to power"; he's literally saying the whole history of Western philosophy is an expression of human will to power, by which we seek to dominate being rather than understand it.

This led to some fascinating analyses. In the 1947 paper *Letter on Humanism*—Heidegger wrote in response to a young French scholar—and Heidegger in that letter, which has been published as an essay, repudiates Sartre's explicit identification of existentialism with humanism. For Sartre, existentialism and humanism are almost the same thing, because, as you remember, in Sartrean existentialism there is no God, nature, no society to guide me and tell me what to do; Sartre has, you might say, a Promethean heroic notion of the human subject—I must choose on my own—and that's what gives human beings our dignity. Existentialism, by negating God in Sartre's version, left us with ourselves; nature in Sartre really doesn't matter, it's just being not consciousness, which is an entirely different kind of thing; and so, far Sartre, humanism and existentialism are pretty much the same thing. That is exactly what Heidegger is now criticizing, because Heidegger now says all humanism did was provide man with a warrant to override and dictate a conceptual scheme to being.

Humanism is certainly traditionally connected with idealism and subjectivity; that is, the notion that the human subject is the center of things, or is the most valuable of things, or is that through which we understand the world, in that only in this center, in human beings, can we find a reflection of true being. This has always been true in the Western religious traditions, namely that I live in a natural world but if I'm created in the image and likeness of God, somehow I have a closer relationship to the origin of all things to being itself than does everything else I find myself surrounded by in nature. In this sense, Sartre's humanism is just an extension, for Heidegger, of the history of Western metaphysics, whose inner meaning was made most explicit in Nietzsche's will to power, as we saw. A "true" humanism, Heidegger says—if we were turn humanism into something that recognized the truth of being—we would recognize that the essence of the human is simply its openness to being.

Heidegger says man is not, and should not conceive him or herself, as the "lord" of being but as the "shepherd" of being. He writes in the conclusion to his essay on humanism, "The thinking that is to come is no longer philosophy, because it thinks more originally than metaphysics, a name identical to philosophy." What that means is philosophy itself, like metaphysics—which, as we've treated it in this course, is traditionally that part of philosophy that tries to understand the nature of things—throughout the Western tradition have placed humanity at the center, rather than being itself; and that must come to an end, he thinks, if we are to think in any new way.

In his 1953 essay, "The Question Concerning Technology," Heidegger writes and produces a quite interesting theory in which he says that technology enframes beings as "standing reserve." Let's explain that for just a moment. What he means by this, by "standing reserve," he simply means—and the German term here is just *Be-stand*—technology treats being as stuff; a good metaphor for standing reserve would be the inventory in a warehouse, all the materials waiting to be used. At the same time, he says technology enframes beings that way; meaning the use of modern technological devices, along with the scientific theories that understand them, justify them, and are used in operating modern technologies, technology in this broad sense imposes a framework or a structure through which we understand the world. In a sense, this treats all being as resource or inventory; a status that covers over the being that is disclosed. What he's saying is we in the modern world no longer experience being as it disclosed itself to earlier epochs of human beings. At all times in history, being has disclosed itself, and also concealed itself; in other words, we understand some things and not others. Heidegger's not claiming that somehow in the past all was disclosed; there's no such thing.

But he is saying that in our age, there is this new threat to our understanding of being: Science and technology are themselves the completion of the task of metaphysics that began with Plato, which treated being through presence or the present, one mode of time, and projects onto this presence the idea, the concept, a creation of the philosophical imagination. In other words, being is then shrunk to what is present, and the present is made dependent on the mind's ideas. Let me give you an example of this, this is a bit abstract. In a typical philosophy class—and I've spoken this way myself, let's say when we were treating Descartes' epistemology, or looking at Hume or at Locke—what I would typically say, what a philosophy professor would typically say, is ok, here's an object, a lectern, how do we know the lectern? What is the lectern? I have certain sense data or experiences I get from the lectern; I have a consciousness; somehow my consciousness represents the lectern; we'd have all sorts of arguments about how that's possible, how that could be, how can it work, does the lectern really exist independent of my own representations of it? All that kind of stuff that philosophers do.

What Heidegger is saying: At the very moment that I frame the question that way, I've already completely obliterated any chance of thinking of being, because what I've done from the beginning is I've shrunk time to the present moment, said, in effect, what's here right now? Here's a physical object, a bit of presence, a thing. It has no other meanings or roles in life, I don't look at its possibilities, I don't look at its history, I don't look at where it's going or where it's been, I take it here now, ignore everything else; I shrink being to the present moment—which for Heidegger is a very bad thing to do—and then I try to use ideas and say, "The ideas presently in my mind are the key to understanding the thing." I both shrink to the present, and at the same time I claim that the concept of "lectern" in my head is somehow the key to understanding this being, this entity, which is being disclosed.

How can we overcome this, our ignoring being as it reveals itself to us? This can only be overcome by returning to the notion of *aletheia*, of truth as unconcealment rather than as accurate representation or propositional truth, all those philosophical ideas we've developed for 2,000 years. Only then can we safeguard the mysterious non-entitative disclosure of being. Being discloses itself; there is mystery in that. Our job is to think that without destroying it; and the philosophical tradition destroys it, or rather destroys the possibility of thinking about it in any deep way.

But—and this is characteristic of the late Heidegger—overcoming technology doesn't mean rejecting or destroying it, he's a bit more sophisticated than that; it means returning to the concealed truth that technology has covered over. That technology was itself a creative act; attending to the creative act of the invention of technology can be a way to understand what lies beneath the technology. Always the aim for Heidegger in this later period is to look back historically, again, to the fork in the road; at some point in the fork in the road, human beings create something novel. That creation can teach us something, because being has disclosed something to us whenever we create something new. But quickly we get so concerned with the created thing, with the new technology, that we forget the being that lies under it. The technology fascinates us and lets our attention pass over without noticing its origin, its having been granted by being. What we need is not the absence of technology—in other words, we don't have to go back to the Stone Age—but sensitiveness to the truth, what he thinks of as the originary *aletheia*; what's originally being disclosed by the creation and use of the technology.

Being itself must grant enframing. Let me stop here for just a second and say Heidegger again is being sophisticated here—it doesn't mean he's being right, but he's being sophisticated—because he's doing something every radical philosopher must do, which is: If things are so different than what everybody else thinks they are, why is everybody else so wrong; what has led us all to be so wrong? That has to be explained, too. Heidegger has to say our technological enframing of the world has itself to have been granted by being, because for him everything is granted by being; so being, which grants enframing, thereby turns itself into the oblivion of itself. In other words, being has granted us marvelous new means by which we are able to ignore being; by which being is more and more obscured. It's our task to turn that moment into unconcealment; in the very heart of our greatest mistakes, that's the place to look to try to understand what we have forgotten and what's been concealed from us. What is needed, then, to do this is not philosophy but what he calls thinking. In thinking technology, we must return to the ancient Greek notion of *technē*, which in Greek simply meant the practical arts—sculpture is *technē*, but so is shoemaking—and the concept of *technē* precedes the distinction between, in effect, fine art and utilitarian relation. He wants to return to that fundamental idea; that's the purpose of his essay on technology, to get us back to that point.

In a later, 1966 essay, "The End of Philosophy and the Task of Thinking," Heidegger makes the remarkable claim that cybernetics or information technology—he would say today the telecommunications revolution—is the final fulfillment of philosophy. Why? Because it is an example of the will to power, understanding reality is pure information. Information is, after all, something immediately accessible to the mind. To try to understand being as if it were information is like trying to say, in Plato's sense, that the true reality is an idea. All of this is wrong, of course, from Heidegger's point of view. Heidegger claims that philosophy's now been completed by science and technology; he's literally claiming contemporary science and technology have finished doing the thing that Plato started doing 2,400 years ago, the thing called philosophy. Information technology completes the Western search for power over being, substitutes the idea or concept for being itself, and reifies being as entity.

What Heidegger wishes for instead is a kind of thinking that will remain when such philosophy ends, a thinking that thinks, as in his language he would put it, the opening of *aletheia*, the unconcealment, which is the source of both being and thinking. The task is to think that; that is, the task is to try to think that source of unconcealment that being accomplishes, which is the source of everything we know. This thinking is—he uses another Greek term—"*ek-static*." The term "ecstasy," which we get from the Greek, originally comes from the root *ek* and *statis*, which simply means "being outside the self." The whole method of thinking by imposing concepts of the self on being—that's what the history of philosophy tried to do—is now being rejected here in favor of something more like ontological poetry; in effect, a way of writing that's no longer propositional, it doesn't look like normal inquiry in logical form with logical propositions. But it is an attempt to write and think the moment of revelation of being by itself.

In looking at all this, some have interpreted Heidegger's late work as a religious and mystical phase in Heidegger's thought, or as a kind of quietism, a retreat from action and public matters; and some have gone further to say that it results from the debacle of his political association with the Nazi regime. Whatever the motivation or inner meaning, Heidegger is certainly calling for an end to what we have called in this course "philosophy" as a mistaken genre, and for its replacement by a kind of open-ended poetic sensitivity to being. If we ask for a more precise formulation than that—if we say, "Heidegger, what exactly do you mean?" he's going to respond, "You are trying to impose on my answer precisely the kind of framework that I've been criticizing all along."

Nevertheless, Heidegger continued to think that in late or postmodern society—by that here I simply mean society in the second half of the 20th century, epitomized in the developed world, and especially by the United States and the Soviet Union during the Cold War, that this new world (the United States and the Soviet Union) embody the technological domination of being, covering over the roots of another path toward listening to being, which he thought had been an undercurrent from ancient Greek to modern German thought, and Heidegger hoped for a return to that undercurrent.

Culture, Hermeneutics, and Structuralism
Lecture 26

For Gadamer, our thought always moves among artifacts and documents bequeathed us by the past. Our language itself is an historical accumulation, each term carrying its past uses.

Martin Heidegger had intimated in his later work that language was the house of being. Now his rival **Ernst Cassirer** reinterpreted Immanuel Kant to make cultural media, like language, the means by which humans organize their experiential world. Simultaneously, novel movements from linguistics, anthropology, and biblical studies were provoking philosophers concerned with the human sciences to see the self as the product of linguistic and cultural meaning, rather than the other way around. Like Heidegger's later work, this was a movement away from humanism.

Ernst Cassirer reinterpreted Immanuel Kant to make cultural media, like language, the means by which humans organize their experiential world.

While Cassirer's work was largely neglected after the Second World War, there are two other schools of thought that also located meanings in culture rather than the self, and these would eventually flourish and have a major impact on later philosophical thought. The great German philosophies of the subject—phenomenology, existentialism, early Marxism, and psychoanalysis—found meaning in the human mind. Now, **hermeneutics** and **structuralism** found meaning in cultural structures. Hermeneutics was a 19th-century science of biblical interpretation; **Hans-Georg Gadamer** now reread the theory of hermeneutics in terms of Heidegger. But the most influential version of the continental turn to language was **structuralism**. First formulated in linguistics by Ferdinand Saussure but famously applied to anthropology by Claude Lévi-Strauss, structuralism holds that the meanings of signifiers are fixed by the differences between signifiers in a system of signs, with each sign defined by its relation to other signs. ■

Names to Know

Cassirer, Ernst (1874–1945): A neo-Kantian German polymath whose philosophy ranged from mathematics and physics to the philosophy of culture and the history of all. His most prominent role was as the premier theorist of culture in the 20th century and author of the three-volume *The Philosophy of Symbolic Forms*.

Gadamer, Hans-Georg (1900–2002): Influenced by Martin Heidegger, Gadamer rehabilitated the 19th-century tradition of biblical interpretation, hermeneutics, as a method of humanistic understanding. His most famous work was *Truth and Method*.

Important Terms

hermeneutics: The science of interpretation invented by biblical scholars in the 19th century, hermeneutics in the 20th century became a philosophy by thinkers like Hans-Georg Gadamer that embedded meanings in historical and cultural traditions.

structuralism: A theoretical approach to the human or social sciences in which the meanings of human actions are derived from networks of signs and/or concepts, for example, in the work of Ferdinand de Saussure and Claude Lévi-Strauss.

Suggested Reading

Cassirer, *The Philosophy of Symbolic Forms*.

de Saussure, *Course in General Linguistics*.

Gadamer, *Truth and Method*.

Lévi-Strauss, *The Raw and the Cooked*.

Questions to Consider

1. Are meanings produced and fixed by historical genesis or by the contemporaneous relations among signs?

2. What place does a structural approach to the human science leave for individual liberty?

Culture, Hermeneutics, and Structuralism
Lecture 26—Transcript

The phenomenologists, psychoanalysts (or followers of Freud), existentialists, and Western Marxists like Adorno and Horkheimer that I talked about in earlier lectures on philosophy in the first half of the 20th century, all took the inner self as the source of meaning, and analyzed its alienation, repression, or neglect in modern culture, modern economies, modern society, etc. You can say, with a fair amount of accuracy, that all these philosophies were "philosophies of the subject," of the inner self, of the self, of that part of us that is somehow in conflict with the outer world; and their view was that we need somehow to find that self, that fundamental layer of experience, that basic authenticity in modern civilization. But at the same time—in the 1930s, '40s, and very clear by the '50s—a different perspective was evolving both in analytic philosophy and in continental philosophy, although my focus in this lecture will be on the continental. The new perspective that was evolving was to view culture and language as the source of the self rather than the other way around. Put it this way: To see meaning—meanings, ideas, whatever philosophy needs to investigate—as somehow determined not by the inner self, the phenomenological experience, authenticity but rather by culture and language, a public reality of signs. This is an enormous switch.

Today we're going to look at some of those European philosophers who were promoting this switch. We're going to begin with one who is often neglected and who didn't play too much of a role in the later development of this perspective, but he deserves mention because he's arguably the most important philosopher of culture of the 20th century, and that is the German philosopher Ernst Cassirer who formulated what we could call a neo-Kantian philosophy of culture. we'll then turn to Swiss linguist Ferdinand de Saussure, a linguist who created a view called structuralism, which is going to have great impact later on; and finally, German philosopher Hans-Georg Gadamer who, following Heidegger, revived the 19th-century field of hermeneutics. On both the European continent and in analytic philosophy, both in England and in North America, language is starting to become the central topic of the 20th century.

Before the war, the German philosopher Ernst Cassirer provided the most comprehensive philosophy of culture in his magnum opus, the three-volume *Philosophy of Symbolic Forms*. As a neo-Kantian—for the moment we can just say as someone with Kantian roots who's applying them in a new area—he largely agreed with Kant's critical idealism, the notion that the mind shapes experience through fundamental forms and concepts; remember, as we spoke of in respect to Kant, using time, space, and causality. For Kant, time, space, and causality are not things in themselves in the world, but they're features of the human organization of experience. Also influenced by Hegel, Cassirer then added a historical component to that Kantian description. Because, Cassirer said—and this is where he starts to break with the Kantian view—human beings are the *animale symbolicum*, the symbolic animal, we construct our world (as Kant thought; we kind of in a certain way construct the world, our mind is organizing experience) not through sheer transcendental machinery, but through symbols and signs. These symbols are linguistic and artistic, historical, mythical, religious, mathematical, and scientific.

Consequently for Cassirer, the Kantian construction of an objective world of common experience is not primarily a subjective matter occurring in the mind, but it is an active public working of human beings through our diverse cultural media. In other words, Cassirer is claiming that when artists paint in a particular historical period, they are influencing and constructing part of the way we understand space, for example; that language plays a role in determining human experience. In other words, the way I experience the world is prestructured by the language I use. The same is true of myth and religion, and even of science; this is also a big step, because he's saying science is yet another symbolic form. You can then ask the question: Does that mean science is no truer than art? He has his own view why science is superior; but nevertheless, science is a symbolic form. This shows how our perception and conception of the world has changed over time from, for example, the period of hunter-gatherers to early agrarian societies, the development of Western culture from the ancient, medieval, and modern periods; in each of these worlds, cultural media are the mechanism by which we make and experience our world.

While Cassirer's work was largely neglected after the Second World War, there are two other schools of thought that also located meanings in culture rather than the self, and these would eventually flourish and have a major impact on later philosophical thought. Let's turn first to the theory of hermeneutics, which was reborn in the work of Hans-Georg Gadamer. Hermeneutics may sound like a frightening word, but, in fact, it was just a name for the 19th century science of biblical interpretation; in other words, in the 19th century, thinkers like the German Schleiermacher and others argued about the best way to interpret the Bible, and the argument they had with each other was called hermeneutics, the study or science of interpretation. What Gadamer did was, having read Heidegger and been influenced by him, to reread or understand the theory of hermeneutics from the 19th century in terms of Heidegger.

For Gadamer, our thought always moves among artifacts and documents bequeathed us by the past. Our language itself is an historical accumulation, each term carrying its past uses. If you want to see this, just go to a very, very good dictionary—let's take the *Oxford English Dictionary*—and you can see for the language that you and I use in everyday life, they may have been used in very different ways but in very specific, particular ways over the past 400, 500, even 1,000 years. Each term carries with it, he says, its past uses; they're part of its meaning. Gadamer explored a whole series of traditional, nonscientific forms of inquiry to show the rich variety of "methods" quite distinct from the scientific method, especially as these different methods that had been employed in the study of history, in the Western historiographical tradition. He thereby elaborated Heidegger's notion that understanding always proceeds from within a "horizon" or context of meanings that we project.

If you go back to our understanding of Heidegger, Heidegger thought, remember, that understanding operates through *Dasein*, in its everyday experience simply projects a kind of context within which things are understood; a context of connections, meanings, and possibilities. What Gadamer does is to say that projection only takes place insofar as we are parts of an historical tradition; so I am bringing a whole historical tradition insofar as I know it and insofar as I'm raised in it, a cultural tradition, to bear on my interpretation of whatever's around me. The notion of horizon, which actually originally comes from Husserl, was used specifically by Heidegger to mean, in effect, "out to my horizon," around me one could imagine as you move through the world there's a kind of "out to your horizon," you are projecting a context for understanding the things in your experience.

What Gadamer sought to oppose was the scientific Enlightenment fear that this tradition-ladenness blocks our understanding of objectivity. Let me pause and try to explain that for a moment. In general, Gadamer's work—especially in his mammoth and widely read book *Truth and Method*—sought to justify the nonscientific methods of other disciplines; in other words, social science disciplines of the history of poetry, the history of art. What Gadamer was saying was we have a tendency all through the Enlightenment period and in the 20th century to regard the method of searching for truth as the method of the natural sciences, and we tried to then expand that elsewhere. What Gadamer wants to say is that's a mistake; these other fields—history, the study of poetry, the study of art—have their own methods. These are legitimate as well, but they're different kinds of methods. The fear that many have had—many in, let's say, the Enlightenment tradition since the 18th century; this is still Gadamer speaking here—is that the human mind, if we understand it as ensconced in tradition and history; in other words, if we say, "Cahoone's mind has been constructed by or is the result of his own personal history inside a culture and an ethnicity inside of a nation," and there's this whole historical background that I bring to bear on the next moment of experience, if that's true (so the fear goes), this would block my understanding of objectivity. In other words, I wouldn't have a neutral sort of direct perception or create neutral scientific theories about the world if I'm an historical creature, if my understanding of the world is tradition-laden, that will be like a filter through which I will see the world; it will block our understanding of objectivity.

But what Gadamer argues is: That would be true only if our only method were the method of the natural sciences; but as he's just said, that's not so. Let's take history in particular, the study of history: All knowledge, in a sense, depends on the study of history; for example, even scientific knowledge from Gadamer's point of view, you have to know something about what Newton's theory was if you're now going to understand how Einstein's theory is better. All knowledge depends in some sense on history; and history must operate by a method wholly different form the natural sciences, in which we have to enter into and empathetically identify with agents of the past. The fact that we ourselves inherit part of our understanding from those we try to historically understand—and this is the key point—is not an impediment to understanding; on the contrary, it's what enables understanding. It's our own interpretive strategies, our very prejudices inherited from the past that provide us a mode of access to the history that was the source of the prejudices. For example, suppose someone were to say, "Oh, Cahoone, you yourself are the product of Western culture. When you try to study ancient Western culture, you're biased by being a member of the culture that you're trying to study, and therefore you won't objectively understand that culture."

Gadamer's claim is the notion of objective understanding used by that critic is itself a mistaken importation from natural science into history, where it shouldn't belong. In fact, my membership in the tradition from which I'm using the Western tradition to understand the Western tradition, that's my mode of access, that's my way in. It's precisely the opposite of the scientific idea of objectivity. It's our involvement with the historical document, the historical artifact, our involvement with it puts us into a dialogue with it, and that dialogue is how we generate historical understanding. This is very crucial: Gadamer's claim is that my involvement with the object—at least in the social sciences and the humanities—does not render my view of it unobjective and so un-useful for cognitive purposes; my involvement with the object makes my understanding of it possible.

What we strive for in our reading of the past is, he says, a "fusion of horizons"; that is, our own contemporary interpretive horizon must fuse with the interpretive horizon of the past artifact or document. In other words, what I'm doing when I try to understand the past, I am taking my worldview that itself is partly a product of the worldview of the people I'm trying to understand through the ancient artifact or document; I'm not trying to replace their view with my own and impose my own modern views—that would be very unhistorical—what I'm trying to do is find a meeting place, fuse, have a dialogue between my modern perspective and the ancient perspective as embodied in that artifact or document. You could say, in effect, that the implications of this view are politically and epistemically conservative. I don't mean in some tremendously strong sense, I don't mean Gadamer has to be a political conservative; but what I mean is this view emphasizes that we think and speak as part of traditions. This same notion will be exploited decades later by the American ethicist Alasdair MacIntyre, who will declare—as we'll see later in the course—that rationality is already and always rationality-in-a-tradition; in other words, reason itself is subordinate to or part of tradition.

But the most influential version of the continental turn to language was structuralism. Structuralism had begun before this—before Gadamer, before Heidegger, even before or at roughly the same time as the middle part of Husserl's career—in the form of Ferdinand Saussure, the Swiss linguist. Saussure first distinguished between what he called *langue*—and this is in French now—or language, and *parole*, or speech. Saussure wanted to first make clear that he was not concerned with the pragmatics of actual speech, but rather with the system of signs in the language; the *langue* and not the *parole*. That's important because a whole bunch of pragmatic considerations about communication come into play in the case of analyzing *parole*; so first of all, he's restricting his attention. He argued, very famously, for what he called the arbitrariness of the sign. Each sign has a purely conventional relation to its referent; that is, in our language, the relationship between a word and the thing the word stands for, or even the concept it stands for, is one that's purely conventional.

This was a rejection of older theories of the origin of language. We haven't talked about this during the course, but it's always been a concern of Western thought, various thinkers throughout history, trying to understand what language is. Why is it that human beings can speak; where did we get this ability? One of the theories of the origin of language was that it emerged from natural cries or from onomatopoeia; for example, using the word "buzz" to represent the sound of the bee. The notion was that somehow primitive human beings in some actual situations were caused to emit a grunt, and the grunt somehow resembled or sounded like the thing that it was a response to, and then out of the grunt came a word. Saussure says one, there's no reason to believe that's true; and two, even if historically it developed that way, that doesn't mean it accounts for the meaning of the word today. In other words, the word "tree" doesn't have any resemblance to the big, leafy things that stand outside my window. The connection between the word "tree" and actual trees must be totally different; it can't be a natural causal connection.

Saussure then distinguished with what he called the signifier and the signified. The signifier is simply a word, like the word "tree." The signified is not an extra mental object, it's a concept. For example, the word "daughter," even if we use it in the phrase, "my daughter," is a signifier not for my actual daughter Rosie, but for the concept "daughter of the speaker." Signifiers are words; signifieds are not things in the world, they're concepts.

Saussure's crucial point—and this is the basis of all later structuralism—was that the meanings of signifiers are fixed by the "differences" or the relations between signifiers in a system of signs. Each sign is defined by its relation to other signs; and, of course, if you look in the dictionary that's true. As he put it, "in language there are only differences." Let's pause for a moment and see what this means: He's trying to say that meaning, the meaning of any term (and implicitly of a sentence) is determined by the relationship between that term and a host of other terms in language. In other words, the meaning of the word "tree" is fixed by the relationship between the word "tree" to a host of other words, which are for types of trees, the relationship between the word "tree" and nature, the relationship between the word "tree" and things that are physically and contingently related to trees (grass, woods, forest, etc.); in other words, he's looking at the system of signs: A word only means because it's part of a system of signs. Unlike in hermeneutics, for example—we just saw with Gadamer's hermeneutics that we're concerned with the history or origin of an artifact or a document that tells us about its meaning—what Saussure is saying is the meaning of a word doesn't come from the word's history, it doesn't matter how the word was invented or where it came from, nor is the meaning of the word a connection between it and the actual stuff in the world that it refers to. That's not what determines meaning; what determines meaning is the relationship between that world and others. The word "daughter" means what it means because it's related to the words "son," "female," "father," "mother," "family"; not equivalent to them, but has a different, specific, particular relationship to each of those other terms, it's part of a system. In effect, "language" means "as a whole system."

Later French writers would apply this structuralism to many different topics in the human sciences. Jacques Lacan, a famous French psychoanalyst, used structuralism to reinterpret Freud's theory of psychoanalysis; and he declared famously: The unconscious is "structured like a language," he claimed. Luis Althusser, another Frenchman, applied structuralism to Marxist theory, making it less historical and more structural. But the most influential of all was the anthropologist Claude Lévi-Strauss. Lévi-Strauss analyzed the meanings of artifacts and customs in non-Western societies in structural terms, and his influence after the Second World War was enormous. Lévi-Strauss would, for example, in trying to understand the significance and meaning of an action or an artifact in a particular culture, he would say you must understand the relationship between it and a whole series of other objects or practices and the concepts that they represent, and that these are organized in a kind of system. It's the role in the system that dictates the meaning of the event or behavior or artifact.

The effect of all this was a movement away from functionalism and behaviorism in the social sciences. Behavior is now understood through its meanings; in other words, compared to, let's say, behaviorists like B. F. Skinner in psychology, who wanted to say we are to understand human behavior as physical responses to stimuli and look at the lawful relations between the response and the stimulus—that's how we understand behavior—structuralists wanted to look at meanings, the actual meanings of words and ideas and concepts; but the meanings and the ideas and the concepts aren't inside the heads of the participants, they're public meanings that are part of the culture. This was also true of that precursor to hermeneutics, something that was called the *Verstehen*—the word in German just means "understanding"—school of interpretive German historiography in the 19th and early 20th centuries. Structuralism was on the same side with the *Verstehen* school and certain other movements in German thought, and against schools like behaviorism. Structuralism saw the determinants of behavior in systems of meanings. But the meaning of a concept, word, practice, or artifact is determined—and this is what makes structuralism special—by its place in a system or network of signs. "Sign" is to be understood very broadly: linguistic signs, artistic signs, any kind of signs; one can easily have a system of hand signs, linguistic signs. The meaning of an individual sign of any kind is relative to the network in which it functions.

Let's think about this philosophically: If this approach is taken far enough, it means that the meanings of my mind—my ideas, thoughts, beliefs, my actions, the meanings of my actions, my gestures—are not dependent on what is in me, on my spirit, on my experience, on my authentic self, but are some kind of an expression of a cultural world of rules and structures of which I'm an occupant, but of which I'm not the origin. The underlying message of both hermeneutics and structuralism meant a break with the German philosophies of alienated subjectivity: phenomenology, existentialism, Western Marxism, and psychoanalysis. Those views held the self to be the origin of meaning. For structuralism and for hermeneutics, the self does not determine or originate meanings, concepts, or ideas; rather, meanings come from systems of signs. These determine the self, rather than being determined by the self.

What this means in a sense is, and this is how it was taken by some structuralists, that the whole idea of "authenticity"—which, arguably, is in Western Marxism, it's certainly in Heideggerian existentialism and in the other existential phenomenologists—it means this notion of authenticity was just a mistaken romantic ideal; there is no authentic self in the sense of a self that has meaning or value or can be understood independently of the system of cultural science in which it operates, there is no such thing. Particularly for structuralism, the way is now open to a truly scientific approach to culture; that is, the structuralists that we've been looking at—that would mean Saussure and Lévi-Strauss—believe we can have a scientific study of the structures of meaning in any culture or any language.

One difference—I should say before continuing—between on the one hand the French structuralists Saussure and Lévi-Strauss, and on the other hand particularly Gadamer's hermeneutics, is while both of them see the culture, language, history as bigger than and as the source of the self, it's structuralism that, in the long run, would have the much more radical implications; for eventually, as we shall see, structuralism would later fuel a truly radical turn among young French philosophers in the 1960s who most properly would be called "poststructuralists." They took on structuralism; they took on structuralism's rejection of humanism, its rejection of the notion of the philosophies of the subject, that the self is at the center; but then they did it several steps further. They're best known, or most precisely known as "poststructuralists"; but more widely in the world, they became known as the "postmodernists," and we'll turn to them in a couple of lectures.

But before we can look at postmodernism, we first must turn to the linguistic turn in analytic philosophy and trace it; and for that we have to turn, of course, to perhaps the most important or most influential philosopher of the 20th century, Wittgenstein.

Wittgenstein's Turn to Ordinary Language
Lecture 27

> Philosophy is a battle against the bewitchment of our intelligence by means of language.
>
> ——Ludwig Wittgenstein

Ludwig Wittgenstein's *Philosophical Investigations* was perhaps the most influential work of 20th-century philosophy. In it, Wittgenstein rejects his own earlier positivism to declare that linguistic meaning is use, dictated not by logic but by the contextual social activities in which sentences operate. Philosophical problems are caused by ripping terms out of their practical context. After Wittgenstein, Englishman J. L. Austin continued to find linguistic error at the base of many supposedly intractable problems.

> **Philosophical problems are caused by ripping terms out of their practical context.**

In a book that resembled a series of short dialogues and puzzles, Wittgenstein criticized the view that meaning lies in the labeling of private mental contents by words defined through public or private ostension. On the contrary, the meanings of words are acquired through the use of sentences in a practical context, as part of human activity. In short, meaning is use. Wittgenstein went on to show that a series of traditional assumptions about language are faulty. Most famously, he rejected the fear that if meanings of words are private correspondences to ideas, they could systematically differ between people. He applied this to, among other topics, the theory of knowledge, showing that skepticism and philosophical arguments against skepticism are equally nonsensical. ■

Name to Know

Wittgenstein, Ludwig (1889–1951): This Austrian was perhaps the most influential philosopher of the 20th century. His early work in logic led to the *Tractatus Logico-Philosophicus*, which influenced the Vienna Circle. After leaving philosophy for many years, he returned to Cambridge to formulate a new philosophy of meaning as used in his *Philosophical Investigations*.

Suggested Reading

Monk, *Wittgenstein*.

Rorty, *The Linguistic Turn*.

Wittgenstein, *On Certainty*.

———, *Philosophical Investigations*.

Questions to Consider

1. What do "language game" and "form of life" mean?

2. Why can there be no such thing as a private language that systematically, and undetectably, differs from the public language of the speaker?

Wittgenstein's Turn to Ordinary Language
Lecture 27—Transcript

Wittgenstein's *Philosophical Investigations* is, with Heidegger's *Being and Time*, one of the two most influential works of philosophy in the 20th century. The book is remarkable. Like his earlier *Tractatus*, which we treated in an earlier lecture, it's organized into several hundred brief statements; but unlike the *Tractatus*, there is no hierarchical, cumulative order. Furthermore, the paragraphs contain dialogues, statements of Wittgenstein and statements of a befuddled critic or interlocutor. In it, Wittgenstein rejects his own earlier theory of language and forms an entirely new one. We will today explore the doctrines of this late work, *Philosophical Investigations*, which didn't reach publication until after Wittgenstein's death, and his last book, *On Certainty*, also published long after he died.

Wittgenstein was a strange fellow. As noted, after his brilliant early philosophical career, and writing the famous *Tractatus*, beloved of the positivists, he believed he had shown there were no significant philosophical problems to solve; so he left the university, left his fame behind, and became a schoolteacher. Highly critical of himself and others, he began at a certain point to think that his early analysis of linguistic meaning might have been wrong, and this caused him to return to the university and to writing philosophy, and to rethink what he had claimed about language in the *Tractatus*.

The result was a new approach to language, which would eventually be called ordinary language philosophy, in contrast to the ideal language philosophy of Frege, Russell, and the positivists. Let's just pause and explain that: The positivists Frege and Russell, their philosophy had grown up out of the new logic created by Frege, and what they wanted to do was create a philosophy in which we have statements about sense data, about our experience of the world in the most primitive sense, most basic sense, most reliable sense that we get from the sciences; then we have a logical apparatus to organize our theories; and we put these together in a perspicuous way. Frege, Russell, and his contemporaries, the positivists that followed him, believed that essentially you couldn't use ordinary language to try to do philosophy; you needed an ideal, logically perspicuous language. Wittgenstein is the person who began to change all that.

Like the continental thinkers we saw in the last lecture, the actual use of language—in effect, you might say culture—began to become the context in which meaning is determined. But, as we'll see, Wittgenstein's approach is very different from either Gadamer or the structuralists; for what makes meaning in Wittgenstein is not tradition (or what some call the diachronic structure; in other words, over time) nor the system of relations among signs at any one moment (or the synchronic structure of signs in a system). For Wittgenstein, rather, the use of language in human activity, in human practice, is what determines meaning; that's his new view.

First we have to see what linguistic meaning is not for Wittgenstein. The meaning of a term is not an essence or set of necessary and sufficient conditions; Wittgenstein points out that most perfectly legitimate uses of a word in everyday language don't have universal and necessary conditions; rules that state with precision what the word means or when it can be used. Most uses of words just have a "family resemblance" meaning; in other words, one trait or one application of the word is coupled with another that is like it in some ways, a third is coupled with it which is like the first in one way and like the second in yet another, the same way that inside a family two members might share the same hair color, two others share not the same hair color but the same-shaped nose, etc. One example he gave of this was what are the necessary and sufficient conditions to call something a "game"? Traditionally, philosophers had said there have to be, even if we don't know it yet; it must be possible by analysis to come up with a list of traits that tell you exactly when something is a game and when it isn't. Wittgenstein is saying there aren't; there is no exact list of conditions, and ordinary language doesn't need them, ordinary language is no worse off for not having that precise list. The word "game" works, and it works in many different circumstances without the help of the philosopher (that's what Wittgenstein is saying).

Thirdly, ostension, or pointing—ostensive's definition is point at something—whether external or internal, is by itself inadequate to fix or teach the meaning of a term. For ostension to work, there must be elaborate stage-setting, and that stage-setting must take a particular form, which is Wittgenstein's main point. Suppose I try to teach a child what the word "ball" means? I'm sitting with my son and I point at a round white volleyball and I say "ball"; does that tell him that the word "ball" means what I mean by a "ball?" How does the child to know the word "ball" doesn't mean "white," or "round," or "something lying on the floor?" Mere ostension cannot define the meaning of a term, and we can't learn through mere ostension; there must be a context or stage-setting that makes it clear it's the ball I'm paying attention to and not these other features of the object I'm pointing at.

But most important, the meaning of a word is not a mental process or referent that accompanies utterance. Wittgenstein calls that view—which is, in fact, just the very most traditional view of language and meaning in the history of Western thought—the "Augustinian view," thereby blaming poor Saint Augustine for a view virtually all philosophers held. It's Wittgenstein's major aim to defeat this view, as we'll see.

Wittgenstein follows Frege in holding that the meaning of a term is its contribution to its sentence; we discussed this a few lectures back. Like Frege and Russell, and also the mature Husserl, Wittgenstein refused to believe that meanings are psychological entities. If you remember, many of the early 20th-century philosophers were trying to get away from John Stuart Mill's attempt to say that meanings and even logic are psychological and in that sense subjective, but common to all human beings. But now Wittgenstein takes a different view than Frege, Russell, Husserl, and a different view than his early *Tractatus*; for Wittgenstein now declares that a word's meaning is a contribution to a sentence, but in particular to the sentence's use, to what the sentence pragmatically does in a context of human activity.

Meanings thus obtain in the role of a term or statement in the context of activity, a practice or, as he called it, a "language game." The famous term "language game" in Wittgenstein simply means some context of activity—playing basketball is a language game, getting your kids breakfast is a language game, saying "I do" as part of a wedding ceremony is a language game—so the practical context of activity fixes the meanings of the words that are used in it; and language games are themselves fixed or constrained by a broader concept, by making a contribution to what Wittgenstein calls a "form of life." Wittgenstein once wrote, "To understand a sentence means to understand a language"; in other words, to understand a sentence you have to understand a whole language. But further he said, "To understand a language means to be master of a technique"; it means to be able to do something, or as he put it elsewhere, "Words are also deeds" (he might have said "sentences" or "deeds").

It appeared to some early readers that what Wittgenstein was doing was arguing for a kind of behaviorism—in other words, taking the view that meaning is simply behavior—or, others thought he was arguing for a kind of skepticism regarding all other views about language as meaning. But most commentators came to see that he was doing neither of these. Wittgenstein is here opposing Platonists, like Russell and Frege, who believed that concepts must be objectively existent (for example, the concepts of numbers must exist independent of their instantiations); and at the same time, he's opposing verificationists like Carnap, the positivist notion of verification. Meaning is not a mental process or a mental entity; intramental pictures do not confer meaning. In other words, he is saying it is not the case that when Cahoone says "The tree is losing its leaves" that the word "tree" has a meaning because I have a little picture of a tree in my head and the word "tree" is a little label I somehow stick on that little image in my head; that's not how words mean. Meaning lies in the use or relation of words in statements to the circumstances of their utterance.

Meaning is also acquired publicly in public action, not through ostension, as we noted before. Ostension can work, there's nothing wrong with ostension; I can teach the child that is a ball, but only with stage-setting. Of course, in real life, that stage-setting is almost always present in the form of a shared activity because, in fact, when I teach the child the word "ball," what do I end up doing? I roll the ball to the kid, the kid rolls it back to me, I bounce it, I move it around, I change it, I use the same description for another ball that's a different color, and gradually the kid gets to recognize, to use the term "ball" in a context of activity that makes it clear what "ball" refers to.

All of this leads to a famous argument that Wittgenstein made in the *Philosophical Investigations*, and that's the argument that there can be no private language. This is going to take a little bit of discussion, but it's a very important problem, because Wittgenstein's new way of looking at language is going to have implications for how we look at the mind. Philosophers of language had sometimes worried, in a skeptical vein, how is it that we can be sure—that you and I can be sure—we mean the same thing by the use of a world? Suppose this lectern looks brown to you and you call it "brown." Suppose I use the word "brown" but I actually in my mind have the color "blue"; in other words, I'm misapplying the word "brown" to the color "blue," and misperceiving this object. How would we ever know this? If you and I are attaching basic terms for qualitative properties of things in the world to different perceived properties, it seems we could be systematically wrong about our meanings and talking past each other most of the time without ever discovering that there was a mistake.

Wittgenstein's approach makes this impossible; that's what he tries to argue in the *Philosophical Investigations*. For the meaning, again, the meaning of a word or sentence is not an internal referent; the meanings of words aren't something in my head, a concept in my head, an idea, an experience. When I speak, I am not putting a verbal sound as a label attached to something going on inside my mind; rather, I am using a verbal sound that has a function in communication and has a place in public behavior. The learning and use of language is governed by public criteria. As Wittgenstein once wrote, he said imagine a person whose memory could not retain what the word "pain" meant … but nevertheless used the word in a way fitting in with our observations of him. In short, what if someone was using the word wrong, thought of the word wrong, attached the word "pain" to a different internal experience, but externally used to word just the way we did so we could never notice the mistake. We might imagine that he means by "pain" some other internal event that we don't mean. Wittgenstein responds to this: "Here I should like to say"—this is one of his most famous quotations—"a wheel that can be turned though nothing else moves with it is not part of the mechanism."

In other words, if I use the word properly and you and I never go wrong in our dealings with each other, that's all it means to know the meaning of the word, and it makes no sense for a philosopher to imagine, "Ah, maybe there's something else going on inside Cahoone's mind that indicates he doesn't understand the use of the word." As long as I use the word publicly the way everyone else does and we never go wrong collectively with each other, we share a language and we share a set of meanings.

Philosophical Investigations was tremendously important—we'll talk a little bit later about this great importance—but in another book, which he was composing right up until the end of his life, until the last few days before he died, Wittgenstein turned this perspective from the *Philosophical Investigations* and he turned it toward questions about knowledge. While it wouldn't quite be right to say that Wittgenstein in his late work has an epistemology, this is as close as we'll get to it; that is, this is his linguistic analysis of philosophical questions about knowledge or epistemology, and this is his last book, *On Certainty*.

He does something very interesting. You may remember we spoke in an earlier lecture about G. E. Moore; and G. E. Moore had given part of the early analytic philosophers an attack on idealism—Hegelian, Bradley, idealism, and skepticism—and in that project, Moore had tried to defend common sense, and insisted that, essentially, "I hold up my hand, and I say 'I know this is my hand.' There is no any sense in trying to doubt that I know this is my hand, rather than to think it's somebody else's hand or not a hand at all." Wittgenstein has a very interesting response, and to understand his response to Moore is to understand Wittgenstein. Wittgenstein agrees with Moore that for me to say "Gee, I'm not sure, maybe this isn't my hand," is nonsense; Moore called that nonsense, and Wittgenstein says, "You're right, G. E., it sure is nonsense for Cahoone to doubt whether this is his hand." However, Wittgenstein also thinks it's nonsense to say "I know this is my hand"; they're both nonsense.

Wait a second, why should they both be nonsense? The second seems to be true; but Wittgenstein says it's nonsense, it's philosophical nonsense. Why? Because we cannot imagine a plausible language game in which anyone can be led to say it. It is clear to say "I am in pain," but it is nonsense to say "I know I am in pain." The only time it wouldn't be nonsense to say "I know I am in pain" is if someone were to actually say to you, "I don't think you're in pain, I don't think you know you're in pain." At that point, it would make sense to say "Of course I do, I know when I'm in pain." What Wittgenstein is saying is a set of words and a statement makes sense in a language game.

If you can't find a normal language game in which they make sense, then the statement doesn't make sense; and now we begin to see the critique he's going to make of all philosophy. He already gave us a critique of philosophy in the *Tractatus*; now he's going to give us an equally nasty critique of philosophy, but it's going to be couched in slightly different terms.

Wittgenstein admits that what he's saying in all of this may sound a bit like "pragmatism"—the pragmatism that we ourselves noted in the work of Pierce, William James, and in John Dewey—and there's some biographical connection here for pragmatism in Wittgenstein, because he presumably learned about the doctrine of pragmatism from his younger friend, the philosopher Frank Ramsey, who was himself a pragmatist, a very interesting philosopher of logic and mathematics who was a pragmatist and died tragically young. But, Wittgenstein continues—talking about whether he's a pragmatist—"Here I am thwarted by a kind of *weltanschauung*"; "*weltanschauung*" means a worldview. He thinks that pragmatism has with it a worldview that he, Wittgenstein, could not accept.

Elsewhere, in a set of writings that were later published under the title *Remarks on the Philosophy of Psychology*, Wittgenstein asks himself, "But aren't you a pragmatist?" and he answers: "NO. For I am not saying that a proposition is true if it is useful … the uses gives the proposition its special sense, the language-game gives it." Essentially what is happening here—and there is real disagreement about interpreting Wittgenstein on this point—but what I would say is Wittgenstein, it is true, wants no theory of truth, and he associates that with pragmatism. Nevertheless, the account he gives of meaning is essentially pragmatic.

Just as in the *Tractatus*, there is no sense in any "deeper" philosophical analysis of the truth of knowledge involved here. Wittgenstein is saying there's no sense in any deeper analysis; all such analysis involves ripping words into a nonpractical context. Let's pause to understand what this means. Remember Moore saying, against the skeptic, "I know this is my hand"; and Wittgenstein, standing in the background, says, "That's nonsense." Why is it nonsense? Because Moore has taken a set of words that make perfect sense in everyday life, but he's moved them into this weird activity called "philosophy." Philosophy rips terms and words out of everyday life and then asks what they mean; that is the mistake of philosophy. The proper task of philosophy for Wittgenstein is, as he said, to "show the fly the way out of the fly-bottle"; that is, the proper task of philosophy is to show how whatever seems like a deep problem of philosophy is actually the result of a misuse of language. From Wittgenstein's point of view, what philosophers have done is mishandled words and sentences and created odd grammatical forms, asked questions that nobody else would ask; but when you do that, you rip the words and sentences out of the everyday practical context that gives them their meaning in their everyday real language games. It's the language games that fix the meanings of terms and sentences; you try to pull the words out of their language games and ask, "What do they mean?" It's not surprising that you can't figure out what they mean because you removed them from the context that gave them meaning in the first place.

Thus, it's still the case that, as Wittgenstein claimed, "Philosophy is a battle against the bewitchment of our intelligence by means of language." As he also said, if I can make one more quick quote here, "The results of philosophy are the uncovering of one or another piece of plain nonsense and of bumps that the understanding has got by running its head up against the limits of language." To pause for a second here: What this means, in effect, is philosophy creates problems where there aren't any. Wittgenstein's not implying there are no problems in the world; Wittgenstein's not saying there aren't aesthetic, religious, moral, and other problems about what to do and how to live; on the contrary, from the days of his early work the *Tractatus*, he said those are the most important problems, but philosophy can't solve them, and philosophy in and of itself is nonsensical.

Here he has to distinguish between the philosophy that is nonsense and then his philosophical therapy that tries to cure the nonsense. If one wants to say, "This seems a bit unfair; he's still doing philosophy, how can he say philosophy is nonsense?" It's just like the metaphor that he used in the *Tractatus*; he said, "My statements in the *Tractatus*, if you understand them properly, you use them to climb the ladder, but once you've climbed to the place you want to be, you kick the ladder way." The use of philosophy as therapy is his kind of philosophy is supposed to show how other philosophers have misused language; and so get rid of, not solve philosophical problems but dissolve them. Thus he can say, "Philosophy may in no way interfere with the actual use of language; it can in the end only describe it. For it cannot give it any foundation either. It leaves everything as it is"; that is, that's it ought to do.

The conclusion of the *Tractatus* still holds good; this is the remarkable thing about Wittgenstein. He's changed the guts, the inner workings, of his view of how language operates very dramatically from his early work; but in terms of what this means about philosophy he ends up the same place: the proper role of philosophy now is merely therapeutic, serving to reveal philosophical statements as linguistic errors.

Wittgenstein's impact was enormous; he's probably the most influential of the 20th century. The narrow impact was the turn of analytic philosophers away from the search for an "ideal" logical language and towards the investigation of "ordinary language" philosophy. This was continued, by the way, by a very important Englishman, J. L. Austin; if we had more time, we'd talk about his philosophic work here. That's the immediate impact, the more technical impact, to transform the way that Anglo-American philosophers thought about language and the kind of language theory they should be seeking, driving us now toward natural, everyday language. But the wider impact was a new nonscientific skepticism about philosophical problems as rooted in the mishandling of language, and a desire to dissolve rather than resolve them through philosophical therapy. The radical implications were not lost on other philosophers either; just as in the late Heidegger, it seemed philosophy as traditionally understood was at an end.

In conclusion we might ask: Who's more radical, Heidegger or Wittgenstein? I don't propose to answer this because it could be answered in very different ways. Heidegger's attack on the whole history of Western thought is an attack on the way we try to think about the ultimate question of the meaning of being, and he concludes that all of philosophy has really just been covering up that meaning and preventing us from experiencing it. In the future, after Heidegger's death, not many people took up Heidegger's late philosophy, with the exception of people like Jacques Derrida—about whom we'll have more later—and certain poststructuralist and postmodernist philosophers; and they indeed took it very radically. Wittgenstein, in one sense, his view is more humble, but in another sense might be more radical, because from

Wittgenstein's point of view, there really is nothing for philosophy at all. If you show the fly the way out of the fly bottle, that's the end of it. If he can show how when someone asks a philosophical question, they've actually made a mistake in the use of words and language, then philosophy gets sort of muffled whenever it pops up. If you want to say that Heidegger is a kind of, in this point, high priest preaching the need to go beyond the Westerns philosophical tradition into a poetic thinking of being and give up the propositional inquiries of philosophy, Wittgenstein is more like a mechanic who's going around and showing when anybody says, "Wait, I need a philosopher; some mistake is made and by just working around their language a little bit." Their problem is solved and you can leave the philosopher at home, you don't need to call the philosopher.

Which is more radical? I don't know; each is radical enough.

Quine and the End of Positivism
Lecture 28

> Quine was a person who had absolutely no feeling whatsoever for existential or religious questions; for him, philosophy had no business going where rational methods could not decide the issue.

Willard Van Orman Quine studied with the positivists but undermined their view. Most famously, he denied Kant's analytic/synthetic distinction, meaning that we cannot separate, except in trivial cases, statements made true by their meanings and those made true by experience: Our theories confront the world as whole systems. Quine agreed with Ludwig Wittgenstein that meaning is public and behavioral. Consequently, translation of terms is holistic. Therefore the meanings of particular pieces of our theories, like terms, are indeterminate; the meanings of the individual terms cannot be reduced to one. This also means that experience cannot determine which metaphysics is the right one; Quine endorses ontological relativity. Like Rudolf Carnap, he accepts that our choice of metaphysics is pragmatic. ■

Name to Know

Quine, Willard Van Orman (1908–2000): Perhaps the most prominent American philosopher of the 20th century, he began as a student of the positivists but went on to undermine many of their doctrines and endorse ontological relativity.

Important Terms

physicalism: The view that reality is physical; this is sometimes used identically with materialism, but properly the physical is a broader category (e.g., vacuums and electromagnetic fields are physical but not material).

reduction, reductionism: In philosophy of science, reduction refers either to explanation of a system's properties as the product of the properties of its components or lower-level entities (explanatory or theoretical reduction) or to the claim that the system is the collection of its parts or lower-level entities (ontological reduction). If reductive explanations are held to be transitive, then this would mean all phenomena are explainable by physics. Some thinkers deny this but maintain ontological reductionism.

Suggested Reading

Floyd and Shieh, *Future Pasts.*

Quine, *Ontological Relativity and Other Essays.*

———, "Two Dogmas of Empiricism."

———, *Word and Object*, chap. 2.

Questions to Consider

1. What is wrong with the analytic/synthetic distinction as traditionally conceived?

2. How is it that we can recognize gavagai yet have different, indeterministic ontologies of it?

Quine and the End of Positivism
Lecture 28—Transcript

Willard Van Orman Quine was a special character, probably one of the few philosophers who, as a young man, crossed the United States by hopping freight trains. Analytic philosophers are not famous for their foreign language skills, but the mature Quine specifically learned Portuguese in order to teach as a visiting professor in Brazil. But Quine was a person who had absolutely no feeling whatsoever for existential or religious questions; for him, philosophy had no business going where rational methods could not decide the issue. He wrote once that he could never remember being depressed for more than half an hour in his life, and even then only when some plan had fallen through, and it took him roughly 30 minutes to come up with a new one.

Quine began his philosophical life with the positivists; but like the relation of Hume to the earlier empiricists, Quine volatilized all the positivists' basic doctrines, without ever abandoning his belief in science as the best method of truth. We will see his attack on what was called the "two dogmas of empiricism," his holism, his thesis on the indeterminacy of translation, and finally his naturalistic epistemology. Quine's long career spanned the transformation of positivism, and this made him perhaps the most important American philosopher of the 20th century, with the possible exception of Dewey.

First of all, Quine accepted what could be called "behaviorist semantics." Behavior is the core of meaning for Quine; he rejects talk of meanings as mental contents. But his behaviorism led in a particularly pragmatic direction. His most fundamental contribution to philosophy was his 1951 attack on what he called "the two dogmas of empiricism"; "empiricism" here means the logical empiricism of his teachers, the positivists. The two dogmas were the analytic/synthetic distinction—which, remember, was invented by Kant long ago—and the reducibility of factual claims to sense-data reports; those are the two dogmas that he wants to attack. Quine showed that except for verbatim translation of one statement by another, we cannot find analytic or empirically irrelevant truth. Remember that "analyticity" or analytic statements, going all the way back to Kant, are supposed to be universally and necessarily true independent of experience, true simply because of the meanings of the words in the statement; or, in effect, true by definition.

Take the famous example, "All bachelors are unmarried." We discussed this back with good old Hume and good old Kant. Both Hume and Kant thought "all bachelors are unmarried" is a necessarily true statement, simply because of the logical relations between the meanings of the words in the sentence; you don't need any experience to tell that it's true. But Quine gets very careful about what this claim of analytic truth means; he argues that the claim of analyticity was essentially the claim of synonymy between the words "bachelor" and "unmarried man" (the claim that they are synonyms). But synonymy is not so easily established. For example, there are other uses of the word "bachelor," in phrases like "bachelor's degree," which are not synonymous with and can't be easily equated to or translated into the term "unmarried."

Thus even seemingly innocuous paraphrase—the difference between "bachelor" and "unmarried man," that difference; and it's a little difference to be sure, he's not claiming it's an enormous difference—but even that seemingly innocuous paraphrase difference brings in considerations of identity that need empirical evidence to adjudicate. Except for trivial cases—and by "trivial cases" I mean simple statements of identity; Quine, of course, thought that the statement "all bachelors are bachelors" is analytic, that's simply a statement of identity—as soon as you step away from simply repeating the same term ("all bachelors are bachelors," "all trees are trees," "all Cahoone are Cahoone") and you have some paraphrased term, there's going to be a set of empirical criteria that allow you to make the second term synonymous with the first. That's all he means, because if that is so, we cannot say that the statement "all bachelors are unmarried" is being made true by meanings along with absolutely no influence from experience. The distinction between statements true by meanings alone—just that the meanings of the words make it true or false—versus statements made true by experience, empirical conditions, what we actually find in the world, facts; that line is porous, it's not a hard and fast line.

This also depends on the philosophy of language. If we understand language as extensional—meaning that meanings depend on their references; that's the notion of "extensional"—then the synonymy of "bachelor" and "unmarried man" is itself contingent and not logically necessary, for it depends on a host of uses of "bachelor." In other words, we are assured merely that "only bachelors are unmarried men" is an empirical truth about a class of things in the world, in the same way as we are assured that the class of creatures "creature with kidneys" and the class of creatures "creature with heart" have the same extension; in other words, all the creatures of the world that are "creatures with kidneys" are also in the box labeled "creatures with heart." But even though they have the same extension, all the same items of reference are in each box, still, the two phrases don't have the same intensional meaning, because it's just not the case that the phrase "creature with kidneys" and "creature with heart" mean the same thing, one uses "kidney," one uses "heart."

At the same time there is another dogma that's connected with the first, as we mentioned: We cannot reduce theoretical statements in science about the factual, real world—these are now synthetic statements, the ones that aren't analytic—to a set of statements about sense data; that's Quine's claim. The law-like statements of science always imply more than what could be reconstructed by simply listing or rehearsing a set of sense data claims. Let's pause just for a moment and see what that means. What's happening in general is the positivists had assumed this distinction between the analytic and the synthetic, and a hard and fast line between them. In the case of synthetic statements this would mean in principle the positivists thought synthetic statements about the world—in other words, the laws of physics or any general claims of science about the world—were nothing but summaries of sense data, facts; in other words, they didn't have any elaborate meaning involved at the analytic level that would complicate them. In effect, you should be able to take a general statement about the physical world, a synthetic statement, and translate it into a kind of list of observations. To say that "all swans are white" means if we saw this kind of an animal, it would be white; if we saw this kind of an animal, it would be white; whenever we find a swan, it would be white. We could summarize statements about factual observations, and that's essentially what the synthetic statement means. He's denying that, too.

This means, against both the analytic/synthetic distinction and the notion of verification—the positivists, remember, wanted to think that the verification of a statement fixes its meaning—our cognition, our theories instead, Quine is telling us, work holistically. Quine wrote, "The dogma of reductionism survives in the supposition that each statement, taken in isolation from its fellows, can admit of confirmation or information at all." That is, Quine is saying this was the traditional reductionist conception that was part of logical empiricism; that you could take any statement out of a whole scientific theory and tell, is it analytic? Is it synthetic? Exactly what's its meaning? In contrast, Quine says, "My countersuggestion … is that our statements about the external world face the tribunal of sense experience not individually but only as a corporate body." This is what is called Quine's epistemic holism.

What this means is Quine is saying, "When I have a scientific theory and I want to know whether it's true or false, it confronts experience"—like experiments in a lab, a sampling that's made in the real world; we observe samples of a population and report on them—"as a whole. This means we can't in principle find direct connections from particular statements internal to the theory, and the stimulus conditions or particular sense data." Put it this way: When the theory is wrong, when the theory makes a prediction that turns out to be false, when recalcitrant experience arises, it will not be clear which of the statements in our theory ought to be thrown out. That decision will have to be, as Carnap suggested, pragmatic.

Let's pause for a moment here and see what's going on (you've seen much of it, but let's add a bit to it): Quine is knocking down a strict dualism, and epistemic dualism, that had been more or less in vogue since Hume and Kant, and then had been made crucial to the work of the logical positivists; the distinction between the analytic or what's true by meaning, or the synthetic or what's true by reduction to observable sense data. That line is porous, and that means in our theory, empirical claims and claims about what words mean are all mixed together. I don't mean they're chaotic, but they're in a tapestry. You can't move one thread out without messing up the rest, and it's not the case that each little place of this tapestry relates to the real world by itself; it relates to it as a part of a whole theory. That means, as we just said, when the theory goes wrong, there's never just one statement in the theory that you can automatically know to reject. On the contrary, we have many choices as to which part of the theory to change; and that means your choice will be pragmatic, meaning you're going to pick to reject out of the theory that statement that, so to speak, causes the least trouble for the theory if it's to be lost. In other words, what does less damage to your theory as a whole, or makes it so the theory remains useful, even when you take this little piece of it out.

Quine illustrates a related issue in a very famous way, and this has to do with his claim of the indeterminacy of meaning. Let's imagine an anthropologist is trying to translate the sentences of a native who he has no language in common with at all; this is a situation of what Quine would call "radical translation," you have to assume the anthropologist and the native haven't been able to talk, they have no language in common. There's no linguistic bridge they can use to try to learn other words. Suppose the native suddenly remarks and points at what the anthropologist knows to be a rabbit; and the native shouts, "Gavagai!" The question is: what does "gavagai" mean?

First of all, as Wittgenstein would point out, simple ostensive definitions do nothing without "stage-setting." That is, if we remember our Wittgenstein, the word "gavagai," you couldn't be sure it didn't mean "running" or "food," or even just "look." It doesn't have to mean "rabbit," it could mean a whole bunch of things. There are certainly some logically possible meanings of the word gavagai that are ruled out by what Quine would call "stimulus situation," which is his fancy way of saying, "What's observed." The native and I each have a background language, a set of beliefs, ideas, and words—you could say we each have a big theory in our heads, each our own separate theory—and we have no access to each other's theory because we don't have any words in common. The native's theory, when it sees this creature running across the forest floor, says "gavagai." My task is to try to figure out what "gavagai" means inside this (the native's) theory. But as I look at gavagai, I immediately think, "It must mean rabbit." But it doesn't have to be, even by Wittgenstein's criteria, because it could easily mean "running," "look," "there goes supper"; it could mean a whole host of things.

Now Quine takes this analysis further: Even if we could agree that gavagai picks out—in other words, that the reference of the word "gavagai" in the native's language is supposed to be something to do with "rabbit"—so suppose the native starts rushing into the brush, and catches the rabbit, brings it back, and says, "Gavagai, gavagai," and then we cook and eat gavagai; gavagai must mean we then say "rabbit." We think our job is done and we understand the meaning of the word "gavagai." But Quine says we're not done yet, and this is what he adds to Wittgenstein: For the native could have in his or her theory that they apply to the world any one of a number of different of ontologies—basic metaphysical theories about what exists—which, when applied to the rabbit, will give it a different meaning. For example, "gavagai" might mean in the native's theory of the world an individual physical object rabbit; that's what it means in our ontology. When I point at the white hopping thing, I say "rabbit," and I mean an individual physical object, a little animal that's called a rabbit. But that's because I tend to think of the world as cut up into individual physical objects; one might almost say in an Aristotelian sense, little substances.

But suppose the native means by "gavagai" not an individual, physical object called a "rabbit" but rather an instantiation of the form of rabbithood. Suppose the native, in other words, is a native Platonist who thinks that actually this reality is an illusion and there are really these eternal forms; this is the form of rabbithood, this is an instance of the form of rabbithood. Or suppose the native thinks this is a process metaphysician, a kind of native Whiteheadian, and says, "Ah, this gavagai is a phase or instance or event of the great process rabbit, or a piece of the great meta-rabbit." All this may seem a little silly, but the point is simply this: There will be no aspect of the observable situation of behavior that the native engages in, in which I seek, or my interaction with the native, which will be able to differentiate among those different ontologies the native might have. The native could hold any one of those ontologies, and we would never know it. Even if we do catch gavagai, cook gavagai, eat gavagai, nevertheless we won't know if what the native thinks gavagai means, we won't know if that's an individual physical object, an instantiation of an eternal form, a phase of an eternal process, we won't know the difference. In other words, reference is, according to Quine, behaviorally inscrutable. There is a point in translating what the native means beyond which I cannot go; there's a level of knowledge of what the native means that I cannot achieve. Translation always remains indeterminate and reference inscrutable.

Furthermore—Quine takes this point a long way—Quine claims not merely that this is our epistemic debility, that the native knows but he or she knows but we don't know what the native knows. He goes further: If the behavioral situation does not distinguish these meanings—and remember Quine is a behavioral semanticist; meanings are behavior—suppose there's nothing the native does, no act, which could allow us to distinguish between these different metaphysics or ontologies that the native might have; that's the indeterminacy. If the behavioral situation does not distinguish these means, then Quine says, "They don't exist." In other words, "there is no fact of the matter" to be wrong about. If language is public and there is no private language, then we know as much of the native's meaning as the native knows. The native doesn't have another secret meaning in his or her head hidden from us that can't be expressed, because Quine has rejected such an idea of meaning. Once we understand the native's behavior, that's all there is to understand; and that means we can't know any more. There is no further meaning in the native's mind that fixes the reference; the reference remains inscrutable behaviorally, and that's the court of last resort. There is no internal, mental sphere to look to decide the question.

What's the metaphysical result of this? It has a metaphysical result, and that's Quine's doctrine of "ontological relativity," which he actually enunciated in a set of essays; the lecture on ontological relativity itself was given in a John Dewey lecture, and Quine recognized that Dewey and the pragmatists had preceded him to some of these points, that he thinks there's a certain kind of pragmatism in his thought. What Quine argued is that reference can only occur in a linguistic framework. We cannot separate our perception or conception of what the objects are from the linguistic framework that interprets them. Consequently, we cannot check the correspondence of framework to data. I'm going to say that again; let's pause and say that again, because it's crucial and we're going to see this again later in another lecture: If I have a framework theory, a set of ideas, a system of beliefs; in this, and I judge reality with this, and I cannot separate my perceptions or my data from the framework. You see what's happening is it's the rejection of the old positivist notion that we can make an absolute distinction between analytic and synthetic, or what is related to the same issue, an absolute distinction between the sense data language that tells us just what sense data we're perceiving, and the theoretical language, the language of the theory; the positivists thought we could separate these. But if these things are all mixing together—analytic and synthetic, and on the other hand the theoretical language and the observation language—then that means, in other words, when I perceive something and report to my scientific team's leader "The meter read five" or "I observed the native eating the rabbit" or "When I report sense data, the report is already organized and affected by the framework language I used to describe it," if that's true, it means the perception and the sense data cannot be independent of the framework; and if they can't be independent, then they can't adjudicate between frameworks. That is Quine's point.

Quine then applies this to all our ontological choices. For example, he says, the choice between—the ultimate metaphysical choice, and he's not afraid of talking about ontology and metaphysics—suppose we want to say "What is the world?" what's our best theory about what constitutes reality? One would be to say—Quine does not go into great detail, he's just interested in sampling possible theories—that everything that exists in the world is a physical object. Another would say all that exists is sense data; that would be Hume's phenomenologism. How to decide between these? The only way to choose among them is, Quine says, pragmatic; that is, to say which works better for our explanatory and manipulative powers. What he's saying is there's nothing we can observe, no fact of the matter independent of the frameworks in which we talk and think and judge that can decide between competing frameworks. The information we get from observation is relative to a conceptual framework we use; a framework that itself only has meaning and was evolved from past observation and past frameworks. The choice among frameworks cannot be decided by any fact of the matter. The choice between them, as Quine said, when it's rational, the choice is merely pragmatic. That is good enough for Quine; it doesn't mean we don't have knowledge, it's not a rejection of our knowledge, but it means our choice of ontology has to, in the end, be a pragmatic choice as to which ontology works better for the theory that seems to fit best so far.

Lastly, there's one more point we wanted to cover in this brief discussion of Quine. In his essay, "Naturalizing Epistemology," Quine made a basic epistemological point: He renounced the goal of justifying all knowledge per se. That goal has been with us since Descartes at least, and it's how

Descartes began his quest for knowledge in the 17th century. Quine takes a different perspective: He says science is our best form of knowledge, and it cannot in principle justify itself. The goal of traditional philosophy, which has been in some respects to try to justify the validity of science and of other kinds of knowledge, is impossible but also unnecessary. This is Quine's abandonment of foundationalism. If it's true, what Quine says is we can use science to study how the human organism acquires knowledge. Let's pause here and see what that means. What Quine's suggesting is this: He admits to himself, "As a philosopher who's wrestled with these questions I come to the conclusion, the best knowledge we have is scientific knowledge." He's not saying it's always right, or even mostly right, but it's the best. OK, then, if that's true, there's no other kind of knowledge that could get underneath it to judge whether it's true or false; that is, if a scientific theory is wrong, the best way to find that out is with more science. Philosophy is no longer in the position; there's no possibility of getting behind science or around science, outside of it, and judging science on some other criteria.

That sounds like we're in a difficult position; but not necessarily, Quine says, because after all, what are we knowers but natural creatures. Human beings, for Quine, are themselves natural creatures evolved from other natural creatures from a Darwinian perspective. Our sensory organs are things in the world, studied by science. Our patterns of thought are things in the mind, studied by psychology, neuropsychology, and cognitive science. Our best knowledge if science, but science itself can study its own roots in the human organism. In other words, we can have a naturalistic epistemology, a theory of knowledge that bases knowledge on our scientific investigation of human cognition and perception.

For anyone who says that to a philosopher, they're going to get a very quick responds. "Wait a second, now you're arguing in a circle," would be the answer. "You're trying to justify knowledge with a scientific account of knowledge, but what justifies your account of science: nothing." Quine responds to this: If somebody thinks this is circular, that's fine; I'm not worried about it. We are—to use the positivist Otto Neurath's metaphor, which Quine likes very much—on a boat at sea and we're trying to repair it as we sail. There are no external foundations to recur to; there's no place else to look for a criterion that says our boat's going wrong or for a means of fixing the boat. Whatever we have is here on the boat with us; that's all we have to work with. The best stuff on the boat we have is science. So if someone objects, Quine is begging the question by using one piece of knowledge, science, to explain another; Quine is simply unimpressed, after having given up the notion for a foundation of knowledge at all. Not giving up knowledge, but giving up the philosophical search for a foundation for knowledge.

We are left then, by Quine, with, as he says, a scientific heritage—that's the sum total of the historical scientific heritage that I have in my head; or among a community of scientists as we try to understand the world, and we have a barrage of sensory stimulation, things that happen as we make our experiments. After the impact of those two things, we make the best choice of ontology we can. The ontology of physical objects, Quine thinks, fits best with the widest variety of our epistemic conditions; thus, he thinks, it makes sense to endorse physicalism. But, he says, there is no further, deeper philosophical justification of it. It works with respect to the best methods we now have available; and once the philosopher has said that, it's time to go home.

New Philosophies of Science
Lecture 29

> Most philosophers of science today reject the seeming irrationalism of Kuhn's account. ... Nevertheless, transition between paradigms remains a crucial issue in accounts of scientific rationality. If Kuhn's notion of incommensurability is, let us say, not fully accepted by scientists in general, everyone has to deal with it in the philosophy of science; in other words, Kuhn has really raised the ante and suggested something that no one suggested before, namely that the very paradigm of rationality, what we call science, might itself have a nonrational core.

The decline of positivist **verificationism**, and the belief that observations statements could be strictly distinguished from theoretical statements, led to new interpretations of scientific knowledge. **Karl Popper**, trying to solve David Hume's problem of induction, concluded that science never confirms its claims at all; it merely disconfirms false alternatives. Philosophers of biology came to object that positivist philosophy of science had ignored sciences other than physics. **Donald Davidson** proposed a notion of supervenience, which seemed more plausible than strict physicalist reductionism. Later, **Thomas S. Kuhn** presented a novel account of the history of science, holding that rather than advancing by patient accretion of discoveries, science advances by revolutions in which a new paradigm replaces its predecessor. This raised the question of how rational the choice between paradigms could be. ■

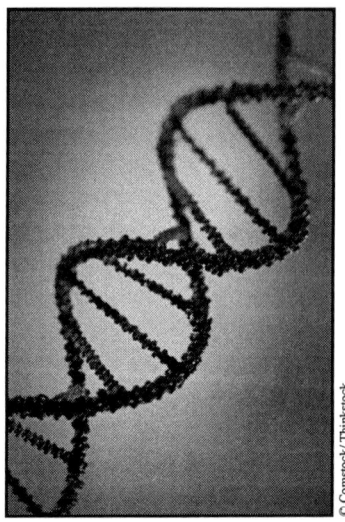

Many philosophers of science considered the discovery of the double-helical structure of DNA an ideal case of reduction.

Names to Know

Davidson, Donald (1917–2003): An American analytic philosopher who made major contributions to a broad range of issues, including the theory of action, radical translation, metaphor, and the notion of supervenience.

Kuhn, Thomas S. (1922–1996): This American historian of science revolutionized his field by arguing in *The Structure of Scientific Revolutions* that science proceeds discontinuously, through periodic revolutions where one paradigm of fundamental concepts is thrown over for another, raising questions about the rationality of theory choice at those moments.

Popper, Karl (1902–1994): An Austrian and then British philosopher of science whose contributions spanned from the logic of induction—where he created falsificationism to answer David Hume—to epistemology to the philosophy of biology to political philosophy (in his book *The Open Society and Its Enemies*). He was one of the most important philosophers of the 20th century.

Important Term

verificationism: The view, held by some logical positivists (e.g., A. J. Ayer), that the meaning of a claim is the observations that would verify or confirm it.

Suggested Reading

Kuhn, *The Structure of Scientific Revolutions*.

Popper, *Conjectures and Refutations*.

Questions to Consider

1. How can induction be justified?

2. How can a rational argument be made from one paradigm to another?

New Philosophies of Science
Lecture 29—Transcript

We've seen in recent lectures that Wittgenstein turned away from ideal language philosophy that was beloved of the positivists, Russell, and Frege toward ordinary language philosophy; and that roughly at the same time, Quine was showing that the positivist view of language and of observation statements, etc., didn't really work. We've seen these changes in philosophy of language in the middle of the 20th century and to some extent in the theory of knowledge, because the former had a direct impact on the latter. What we want to do in today's lecture is chart what this change, this sea change, would mean in the philosophy of science and the philosopher's view of science.

Not only Quine, but other philosophers of science, had recognized that observation statements can't be independent of theoretical statements. This was a major blow, of course, to the positivist interpretation of science. For now that observation statements are embedded with theories—they can't be extricated from theories—the former (observation statements) can't cleanly decide between the latter (the theories). But more changes were to come: Karl Popper, a very important philosopher of science, was to offer a major alternative to the view that truth is verification. At the same time, the positivist notion of reduction to physics would be challenged by Donald Davidson's notion of supervenience. Then finally, Thomas Kuhn would come along in the early 1960s and change everything with a new account of scientific progress.

Ever since Hume, philosophers of science had been bedeviled by the problem of proving the validity of induction. If you remember, "induction," broadly speaking, is our ability to infer from a set of occurrences, like a sample, to a true statement about a general population or a general conclusion. Remember that Hume had argued that there is no rational proof of the validity of induction. More narrowly, we could put it this way: We might say that if we sample several marbles from a large container into which we cannot see, and we draw five marbles and they're all black. If we're asked what we think is the color of the other marbles in the container, we'll induce that the rest of the marbles are probably black, too; not certainly black, but probably. The question is: How do we know that? The marbles are all separate entities.

Each selection that I make—this handful, another handful, another—is independent of the others. Why should the blackness of the chosen handful be somehow connected to the color of the yet unchosen? In other words, as Hume pointed out, it doesn't seem clear—he put it more strongly, he said induction is irrational, and it's merely a matter of habit—though we all believe in induction and there aren't any philosophers, more or less, who say induction if false, the problem is we all believe it, we all use it, but we can't see what the proof or argument is to show that it's valid.

Karl Popper—who was one of the most important philosophers of science in the 20th century, and he was around rather earlier in the century, born in 1902, and doing important work already in the 1930s and '40s—attempted to answer this question, the problem of induction, in a way that would eventually alter how we regard all scientific conclusions. His move was deceptively simple: He said experience or observations do not confirm scientific or inductive hypotheses; they don't. This sounds pretty bad; this sounds like giving in. he says, "No, it's not, because the function of induction is not to confirm, it is to disconfirm hypotheses. We formulate a scientific hypothesis based on a sample of experiences, and we assert its "truth"; but that means nothing more than that it has yet to be disconfirmed. It's our best guess up until now. In fact, for logical reasons as well—which we're not going to go into the complicated arguments here—Popper concludes evidence really can't confirm any theory, it can only "falsify" a theory; and this would mean that scientific claims are highly fallible. This theory, Popper's own theory, is called his falsificationism, but it's also true that he's a fallibilist, as was Charles Sanders Peirce, the inventor of the theory of pragmatism; "fallibilism" meaning that all our judgments are fallible. Nothing in Popper's falsificationism or his fallibilism undermines realism. In other words, they don't undermine our claim that the products of scientific inquiry, the theories we come up with that have survived tests of falsification, nothing in his work prevents us from saying those theories that have survived are our best guess as to what is true, he just wants to say we should never regard the theory of the moment, our best guess, as if it's been confirmed; it's never confirmed, it's simply that it hasn't been falsified yet, it's the one left standing.

This theory, which not everyone accepted, became an important way in the mid-20th century that philosophers of science could think about scientific claims while at the same time they were recognizing the positivist justification of science was falling away. In a related vein, positivism had always endorsed physicalist reductionism; that is, the view that all scientific knowledge should in principle be reducible to physics as the most basic science. You can see why if we pause for a moment to consider that. In other words, it looks like—or at least some people might say—my mental operations are derived from my neurology, the neurology of my brain and central nervous system, in interaction, of course, with an environment and a whole host of complicated things. But if we knew more, we should be able to find—so many people have thought—some explanation for my thoughts, beliefs, ideas, and actions in my neurology. That neurology is part of biology, the study of physical organisms, of which I'm one. Physical organisms are composed of materials studied by chemistry, so it should be that in looking at chemistry we should find explanations for biological organisms and the events that take place in them. But what is chemistry, after all, but a discussion of the properties of atoms, and atoms obey the laws of physics. The general view was that physics is the broadest, most comprehensive, most fundamental science; and so in principle, even though no positivist ever claimed as of today we should be explain somebody's thoughts from physics, no one has ever made that claim. But the claim was: in principle, we should be able to eventually; that's physicalist reductionism.

There were always dissenters from physicalist reductionism, the most notable I've mentioned before in a lecture, and these were the British emergentists who claimed that, as you may remember, nature is divided in a hierarchy of levels, that novel phenomena appear; that, in other words, you can take a group of entities of a certain description like atoms, but when you put them together in a complex form, the whole has properties that are more than, so to speak, the sum of the parts. In effect, what the emergentists said was, for example, the properties of chemistry can't be deduced from the properties of physical systems; the properties of biology can't be deduced from the properties of chemical systems. Each is dependent on the other—the biology is dependent on the chemistry and is dependent on the physics—but nevertheless, there are novel properties at each level that are irreducible to the lower level. Emergentism fell from favor after the 1920s, due jointly to the success of positivism—which was then becoming the major theory of science—and also because of quantum mechanics, because quantum mechanics, the full theory of which was achieved in the late 1920s right up to early 1930, provided scientists for the first time with a way of explaining atomic structure, and the chemistry of an atom is based in its atomic structure. The success of quantum mechanics seemed to promise that chemistry could be reduced to physics.

Nagel, one of the positivists, in trying to support physical reductionism proposed a complicated set of "bridge laws" that could be used to show how higher level, more complex sciences could be translated into, hence reduced to, the laws of physics. Just to say what this means in general, each of the sciences has a different language and a different set of basic concepts. If you're going to claim that everything's really physics or everything in principle should be reducible to physics, you have to actually show how you can translate the terms of biology and the terms of chemistry into statements about physical entities, so that translation is necessary for a reduction to work. Some reductions were considered to be obvious success cases. The chief examples are: the reduction of classical thermodynamics to statistical mechanics; classical thermodynamics of the 19th century was eventually shown by Volkmann to be explainable through the statistical mechanics of atoms moving inside of gasses. Another example would be many people would say that Newtonian mechanics has been successfully reduced to Einstein's relativistic mechanics; in other words, the relativistic mechanics tells you why the Newtonian mechanics worked, and you can substitute the relativistic mechanics for the Newtonian mechanics and, obviously, the relativistic mechanics explains more than Newton ever did explain. These were supposed to be prime examples of successful reduction; but nevertheless, in the philosophical analysis of each of these cases, there remain serious technical problems in the formulation of the bridge laws, often making reducibility an open question. It wasn't clear that the positivist program of reduction could really work.

Later on, in the 1970s, the philosopher Donald Davidson introduced the notion of supervenience; actually the term "supervenience" had come from one of the British emergentists, but Davidson introduced it in the philosophy of mind. The reason that philosophy of mind matters—and we're not saying much about the philosophy of mind, which is a very, very big and technical subject of its own; we're not saying much about that in these lectures, but in this case there's an important connection with what we're doing—obviously for some people the question of whether more higher or more complex sciences can be reduced to lower, that especially cuts or becomes especially important when we come to the question of mind and whether psychology, whether the human mind, can be understood and reduced to neurology or biology. What Davidson did was give us the notion of supervenience. Supervenience asserts that while any change in mental events or properties must presuppose a change in neural events or properties, the mental events or properties could still not be reduced to, or explained by, neural events alone. For example, if my son Harry becomes annoyed with me, the arising of that mental state of annoyance necessarily implies that something happened in his brain, even though the latter (the brain state) can't explain the former. While this was, as noted, focused on the mind, the notion of supervenience could in principle apply to other natural sciences like chemistry and biology.

The point is: Davidson provided an option for philosophers who wanted to deny reductionism—in other words, move away from the old physicalist reductionism—without turning to what they regarded as an unscientific or mystical notion of emergence. To sort of reiterate that point, Davidson simply asserted that there is a special kind of dependency relationship between mental events and physical events like neurological events in the brain such that whenever there's a change or difference at the mental level there must be a change or difference at the physical level; you can't have a higher level change without a lower level event or change. This is a way of asserting dependence of mind on brain. Nevertheless, Davidson said, we still need two different sciences: one to study mental events, call it psychology; and one to study physical events in the brain, call it neurology.

Many came to accept that while ontological reductionism must be true—that would mean that all realities are constituted by the elementary particles of physics, so that physicalistic reductionism is true ontologically in terms of what stuff is made of—but nevertheless, many continued to say that explanatory or theoretical reductionism is false; in other words, we shouldn't ever expect to be able to substitute physical explanation for nonphysical, for example psychological, explanation. This is the kind of halfway position, in fact, that many philosophers hold to this very day; namely that in principle, I, Cahoone, am nothing but quarks and electrons; in other words, a collection of the tiniest little particles that physics has come up with. That's what I am, and there's nothing else in me but that. However, they would say, you're crazy if you ever think we'll be able to explain my biological processes or my mental processes by looking at quarks or electrons because the difference in complexity is just so enormous. Sciences and explanations get to be pluralistic, but the ontology or the theory of what actually exists is reductionistic, physicalistic.

At the same time, as Popper himself helped to establish, the philosophy of biology came of age in the second half of the 20th century. Early 20th century philosophy of science had focused almost entirely on physics, which the positivists regarded as the most basic science. But philosophers of biology in the 1960s and thereafter began to jump up on their hind legs and say that biological explanation in principle isn't reducible to physical explanation, and that philosophy of science, if it's only based in physics, is failing to understand biology; it's imposing a misleading model on our understanding of other sciences. Let's take just one example, and it's perhaps the most famous: purpose or teleological causation. We remember back from the very beginning of this course, one of the great achievements, shall we say, of the scientific revolution of the 17th century was to banish Aristotle's notion of final causes, goals or final causes, from physical explanation. It may be that physicists are happy, and perhaps chemists, with that banishment of teleological causation, but biologists are much more ambivalent about it; it seems that they need to keep some kind of final causes.

Despite the discovery of the double helix of DNA, which encouraged some to think that biological explanation could all be genetic and all be chemical—the discovery of the double helix gave the implication that it seemed again, as quantum mechanics had done in the 1920s and the early '30s, it now seemed biology really is just chemistry or could be reduced to chemistry—many biologists in the '60s, '70s, and the '80s began to think about this quite differently: they begin to separate their notion of purpose from mental purpose; or as Colin Pittendregh put it, teleonomic versus teleological causality. Let me explain those terms: They began to say teleological causality would mean when a creature with a mind has an idea, and that idea has a causal relationship to what it does; in other words, I say, "Ah, I'm hungry and I need to eat," and then I rush off to the store to get something to eat. That's teleological causality. But what Pittendregh wanted to claim is that's the wrong model to use with, let's say, understanding why ants build an ant hill or why mice build a nest. Everybody agreed we can't assume they have minds and ideas in their minds as purposes, but some biologists and philosophers of biology wished to retain the idea that there is still some kind of telic, now called teleonomic, or a different kind of final causation, involved in biology.

We can put it very simply and elegantly as the philosopher of biology Ernst Mayr put it. He said the evolutionary biologist does not merely say the following: The wood thrush flies south and thereby escapes the winter; that statement's true, the wood thrush does fly south, and thereby the wood thrush escapes the winter. But, Mayr says, if that's all the biologist said, a crucial bit of biological information would have been lost; because what the biologist really wants to say is the wood thrush flies south in order to escape the winter. The "in order to" is not mental or personal, it's not that the wood thrush is thinking, "Hmm, I have to go to Alabama now because it's going to get cold," it's that the wood thrush has a genetic program that it has acquired from evolution. It's acquired it in order to survive the winter; so there's a biological "in order to"—which is a kind of final causation, teleonomy—that Mayr would say biologists can't get rid of.

It appeared that the sciences of more complex phenomena could not so easily be reduced to physics. Many philosophers came to believe, as I've said before, in an "ontological reductionism", but not an "explanatory reductionism"; believing that, again, the complexity of larger systems could never be given by physics. Supervenience and emergence were invoked to describe this inability. At this point in the mid-to-later 20th century, we see a loosening up of the views of the philosophy of science, partly due to changes in epistemology, partly due to Quine's work, Wittgenstein, Popper's notion of falsificationism, the general death of positivism you might say, the development of the philosophy of biology making everything more complicated. But now came the real shock: The biggest blow to earlier philosophy of science came, oddly enough, from the history of science, and in particular, from Thomas Kuhn's 1962 *The Structure of Scientific Revolutions*.

Kuhn's target in that book—it's a book about the history of science—was what was typically called the "Whig" interpretation of the history of science. We don't have to worry about what that means in terms of the British political party, but essentially what the Whig interpretation held was that science proceeds cumulatively and inevitably through the linear addition of discovery and argument based on a background foundation of set of concepts and assumptions. This is the kind of science which, at least if you're my age or older, you learned and probably many people still learn in their sciences classes: Namely, science proceeds by putting one brick on top of another brick. You get a foundation for your science, each experimentalist or theorist adds knowledge, and we gradually build, build, build, build. Kuhn argued that such is a plausible description only of a part, and in fact the least interesting part, of the development of science. For while what he will call "normal" science in most historical periods does proceed through the patient accumulation of fact, over time there gradually develops cracks or fissures; unsolvable problem begin to accumulate in this structure being built by normal science. When these cracks become grave enough, a scientific "revolution" takes place; nothing incremental, but a sharp break involving not the addition of one discovery or one little argument, but the wholesale replacement of what he called the "paradigm." If you've heard the word "paradigm" in your life, it's probably because it came from this book of Kuhn's, which made it famous.

In a scientific revolution, the whole paradigm, meaning the fundamental concepts and practices of a science in a period of time, gets rejected. One paradigm is radically overthrown by another. Examples were: the Copernican, Newtonian worldview was overthrown by Einsteinian; and quantum mechanics was a revolution against earlier theories of matter. The first lesson of Kuhn is science doesn't proceed continuously, but continuously for a while and then discontinuously, continuous for a while and discontinuously; so normal science is performed when there's a single trusted paradigm: Everyone does their work inside the paradigm, but at a certain point things break down and a new paradigm comes in. Scientific change is thus partly discontinuous; it's not the patient accretion or the construction of a building higher and higher above its foundation. It periodically molts its exoskeleton and occupies a new foundation before returning to a period of "normal" science.

That sounds very interesting, maybe it's even true, but here's where the philosophical problems start to arise. Kuhn held that the meanings of the terms used in observation and theory in any period of normal science are dependent on that holistic paradigm. The terms used by normal science are woven into the paradigm; in other words, they only have meaning and can be applied in that paradigm. If that's true, then different paradigms must imply that the terms they use have different meanings, as if they were two different languages. In other words, what the Einsteinian meant by mass is not what the Newtonian meant by mass. If that's true, the question is: How could experiments or any kinds of observations decide between the paradigms? It's the same problem that we've already seen: If the observation language isn't independent of theories, if they're stuck together, then any new observation already has some theory with it; observations are no longer neutral judges of which theory is true.

Indeed, the way that Kuhn expressed this problem is quite radical. The question is whether paradigms are incommensurable; and what he meant by that was mutually untranslatable, where you literally could not translate the notion of Einsteinian mass into the notion of Newtonian mass or vice versa. The image here would be that each paradigm just cuts up the world differently, and then there's no way to translate, no simple way to translate, the terms of one period of science to another. If that were true, it would mean there would be no logical inference across paradigms. This would mean, literally, there could be no rational argument from the old paradigm to the new one; the decision to adopt the new one would have to be an irrational leap, or sociologically explained, and Kuhn is not afraid to say it: Most of the time the new paradigm is established when the holders of the older paradigm die off. Young people from graduate schools that have learned the new paradigm, they get jobs, they get tenure in physics departments; the new paradigm takes hold. That's perfectly fine as a sociological explanation, but it kind of implies that theory change isn't rational; that's a problem.

Most philosophers of science today reject the seeming irrationalism of Kuhn's account, in other words, the hardcore implications of incommensurability between the paradigms. That's a big thing to say: not just that the paradigms are different, but that they're incommensurable; that you can't translate from one to the other. Nevertheless, transition between paradigms remains a crucial issue in accounts of scientific rationality. If Kuhn's notion of incommensurability is, let us say, not fully accepted by scientists in general, everyone has to deal with it in the philosophy of science; in other words, Kuhn has really raised the ante and suggested something that no one suggested before, namely that the very paradigm of rationality, what we call "science," might itself have a nonrational core.

Derrida's Deconstruction of Philosophy
Lecture 30

> Derrida's key claim is that a sign and its meaning are members of both a diachronic or temporal series of that sign's occurrences, and the synchronic or simultaneous pattern of related signs in the language; the reference to both of these are essential to the sign's meaning.

Postmodernism was the most radical critique of modern, or any other, philosophy. One of the most famously difficult of writers, **Jacques Derrida** was the most prominent inspiration of postmodernism in philosophy. More precisely a **poststructuralist**, Derrida probed the implications of a structuralist view of the human sciences and philosophy, albeit one that denied structuralism's scientific aspirations. All use of linguistic signs produces multiple meanings. Writing, distinct from speech, is particularly troublesome in severing meaning from the presence of the author and hence is particularly infiltrated by "differance," or the unending production of differences in meaning. Philosophic writing tries to deny or repress this multiplicity in order to achieve fixed, unitary meaning, but it can never succeed. Derrida deconstructs works of philosophy, showing how their very attempts to fix meaning are self-undermining. ■

> Derrida deconstructs works of philosophy, showing how their very attempts to fix meaning are self-undermining.

Name to Know

Derrida, Jacques (1930–2004): A French poststructuralist and the inventor of deconstruction, a radical philosophy of reading philosophical texts as having multiple, indeterminable meanings. He was one of the main instigators of postmodernism in philosophy.

Important Terms

postmodernism: A family of philosophical, artistic, and social movements that either hold that contemporary advanced societies have abandoned key features of modernity or hold that all presentation of reality (e.g., perception) presumes representation by signs. Most famously defined by Jean-François Lyotard in his *The Postmodern Condition: A Report on Knowledge.*

poststructuralism: The French postmodernist philosophers of the 1960s, like Jacques Derrida and Michel Foucault, are more precisely termed poststructuralists, who apply structuralism reflexively to the theories of the human sciences and philosophy, leading to radical results.

Suggested Reading

Derrida, "Differance."

———, *Of Grammatology.*

———, "Structure, Sign and Play."

Descombes, *Modern French Philosophy.*

Questions to Consider

1. Why has philosophy traditionally tried to reduce writing to speech?

2. What job is left for philosophy to do?

Derrida's Deconstruction of Philosophy
Lecture 30—Transcript

While analytic philosophy was busy undermining all its past hopes, continental philosophy was not idle. It was about to unleash the most radical critique of modern philosophy, or of any philosophy whatsoever. This broad movement would come to be called "postmodernism," but its early core was really better called "poststructuralism," and its leader was Jacques Derrida. What was about to happen is that the philosophical tradition of the 20th century in Europe that began in one sense with Husserl, was fed also by Nietzsche and Kierkegaard, which then bloomed in Heidegger, took another strange turn in Heidegger's late work; the Husserl, the early and the later Heidegger, that whole tradition is now going to be subjected to a deep internal criticism to members of the tradition who'd been schooled on structuralism from Saussure and Lévi-Strauss and had taken structuralism to a new level. It's an internal critique of the continental tradition; we're going to see how far that critique goes.

Born Algerian and Jewish, Derrida was one of a young group of French philosophers who came of age in the 1960s, including names like Michel Foucault, Gilles Deleuze, Luce Irigaray, Jean Baudrillard, and Jean-François Lyotard, and others. They revolted against the humanist existentialism and Marxism common in France, although that doesn't mean they gave up leftist or socialist-oriented politics, but they did attack Marxism and its theory of history. This means they so loathed Sartre, who represented for them the old guard; and like so many French intellectuals they were politically radicalized, first and foremost by the French colonial war in Algeria, then by the American war in Vietnam, climaxing in the nearly worldwide student revolt of the spring of 1968, which hit the Parisian academic world particularly hard.

Intellectually, these new young philosophers were heavily influenced by psychoanalysis, by Heidegger, and by Nietzsche, but most of all by structuralism. Remember that structuralism holds that the meaning of signs is structurally determined by the difference of all signs from each other in a network; it's the synchronic relation among signs, not their history, and not their relation to objects in the world that determines their meaning. What the new young philosophers did was they turned structuralism against itself; that is, they began to apply structuralists' principles to the "human sciences" as they were called, including philosophy, taking those sciences as structures of signs whose meanings are defined by differences. Let me just explain that a bit more: Structuralism, originating from Saussure and then being made so famous in France by Claude Lévi-Strauss applying it to anthropology, but that implied structuralism could be applied to sociology, psychology, or a whole bunch of fields. It seemed to some structuralists in the 1950s and early 60s that structuralism was the method for the study of the human sciences; in other words, the sciences of the human beings, literature, and societies, not the natural sciences but the human sciences. It looked as if structuralism was going to be the next best hope of people who wanted a scientific way to study human matters, the humanities, history, anthropology, culture, but they wanted a scientific method that was not at all like the natural scientific method. What the poststructuralists do, this young group says, in effect, your sciences, human sciences analyzing the world, they too are structures of science that we are now going to study; in other words, they applied a self-reflexive critique of the new structuralist-inspired human sciences by the theory of structuralism.

Their question was (I'll jump ahead to the more radical way that they put it): What if all writing about human beings—sociology, anthropology, and philosophy—were to self-consciously understand itself through a structuralist analysis? Just hold that in the back of your mind as we begin looking at the view of Jacques Derrida. Derrida's work, which is very complicated: One way to begin examining it is to look at the theory of signs, or as we say semiosis; "semiosis" just means sign-using or the study of signs. Remember from Saussure that semiosis uses arbitrary signs; so certainly Derrida accepts that: The signs we use in language are arbitrary, they're determined by human convention; they have no connection to the physical events of the world outside of themselves. Secondly, signs are what Derrida would call exterior or material, they're not solely mental. What he means is they are sounds or marks on a page. When Derrida refers to a sign, he's talking about what I say (my words, my propositions) and also what I write, or any other kind of sign; marks, pictures, all these can be signs. He's not talking about ideas in my head. Each sign must be—and this is a basic criterion—repeatable, identifiable as the same sign. In other words, it has to be the case that when

I use the word "tree" in one sentence and five minutes later I use the word "tree" in another, there has to be something enough common between them that I can say it's the same word.

Derrida's key claim is that a sign and its meaning are members of both a diachronic or temporal series of that sign's occurrences, and the synchronic or simultaneous pattern of related signs in the language; the reference to both of these are essential to the sign's meaning. The meaning of each sign is relative to this combination of present and absent signs. Let's pause for a second. That means when I use the word "marriage," that word "marriage" exists, you might say, in two different lines: one is the historical uses of the word "marriage" by me, by other English speakers, by people in my culture. The word "marriage" today is tinged by all the meanings I've heard attributed to it and all the meanings that it's had in the past; the word "marriage" has accumulated meanings over the past, it has a history. That's the diachronic line. It's also, according to the structuralists, true that "marriage" only has meaning because it's related at this moment, not temporally or historically, to a whole bunch of other words in the English language that are related to it—the word "husband," the word "wife," the word "children," the word "family"—all this system of words; if that system was different, this word would be different. The meaning is determined by both the diachronic or historical, and the synchronic or structural location, shall we say, of the sign.

The point is that the meaning of the sign is constituted in both these ways, and that means it's relative to all uses of that sign. The sign's meaning is, as Derrida puts it, "deferred" or "differs," in that the meaning refers and is relative to past uses of the sign, past contexts of use, and the nonpresent related signs in the language. That is, the sign's reference to nonpresent signs constitutes the meaning of the sign. That's an odd way of talking, but if you think for a moment, it's not a bizarre thing to say. The word "marriage" only means, the structuralists have told us, because it's related to a whole bunch of other words. Those other words aren't being said right now; in other words, they're absent. The word "marriage" wouldn't mean if it wasn't related to a whole bunch of absent words. Furthermore, the word wouldn't mean if it didn't have a history of signs that are also, at the present, absent; they just aren't being spoken right now. In other words, every word has a kind of aura about it trailing behind it all these other uses of itself and related terms that are part of what give us meaning. This sign only means because many, many, many, and indefinitely many other signs also mean; each sign implicates all these others.

The meaning of a sign for Derrida—and this is a crucial point—is always another sign. Signs thus generate more signs. If you try to figure out the meaning of a linguistic sign, you go to a dictionary and what do you get? More signs; and if you don't know their meaning, you look them up, you get more signs. Signs thus generate more signs; they are relative to the ones they generate. Each sign is the sign of a sign. This also means that signs are, to use Derrida's word, polysemic; they're inexhaustible. Every sign has an indefinitely large number of meanings. Think of all the different ways that the word "marriage" could be used in every dictionary you've seen, in every legal document, in any jerk you've ever heard; all the variance on the meaning of "marriage." Derrida is saying when I use the word "marriage," if I were to try to say what its full meaning is I would have to cite all those other uses that all play some role in determining the meaning of the word "marriage" when I use it.

We have no reason to privilege any of these multiple meanings of a sign as the meaning. By itself, the sign means all of these other meanings; the sign's meaning is literally incomplete without all these references, it includes them all. But no single usage of a sign can do that; therefore, Derrida's fundamental point is that sign's meaning is nonpresent; in other words, it's not there, it's absent, you could say if you wish that it's implicit. We, as speakers, cannot hope to provide what the philosopher hopes: a direct, unmediated contact between the user of a sign and the object, referent, or meaning of the signs they use. Literally, he's saying in a certain sense: I don't know what I mean. I can't, because meaning has to do with the signs, not what's in my head, not what I hope, not what I want it to mean; but what it actually means has to do with the words, and the words have their history and are part of a synchronic arrangement of science. All that baggage would have to be explicated to say in full what any word means. This means, of course, that whenever we use signs, our signs carry far more meanings than we would want to communicate. In a sense what Derrida is saying is if we really paid attention, meaning is just uncontrollable; it's generative: The sign creates more signs and more signs, and you could never encapsulate all the meanings of a commonly-used sign. When we communicate, though, what that means is we must suppress unwanted meanings. The sign-user is literally in the business of trying to repress, and that means—to put it in a somewhat more dramatic way—every statement, spoken or written, is a lie for Derrida. It's a lie because in the very use of words, I have to pretend that there isn't complexity behind everything I'm saying, so that I can pretend and you can pretend that what I'm saying is simple, direct, and immediately understood.

The final and crucial philosophical claim to this introduction to what Derrida is doing is: All presentation presupposes representation. What we've just said is: We just gave this very complicated theory of what signs are; they're complicated, they're uncontrollable. That's bad enough, you might say, but now that theory of science takes on great importance, because what Derrida says is all my contact with the world, all my perception, my sensation, my cognition, presupposes signs. All perception presupposes signs; all cognitive operations involve signs. We have no immediate cognition of the presence of objects without signs; everything operates through signs.

Let's pause a moment. This might seem absurd; you might say, "The floor is the floor; I'm standing on the floor, I feel the floor, I perceive the floor." Derrida does not have to deny that the floor is there, but what he wants to say is everything I think I know about the floor is already affected by a sign, a concept, a word by representation. When I call it "the floor," I'm using words. To try to somehow describe what I'm experiencing without using any concepts or words, what would I end up with? In principle, I'd probably end up with something like the sense data of the positivist, and then you look at the trouble they got into. The point is: Whatever the human mind experiences, because the mind operates with signs, everything is mediated by a sign. Once this is accepted, it means all cognition, perception, and knowledge are marked by and infected by the generative polysemia, the many meanings, and non-presence of signs.

This is what led Derrida to the famous statement: There is nothing outside the text. Some people have thought that he meant there's no reality outside books or speech, but he didn't mean that. What he meant was there's nothing outside context; in other words, there's nothing we experience, know, or contact that isn't in a context. What's the context? Signs are part of the context; language, and the signs through which humans communicate with each other, are part of the context. For us, there's nothing without signs. He's not saying signs are everything; but there's nothing without signs.

That was Derrida's theory of signs and of its importance; but his primary aim was to apply these insights to one type of communication in particular, to writing, and to philosophical writing especially. Writing shares all the features of semiosis we just described, but writing exposes them in a particularly naked way, and it's for this reason that Derrida comes up with this theory; he expresses it in a book called *Of Grammatology*. Derrida says philosophers have always been frightened of writing, have tried to reduce writing to speech. This counts a little strange, but it's a very interesting theory. Writing is distinctive, for it's the inscription of durable signs that exist independent of the presence of the author. Speech isn't like that, except, of course, once we have electronic recording of speech, that's different; but without electronic recording of speech, the writing of a sign is quite a distinctive way of transferring information. The author is always absent. In other words, if I write a sentence on a piece of paper and leave it here for 100 years, someone can read it. I'll literally be dead when it's being read; my meaning persists, or some kind of meaning, even when the author's absent. This is why deconstructionists or followers of Derrida often say, "Every author is a dead author." What that means is once you put it in writing, you no longer control it; it's out in the world, it's a public sign. It will be interpreted by readers as they will interpret, and it has nothing to do with your intentions; what you wanted to say is irrelevant, what's relevant is what you did write.

Philosophy has tried to imagine that writing is derivative of speech, because speech appears to give signs presence: The speaker and hearer are in almost direct contact, the speaker emits signs literally with the breath of life. "Phonocentrism" is Derrida's name for the privilege of speech over writing. Western philosophy has always tried to interpret signs through the idea of speech, because it's more comfortable to talk about speech because speech has a closer relationship to the life and consciousness and experience of the speaker than writing does; the relation of writing is more different. In this, Derrida coined a famous technical term: differance. Really, this is just the notion "difference" in French. The French word for "difference" is spelled just like the English word except for the addition of an accent. Derrida takes that word "difference," spelled the same way in English and French, and he substitutes for the second "e" an "a," so an "-ance" rather than an "-ence." In French pronunciation, that's pronounced exactly the same; it's pronounced as an "e" would be pronounced. The point is that he has made a word ("differance") that's literally not a word in the French language at all—there is no such word in the French language—yet its distinctiveness can only be seen in writing, not heard in speech. What this means—this is a clever little move of Derrida's—for Derrida is the unending, polysemic differences invoked by every sign. As he says, "We provisionally give the name *differance* to this sameness which is not identical." If you wanted to say—Derrida would never want to say—what is everything? What is the basic for everything? Even such an attempt, for him, makes no sense; the philosophical search to try to constitute the universe of the world makes no sense. But if you wanted to pick some term in Derrida and say, "For him, what is everything," everything is differences.

Philosophy in the last 2,000 years (Western philosophy) has tried to control the meanings of words. Derrida names logocentrism as the dominant metaphysics of the history of Western philosophy. It insists that signs presuppose a direct or immediate relationship to an object or a content; that is, what he calls "the transcendental signified." Philosophy needs to fix meanings; and to do so, it resorts to writing, which renders difference most intractable. Writing is dangerous for philosophy, for it exacerbates the difference philosophy is determined to control between the sign on the one hand, and both the speaker and the signified object on the other. Derrida's point is that this control is impossible.

The word "deconstruction," as it's used in talking about Derrida, has a very particular role. Deconstruction is Derrida's method of critically reading logocentric texts; in other words, texts through the history of philosophy that are trying to nail down the meaning of words, usually by saying that a word or a statement in writing or speech has a direct, immediate, privileged relationship to an object in the world (transcendental signified). That attempt—all philosophers have been trying to do it for 2,500 years—is always mistaken and can't be done. Deconstruction is his method of taking any book or any piece of writing of that tradition of Western philosophy and taking it apart.

What Derrida actually does in his writing, at least his most prominent writing, is Derrida rarely wrote essays or books to express a view, what he did instead was always work reactively, or if you will, negatively: Take a work of philosophy and start to pick it apart. This is the typical way deconstruction worked: You look at philosopher's work, you look at their main points and big distinctions, you pick a distinction that appears marginal to the text but which, once you pull on it, you show that the whole text comes apart; in other words, that the basic conceptual dichotomies or distinctions made by the text are unstable, they don't make sense. One side implies the other; two things are distinguished: A is distinguished from B, but it turns out under Derrida's analysis B has A in it and can't be understood otherwise, and vice versa (A has B in it and can't be understood otherwise). Like, for example, appearance in reality, mind in body, the ideal in the empirical; the point of his deconstruction is to show how references to terms that are typically in the history of philosophy placed, according to Derrida, in hierarchical forms. For example, typically a philosopher might distinguish between reality and appearance. There's reality and appearance; the philosopher wants to know the reality, not just appearance. Reality's better than appearance. This is a hierarchical distinction for Derrida.

He's going to show that the devalued term "appearance" actually is crucial to defining and understanding the privileged term "reality"; and the result is he's going to undo the logical independence, the independent meaning, of the privileged term. The privileged term actually presupposes the demoted term, for example, appearance; if we pull on that thread, neither term means what it was supposed to mean.

For a very quick example, we could turn to his book *Speech and Phenomena*, where Derrida examines Husserl's book the *Logical Investigations*. Husserl had distinguished two kinds of signs, which we describe very quickly called expressions and indices. By expressions, Husserl just meant regular linguistic signs, like "tree"; and "tree" has meaning by this conventional relationship to something outside the mind, the tree in the real world. Indications are what Husserl called exterior, nonlinguistic phenomena that have a causal relationship to the object that they mean; for example, a weathervane. A weathervane tells you where the wind is blowing because it's blown by the very wind that it's a sign for. Husserl tried to say that indicators like weathervanes are deficient signs, because the true expressions or expressive signs, their meaning is an idea in the mind of a person, and therefore the true signs. In a novel analysis, Derrida tires to show, as he looks at how Husserl distinguishes these two kinds of signs, that Husserl's conception of the indicative sign is actually the basis for his understanding of the expressive sign; that the expressive sign, which is supposed to be the authentic or truest sign is actually dependent on the notion of the indicative sign. The whole distinction collapses. That's the idea that Derrida's trying to show: that in effect, the empirical and the ideal can't be separated.

Derrida performed many deconstructions of texts in philosophy; he wrote on other continental figures like Lévinas that we haven't seen, but on many we have seen: Husserl, Hegel, Rousseau, Heidegger, Marx; all of them. He tries to show the complex, dialectical nature of each text, and philosophically deny every attempt they make to get at the origin of meaning or the pure immediate relation of a sign to its object. Derrida's writing is famously difficult, brutally difficult; and for many philosophers, they think this is simply an attempt at obfuscation to try to hide the fact that he really has nothing to say. But whatever one's view of Derrida, I think one has to say that's false. Derrida's weird way of writing comes essentially from this: a recognition or the question, how can you write when you accept that writing is lying? That is, Derrida's strange style comes from the self-reflexive awareness that all uses of signs are dissimulative, an attempt to suppress the play of signs, yet you have to say that in signs; so how do you do that? This creates a great difficulty in his texts.

At any rate, Derrida is clear about one thing: He claims that there is no escape from the language of logocentrism, for him or anyone else. In other words, we cannot stop trying to suppress meanings; trying to attach our terms to transcendental signifieds; trying to privilege some of our signs as having an immediate, present relation to whatever exists independent of signs. We can't help doing that; we will always do it. What, then, is the point of his writing? It's in effect to play with these logocentric texts, to grant ourselves some limited degree of freedom within them; in other words, to loosen up the hold of the picture these texts promote on our minds. At the same time, Derrida simply doesn't think that any philosophical question is finished, or reliably answered; they can only be endlessly discussed. There's no point where justification is reached and truth has been established. At one point, I saw Derrida giving a response to the work of another well-known philosopher. The philosopher went through and gave certain arguments for why he thought Derrida was wrong, and Derrida's first response was to say, "Oh, I see; all finished" (slapping his hands against each other). From Derrida's point of view, there is no such thing as the end of a philosophical question at all.

Derrida is certainly a polarizing figure; many Anglo-American philosophers, analytic philosophers, consider him not a philosopher at all, others fear him as a kind of nihilist. But for some philosophers with continental philosophical training, some of them consider him the most radical internal critic of the tradition that's yet been produced. His greatest influence was actually not in philosophy but in literary criticism.

Some people had a political concern about Derrida; that is, some considered him a dangerous radical in a social or political sense, that his conclusions would undermine any commitment to a good society, or democracy, or liberal republican society. Politically, like almost all French intellectuals of the second half of the 20th century, Derrida was a man of the left, but not the Marxist left; and he was once arrested in Communist Czechoslovakia, before the fall of the Berlin Wall, for participating in an unapproved conference. Months before his death in 2004, Derrida, in fact, made it clear in a little essay that he sought to defend "our Enlightenment heritage"; it sounds rather bizarre. But one might think here of Hume: Remember, Hume was a radical skeptic if there ever was one, but he nevertheless produced a moral theory and endorsed a lawful politics on the basis of his skepticism. Sometimes, if the philosophical critique is sufficiently radical, it simply leaves us where we were before. To think of Derrida as undermining Western civilization or the Enlightenment is perhaps an exaggeration.

The Challenge of Postmodernism
Lecture 31

Some postmodernists become what we could call postcritical. This is a different group of postmodernists. By postcritical I mean ... that this group of postmodernists came to apply their radical critique of political and social norms so fully that they undermined the use of those norms to criticize the status quo.

Jacques Derrida and other French poststructuralists fueled a new movement in philosophy: postmodernism. Postmodernists deny presence or immediate relation of our ideas, perceptions, or representations to objectivity. All presentation presupposes representation or the use of signs, which are constructed by us. Some postmodernists make the historical claim that contemporary society or knowledge function without the need for authenticity or unity that earlier, modern society and thought required. Thus **Jean-François Lyotard** argued that contemporary science no longer seeks, nor requires, a unified picture of the world, while Jean Baudrillard claimed that we literally no longer interact with reality, but with a hyperreality of simulations.

> **Postmodernists deny presence or immediate relation of our ideas, perceptions, or representations to objectivity.**

Others, inspired by **Michel Foucault**, argued that social normalcy is constructed by repressing social deviants and the identity of majority cultures by the suppression of minorities. Feminists like **Iris Marion Young**, Susan Bordo, and **Sandra Harding**, postcolonial writers like **Gayatri Chakravorty Spivak**, and Americanist philosopher of race **Cornel West** find in the postmodernists a means of social critique. But the question remains, is the postmodern critique so radical that not only the status quo, but any normative ideal used to lead reform, must fall before it? ■

Names to Know

Foucault, Michel (1926–1984): Along with Jacques Derrida, he is one of the two most influential poststructuralists and creators of philosophical postmodernism. Unlike Derrida, his work was essentially historical; he sought to portray how the language of the human sciences since the 16th century had constituted modern human being. He was heavily influenced by Friedrich Nietzsche's notions of genealogy and power.

Harding, Sandra (b. 1935): An American philosopher best known for her contributions to feminist epistemology, she argues that modern theory of knowledge and science privileged a masculinist conception of knowledge as objective and based in distance rather than interaction.

Lyotard, Jean-François (1924–1998): This French poststructuralist's work was closest to political and legal theory, and his *The Postmodern Condition: A Report on Knowledge* became the most famous definition of philosophical and social postmodernism in the 1980s.

Spivak, Gayatri Chakravorty (b. 1942): This postcolonial philosopher was born in India and educated there and in the United States. She incorporates feminist, Marxist, and Derridean perspectives to demonstrate how the literature of the colonial European powers constructs and subjugates the subaltern: women, the poor, and the non-Western.

West, Cornel (b. 1953): This prominent African American philosopher and minister has worked in many areas of philosophy and as a public philosopher in the Jamesian and Deweyan tradition. As author of *The American Evasion of Philosophy*, he argues for a "prophetic pragmatism" on the basis of the Americanist tradition.

Young, Iris Marion (1949–2006): This American feminist political philosopher was influenced by poststructuralist thought and was the author of many books, including *Justice and the Politics of Difference* and *"Throwing Like a Girl" and Other Essays in Feminist Philosophy and Social Theory*.

Suggested Reading

Baudrillard, *America*.

Cahoone, "From Feminist Empiricism," "The Scaling of Bodies," "A Genealogy of Modern Racism," "Can the Subaltern Speak?" and "The Cartesian Masculinization of Thought" in *From Modernism to Postmodernism*.

Foucault, "Truth and Power," in *The Foucault Reader*.

Lyotard, *The Postmodern Condition*.

Questions to Consider

1. Has reason (or rationality), as a norm and ideal, itself been a tool of social repression?

2. What notion of freedom, equality, or liberation that might be opposed to the established status quo would not be open to deconstruction?

The Challenge of Postmodernism
Lecture 31—Transcript

Having examined one of postmodernism's most famous instigators, Jacques Derrida, it's now time to try to understand the term "postmodernism" in German. The term has a complex history. It was first used in 1917 by Rudolf Pannwitz, a German thinker, to refer to what he considered the post-Nietzschean nihilism of the 20th century. Then it came into use in literature and most famously in architecture, in each case indicating the obsolescence of earlier "modernist" movements in art and in architecture the earlier 20th century; so postmodernism indicated a kind of post-1950s artistic and architectural style. But then the term came to be adopted in the late 1960s and '70s in philosophy and also in social theory as a name for something about the new post-Second World War period.

For some, the term "postmodern" is a historical claim that post–World War II advanced societies have entered a new cultural-social period where older, modern notions no longer apply. Postmodern in this form is a name for the culture of postindustrial societies; that's how some people use it, especially in the social sciences. For others, it signifies a political critique of the modern as a period of oppression and imperialism that more recent thinkers wish to criticize and supersede. Certainly much of postmodern writing appears as radical as radical could be; but must it be? Is it really radical? Let's talk about postmodernism in general.

Virtually all postmodernists accept a couple of basic ideas: One, that perception and cognition presuppose signs and representation; this is exactly what we saw in Derrida. That is, from the postmodern perspective, there is no direct, immediate, or incorrigible access of mind to the world. All knowledge and cognition, and action, is mediated by signs, by language, by culture, by representations. Second, postmodernists also hold that what other philosophers have traditionally taken to be the fundamental units or unities of reality—substance, self, God, knowledge itself, the notion of reality versus appearance—postmodernists look at these terms as attempts to mask differences and to suppress them; that is, these terms, postmodernists believe, are mistaken attempts to reduce the pluralistic, playful complexity of the world and put it into very narrow categories, and, as we'll see, often for political or social reason.

One feature of some postmodernism is directly historical, and for that we can turn to the French writer Jean-François Lyotard. Lyotard makes the argument that the advanced societies—he means developed societies—after World War II, we can call them postindustrial societies, no longer possess nor require what he called "metanarratives" of legitimation, like Marxism or a Hegelian notion of an integrated moral state, or progress.

These postindustrial societies are postmodern. The disparate practical-linguistic contexts of social activity, Lyotard holds, justify themselves by achieving their own goals. In short, what's being claimed by Lyotard is: Ours is the first civilization that no longer has any unity, and it doesn't need it, either. That's crucial; if Lyotard was to say, "Our society has no unity and that's a terrible thing and we need to get it back," he'd sound like a conservative; but the postmodernist says, "We have no unity, and we don't need it."

For Lyotard, the life of social members is contextualized by practical linguistic contexts, Wittgensteinian language-games, with their own internal norms. Society functions without a high level of coordination among those games. Let's pause and see what this means: You go to work; there's a set of practical rules and linguistic rules about what can be said and done in the workplace. You go to church and participate in a different language game. There's the family setting in your home; there are professional organizations you participate in; there's the rules that govern the deployment of mass culture throughout society. All of these contexts of life, from the postmodern point of view, have their own distinct, separate rules—they're, in Lyotard's sense, language games—and there's no need to have an overarching set of rules that unifies them. Postmodern society, the implication is, is fragmented, and it works as fragmented; the fragmentation is not a problem to be solved.

Lyotard claims this as well about science itself. Postmodern science, according to him, is a proliferation of independent research programs that cannot be integrated. The whole notion of the unity of science—which is something that was certainly promoted by the positivists—is, for him, anachronistic. Distinctive sciences are, for him, even incommensurable; their modes of knowledge cannot be integrated, and we shouldn't try to integrate them. In other words, to expand on this a bit, not only is it the case that physics, chemistry, biology, engineering, meteorology, psychology, and cognitive science each have their own research programs, but even within them fields and subfields have their own research programs creating and producing knowledge, Lyotard would say, and this postmodern practice of science neither needs or really could tolerate an attempt to unify and integrate the views, the conclusions, of all of the sciences.

In short, postmodern society and its disciplines of inquiry are all radically fragmented. Conservatives may make, as I said, the same criticism; but for Lyotard this fragmentation is both inevitable and desirable. Why desirable? Because, from the point of view of Lyotard as a postmodernist, it is unity and consensus that are the great dangers to human freedom; individuality and freedom thrive in the transitions between language games. In other words, fragmentation is, in a sense, good; and unity and integration would always mean the suppression of some differences and the rule or power of a few.

Lyotard wrings a normative implication from his sociological description: "A recognition of the heteromorphous nature of language games ... [what he means by that is simply that language games are very different from each other] obviously implies a renunciation of terror, which assume [language games] are isomorphic and tries to make them so." That is, what Lyotard's claiming is, terror or the heart of authoritarian rule in society, the loss of freedom, comes from the attempt to make all language games function according to the same rules. It's the fragmentation and differences among language games that make freedom possible.

At the same time, postmodern techniques of analysis have often been wielded for political purposes; you can already get a taste of that from what Lyotard has just said. But most of these trade on the work of another French postmodernist and poststructuralist, Michel Foucault. Foucault was a critic of the way human sciences, like psychiatry and penology, had been used to define deviance, and then segregate aberrant humans in order to construct a notion of normal selfhood. As noted earlier, Foucault once quipped that man was invented in the 16th century. What he meant by that is a typical structuralist or poststructuralist thing to say; what he meant was that, following structuralism, "man" is a signifier (it's a word), which is constituted by a set of discourses; that is, by the linguistic and practical activities human beings engage in. The ones Foucault is most interested in, most notable, are those of the human sciences, like psychology, medicine, psychiatry, and penology.

When Foucault says that man was invented in the 16th century, what he means is it's only since the 16th century that Western society invented a new set of sciences of being human—like psychology, psychiatry, etc.—and these sciences describe human being in a certain way. In Foucault's way of describing it, those sciences constructed a normative, normalizing picture of what it means to be human.

Foucault's approach was taken up, sometimes along with Derrida's, to argue that Europeans had, in the modern period, in the imperial age, repressed non-whites to "construct" their own racial and class identity as a preferred category, just as males had repressed women in order to "construct" an ideal of masculinity as the repository of political power. You may here in this a little echo of the views of Adorno and Horkheimer from their book *Dialectic of Enlightenment*. The notion is that a class of people, in order to feel secure about their own identity, need some other class to rule, and they need to be able to constitute, construct, or imagine the selves of those other people as being very different; in effect, projecting their own unattractive qualities onto this group so they can constitute themselves as different.

Foucault went on in his career to do a variety of work, especially in the historical analysis of sexuality, and the study of sexuality as a set of techniques for constructing and controlling the self. Politically, we could say that Foucault was a left-Nietzschean; following Nietzsche, Foucault accepts that all life, including inquiry into truth, is power. In other words, science, the social science, is seeking power. If all science is power and all knowledge is power, how are we to seek knowledge and yet have a society of freedom? For Foucault, a bit like Lyotard, the goal of social liberation is not to transcend power relationships—because you can't do that—but to loosen them up, to fragment them, to make sure there are no overwhelming centers of power.

Foucault was, with Derrida, one of the most famous representatives of the postmodern movement. Foucault represented the social and political side, particularly by exploring sexuality, which he also did in his personal life as well as in his intellectual life. Foucault died of AIDS in 1984. Derrida represented the more cognitive, epistemological, and philosophy of language implications of postmodernism; Foucault was the high priest of the political side of postmodernism.

Their thought, and the work of the other French poststructuralists, spawned a slew of political formulations, especially in the United States. For example, feminist epistemologists like Sandra Harding and Susan Bordo argue that modern epistemology—and she means Descartes, Bacon, Galileo; everybody since the 17th century—has expressed a gendered, or characteristically male, conception of knowledge. A feminist alternative might see knowledge as arising out of the interaction of inquirer with the subject matter—a more interactive model of coming to know—rather than the scientific ideal of maintaining an "objective" distance (if we understand it that way) from the object of knowledge. They extended this to a critique of classical epistemology: Reason itself, it was held by some, was a male construction based on the political need to maintain power in male hands.

Continuing this line of thought, the postcolonial philosopher Gayatri Spivak takes even Foucault to task for Eurocentrism; for defining "human being" in terms that primarily are modern Western, that are the result of imperialism. African American philosophy also made a contribution: The well-known Harvard professor Cornel West shows how the very notions of reason and of rights, which were used since the Enlightenment and which certainly had some role in the development of human freedom, were nevertheless projected by the ruling classes of the West as the guarantors of their own liberty and equality, but were simultaneously used to repress racial minorities. Iris Marion Young analyzed the way that political and cultural arrangements "scale" the bodies of the rulers and the ruled, designating some as "abject," revolting, disgusting by way of maintaining the identity of the "best." She calls instead for a pluralistic "politics of difference."

So the common claim of postmodernists in this political sense is that the very norms modern writers and philosophers like to think of as guaranteeing a decent progressive society—norms like truth, morality, reason, beauty, individuality, rights themselves; all these notions that have been fought for and thought of by modern philosophers as crucial to the morality of the modern era—the postmodern thinkers I've just described regard these as tools of repression; that, in effect, the use of these notions, despite the best appearances, have, in fact, been employed to repress whole segments of society. Take an example: In traditional liberal democracy, we have the notion of the "melting pot" of assimilation in the United States, the ideal of equality. These were actually not simply applied, or when put into practice, they required that the "other"—this is a common postmodernist term; when I try to define myself or my class or gender or racial group tries to define itself and solidify its sense of self, it must do it by contrasting itself with an "other," those "others"; let's say women, racial, ethnic, and religious minorities, homosexuals—and the way we do this is we essentially strip ourselves of qualities we feel are unattractive, we project and attach those onto the other group, and we have to deny that there's any commonality between self and other. The antidote to all is, from the point of view of postmodernism, a recognition of difference or diversity, and an embrace of diversity, often found at the margins of official discourse.

Let me add just one little point to this; I'll give you an example: Back in the 1960s, when Lyndon Johnson at one point in his support for the civil rights movement, remember he introduced at one point Martin Luther King to a popular audience. He said, "Martin Luther King Jr. is a credit to his race, the human race." From a certain older point of view, him saying that is morally good because he's asserting that he himself Lyndon Johnson and Martin Luther King Jr. have this commonality: they're both human beings, part of the same species, they're the same. But from the postmodernist perspective, Johnson's remarks are not quite so attractive, because, in effect, from the postmodern perspective, postmodernists would say, "Are you saying that the differences between yourself and Martin Luther King Jr. have to be ignored for him to be equal? Shouldn't we instead say, 'Martin Luther King Jr. comes from a different race, a different social background worlds away from my own,' (Lyndon Johnson might have said), 'and nevertheless, we are worthy of equal respect.'" It's this trying to wipe away differences and trying to regard people as same that's regarded from the postmodernist and poststructuralist point of view as a sin against the reality of difference.

The philosophical issue between the postmodernists and their progressive political allies—in other words, more traditional liberals who support a liberalism of rights and individualism, classical liberalism, progressives concerned about trying to increase government control over wealth and government concern for the poor—in other words, the politics of class, which is more traditional politics in the United States; the postmodernists were more concerned with politics of identity, identity politics, what type of person are you, less concerned with dollars and sense, you might say, and more concerned with skin, gender, and with sexual orientation. In doing this, the postmodernists were then sometimes criticized by their more traditional liberal friends because if the postmodernists attack every form of unity, every norm that can be asserted and every goal by which we would unify society in some way, then traditional liberals fear that this would actually take away support from the kind of social movements they most desire. There's always been a bit of a friendship of convenience but yet conflict between traditional liberals and progressives and postmodern liberals and progressives.

Lastly, some postmodernists become what we could call "postcritical." This is a different group of postmodernists. By "postcritical" I mean—and I'm being a little unfair; every philosopher is critical of something, so they certainly did not lack criticism of some other ideas—is that this group of postmodernists came to apply their radical critique of political and social norms so fully that they undermined the use of those norms to criticize the status quo. Let's take as an example Frenchman Jean Baudrillard; Baudrillard's a postmodern sociologist and cultural critic. Baudrillard's views were not at all critical, but rather an ironic celebration of mass culture. Postmodern society for Baudrillard—and one of his most important examples was the United States—has abandoned reality altogether in its massive production and consumption of signs, from film, television, recorded music, the print media, and the internet. Baudrillard's claim was that we in the modern societies of the Earth now inhabit what he calls a hyperreality, a condition in which a relation to reality has not only been replaced by a relation to signs—in other words, we deal with the advertisement, not the thing—but where those signs are mainly what he called "simulacra," meaning signs that don't actually purport to represent anything at all. In such a condition, our criterion of the "real" is whether something can be reproduced or signed.

In other words, Baudrillard was claiming something extremely radical; so radical that it seems essentially it unhinges any possible political critique of society that you might produce. From Baudrillard's point of view, people on the left, the right, the center, other postmodern social critics, the most conservative elements of society, everybody is dwelling in a world of hyperreality, where all they see are the products of mass culture and they no longer can get through or reach through those cultural images to the reality behind them.

A somewhat similar, although much more scientific, view was developed by the German sociologist Niklas Luhmann. Luhmann radicalized Max Weber's distinction of social action into instrumental spheres governed by disparate values. As you may remember when we discussed Weber, Weber was the first person to actually give voice to this basic idea that in modern society or in late modern society, the 20th century, that lacking religion as a way to give a total integration to our view of the world, we modern people are left with a bunch of different competing, ultimate values, none of which can be reduced to the other and none of which can gain an obvious superiority to the other. In other words, I am committed to the value of my family life, the value of my country, the value of my profession; each of these roles that I occupy has rules I need to follow and value, but which takes precedence over which? How to integrate them all? Weber says in the modern world there is no way; you must merely choose among them, and you can't help but, in Weber's terminology, sin against one value while trying to promote another value.

Luhmann took this even much further, arguing that essentially modern society has nothing like unity at all; there's nothing in modern society—in this way he's speaking much like Lyotard—that modern society does not present what traditional sociology would have thought as a collective consciousness or a collective culture or a common point of view that plays a normative role in determining social behavior. That's not how we act; we move between social situations, we follow the rules of those situations, there is no way to integrate them.

Baudrillard's work, and Luhmann's, illustrates a problem, which many of the writers acknowledge. Poststructuralism—or postmodernism more broadly—may provide the means to critique the status quo, but can it provide the resources for a normative solution, a theory of justice or rights or identity, necessary to justify an alternative? In other words, if the postmodern critique attacks every statement that a policymaker or a philosopher or a social theorist might make—any time any of these persons tries to say, "This is what's wrong with society, and this is what we ought to do; this is the definition of society"—if postmodernism gives an external critique of those norms and idea, which they can using the radical ideas of Foucault and Derrida, it would seem that they would simply unhinge any positive statements we might make at all; in other words, that they would leave us with the ability to criticize everything, but to say or do nothing.

For if we are to change society in which ever way we think is best, this would seem to require justifications of unity, identity, and privileged conditions that postmodernism must, by its very nature, undermine. Can the critical beast of postmodernism be brought to heel; or must it, having chewed up the opposition, actually starting gnawing on itself? This is the internal problem of critical postmodernism. That is, and we've seen this before—this problem was raised partly by Adorno and Horkheimer, and in some of the other lectures in this course—if the mode of philosophical criticism you engage is radical enough so that it not only criticizes first the views it opposes, but then the basis for any view whatsoever, does it simply leave everything where it is? Because any norm or ideal that could be used to change the world would be in principle just as open to postmodern criticism as the world is itself.

But there's one more major figure associated with postmodernism in philosophy who is not a continental philosopher at all; someone trained as an analytic philosopher, as a matter of fact, but who also learned lessons from the continentals just while he, at the same time, went to school with the American pragmatists, mixing all these together into a decidedly American version of the postmodern stew. In the process, he became the most famous philosopher in the world for the last 30 years. I'm speaking of Richard Rorty, and it's to his work we'll turn next.

Rorty and the End of Philosophy
Lecture 32

> Rorty remains deeply controversial; loved by some, disliked by most perhaps. At the very least, we can say that Rorty really did announce more clearly than any other philosopher of the mid- to late 20th century the end of foundationalism. ... The deeper question we're left with is, is philosophy wedded to that foundationalist project? If it is ... then philosophy as we understood it is at an end.

In the later Martin Heidegger, in hermeneutics and structuralism, in Willard Van Orman Quine and Thomas S. Kuhn, we begin to see the end of a conception of first philosophy that had been active since at least René Descartes: foundationalism. The attempt to justify epistemic realism, or our objective knowledge of the world, by identifying indubitable first principles or incorrigible sense data has ended. Now there are no nontrivial first principles that are indubitable or that can be noncircularly justified, and all statements of sense data are themselves infiltrated by theories and perspectives unjustified by that very data.

> **All statements of sense data are themselves infiltrated by theories and perspectives unjustified by that very data.**

There is no, as Thomas Nagel put it, "view from nowhere," or as **Hilary Putnam** put it, "God's Eye view" of the world. Likewise, as **Joseph Margolis** points out, the Kantian notion that a universal and necessary inventory of human projections onto the world, or a pure, presuppositionless account of experience, is just as impossible. We no more have a foundational theory of our own knowing apparatus than we do of what it knows. The point is that foundationalism is dead. The person who wrote the obituary was **Richard Rorty**. The most famous American contributor to postmodernist philosophy, Rorty argued that the search for the foundations of knowledge is a bankrupt enterprise, that traditional philosophy is well forgotten; knowledge is simply whatever the verification procedures of society say it is. ∎

Names to Know

Margolis, Joseph (b. 1924): An American philosopher with the rare ability to work deeply in all three 20th-century traditions: analysis, continental philosophy, and pragmatism. He is the author of many books seeking a pragmatist view of knowledge that accepts relativism but does not undermine a realist interpretation of science.

Putnam, Hilary (b. 1926): A major American analytic philosopher of language and of mind, he was an early proponent of functionalism in the philosophy of mind. His later thought was heavily influenced by pragmatism and the work of J. L. Austin.

Rorty, Richard (1931–2007): An analytic philosopher who came to critique the whole genre of analytic and continental philosophy. He was the most famous critic of foundationalism and regarded himself as a radical pragmatist.

Suggested Reading

Rorty, *Consequences of Pragmatism*.

———, *Objectivity, Relativism, and Truth*.

———, *Philosophy and the Mirror of Nature*.

Questions to Consider

1. For Rorty, is pragmatism realist, antirealist, or neither?

2. For Rorty, what is the difference between the truth of everyday claims and the truth of philosophical claims?

Rorty and the End of Philosophy
Lecture 32—Transcript

In the last lecture, we had a bit of a sojourn into political philosophy, because postmodernism certainly did generate a certain amount of political thought and political writing; and as we saw, it was mostly political thought of the left—poststructuralism and postmodernism are famously associated with the left—but not exclusively so, because we also saw at the end Niklas Luhmann's thought, which is sometimes actually thought of as conservative; so it's not absolutely necessary that poststructuralism go in the left-wing direction, although it typically does. Today we're going to leave politics behind and get back to the theory of knowledge, because here today we're going to look at the work of Richard Rorty.

Richard Rorty was the most well-known philosopher in America in the late 20th century, highly admired and often vilified. After training as an analytic philosopher, in mid-career Rorty's work took an intriguing turn; and that came with his 1979 book, *Philosophy and the Mirror of Nature*. This had a tremendous impact, and the rest of Rorty's career was actually spent elaborating and justifying the argument of that book. In effect, Rorty came to represent the American wing of the postmodern movement; that is, a unique pragmatic form of postmodernism. We will examine his argument and its significance.

The task of *Philosophy and the Mirror of Nature* was complex. First, Rorty wanted to argue that the Cartesian-Lockean-Kantian project of foundationalism—that is, the attempt to justify our realistically true knowledge of the world—was wrongheaded and impossible; that's one point he wanted to make. In particular, Rorty argued that there can be no noncircular justification of any metaphysical or epistemological point of view. Given the lack of immediate relation of cognition to its objects—which, as we've seen, many of the 20th century thinkers we've reviewed have agreed with that—our cognition is always mediated by what Rorty called a "final vocabulary" of theories, propositions, signs, and even culture, which we bring to experience. But this means there can be no noncircular justification of that vocabulary. If the final vocabulary—he uses the term "final" just to mean the biggest or the most complete vocabulary I have; the widest possible set of my beliefs, ideas, terms, language—always mediates between our statements of what we perceive, or of what are our ultimate cognitive capacities are, and their objects, then the relation of the vocabulary to naked reality can never be checked. I can put it this way in a very simplistic sense: If I am wearing rose-colored glasses, everything looks rosy; and if I can't take the glasses off, how can I ever check to see if reality is really rose-colored or not?

Rorty coupled this argument to a unique historical account that is perhaps equally important for understanding early 20th century philosophy. Here's what Rorty said. Early 20th century philosophy had continued the foundationalist project of early modern philosophy—in other words, the project of Descartes, Locke, Kant, and others—and it had done it in two particularly radical forms: Husserlian phenomenology on the one hand, and logical positivism on the other. What Rorty is saying is that both the early continental philosophers (phenomenologists) and the early analytic philosophers (in particular the positivists) both tried to ground knowledge, find a foundation for knowledge, on the one hand in a transcendental account of pure experience, and on the other hand in a combination of physicalistically caused sense data and logic. But, Rorty points out, by mid-century, each project ended in bankruptcy; and that bankruptcy was the result of its own internal critique. All descriptions of ultimate evidence or sense data are themselves caught up in theoretical disputes, hence the evidence and sense data cannot decide among them.

That was the verdict we ran into in looking at Quine and others in criticizing the basic ideas of the positivist program. That message was also seem in later representatives of continental traditions; because just as Quine and Wittgenstein undermined the logical positivists, Heidegger, Gadamer, and Derrida undermined Husserl. In each case, they undermined the initial foundational hopes of the discipline.

To pause for a moment: What Rorty is saying is that there's a beautiful parallel development of these two major schools of thought of 20th century philosophy; schools that, to some extent, claim that they have nothing in common and that have attacked each other and regarded themselves, as I once said, as playing two completely different kinds of games without much in common. But Rorty's saying they had a lot in common: They had an early phase, continental and analytic, in which they tried to do what Descartes wanted but do it even better, more radically, and find the ultimate science that would found all knowledge. But in each case, the later contributors to that tradition discovered problems in their fundamental ideas until that school came, in each case, to undermine itself. That's an interesting theory; it has something to be said for it.

There was one more component to Rorty's argument: He claimed there was one school of thought that had never accepted the foundationalist defenses of realism. The recent self-criticisms of phenomenology by Heidegger and Derrida, and of analytic philosophy by Quine and Wittgenstein, can both be seen to be incorporating insights that in effect lead them back to that third tradition, which had never quite gotten on to the foundationalist project. What's the name of that tradition? Pragmatism. Rorty is claiming that pragmatism is an alternative to these two forms of foundationalism, and that historically as these two forms of foundationalism, analytic and continental philosophy, realized their own difficulty they had tended to take on certain resources from pragmatism.

In later writings Rorty made this epistemological position more clear. He rejected what he calls "representationalism." Representationalism is the notion that our language represents reality. From this perspective—that is, from Rorty's—both realism and antirealism are answers to a mistaken question. In other words, let me explain: Typically philosophers have tried to ask—especially in the 20th century where language became kind of the central medium or location for philosophical questions about human knowledge on both sides of the Atlantic Ocean—the questions about language that turned into questions about, "How do we know that our words hook onto reality, hook onto the real world, that my descriptions of the world are true? What's the relationship between knowledge and reality?" Realists meant to say, "Well, there is some way that our ideas really do correspond to reality," and antirealists said, "No, we can't show our language corresponds to reality, we can only show that our language corresponds to itself; that is, one bit of language corresponds to another, we can't actually show it corresponds to reality."

Rorty is claiming both are false; or more than false, he's saying both of them are answers to a mistaken question. We cannot examine the relation of our statements to reality. You might say that's crazy. If I say to my wife, "Betsy, my keys are on the counter," and she says, "No, they're not," hasn't my statement been tested against reality? Rorty agrees; but it's tested by other statements, my wife's statements. In other words, language is the medium in which we express the evidence of reality, and one bit of language tries to correct another bit of language. But what we cannot do is stand outside of language altogether and ask, "Does language as a whole map onto the world?" to put it differently, Rorty says nothing makes our beliefs true; he rejects that whole notion of truth. In fact, Rorty came to recognize that he was rejecting the very account of truth altogether. In other words, Rorty is saying it's a mistake for philosophers to try to define "true."

For Rorty, the predicate "true" functions only as a compliment we pay, as he says, an endorsement of, whatever statements survive our verification procedures. Those procedures are public and social. All people in all cultures in all societies have ways of trying to figure out whose statements are right and whose are wrong; they have procedures for doing that, like testing. When your views past those tests, we call them "true"; "true" doesn't mean anything more than that. Additionally, Rorty accepts Donald Davidson's claim that "belief is by nature veridical"; that is, by nature truthful. What Davidson meant was not that all our beliefs are individually true; he meant that the whole interaction between the human organism and the environment is designed to create true beliefs. Beliefs are the way we deal with reality; our beliefs are generated as our best grasp of the real, and there's no further justification of them beyond the tests we typically employ in our language to generate them.

Any philosophical attempt to give a theory or account of truth beyond this is wrong-headed. This is a major claim; we'll pause just for a minute to say something about this. As Rorty got older in the years after 1979 and *Philosophy and the Mirror of Nature*, he kept reformulating his view—never changing it in fundamental ways but reformulating it—to try to say more and more precisely what it is he's rejecting; and this is one of the best ways to put it: There is really nothing philosophically interesting about the concept of truth at all (that's what he's claiming); and all philosophical attempts to get at the notion of truth, to prove that we have some truth are mistaken. Why? For a variety of reasons, but the biggest one we've already mentioned; here's what we cannot do: We cannot say, "Here I am." I have a series of capacities for trying to understand the world. They're thoroughly linguistic—they're all wrapped up with my public culture, with my language, it's in language that I state whatever evidence it is I take from the world—so I have this big, you might say, means by which I know the world, and it generates a certain amount of knowledge from things. Fine; Rorty has no objection to all that. He is not a skeptic about everyday knowledge or scientific knowledge. Indeed, Rorty says, there's no problems with everyday and scientific knowledge; the only problem is with the philosophers' attempt to prove that we have some. That's when we fall into problems; because the philosopher, in order to prove that we have knowledge, what would the philosopher have to do? The philosopher would have to leap out of the human condition, find some neutral place to stand, view the universe as it is in a thing in itself, and then view how human beings understand the universe. That is not possible; it can't happen. The only way anybody can know the world is through the means by which they know the world; we cannot step outside those means and judge them. From Rorty's perspective, as he once put it, "Philosophy is dead"; that is, philosophy that tries to figure out the underpinnings of all knowledge is finished. It never made any sense, and we should just stop doing it.

Rory interprets his own view as pragmatism. Let's examine that for a moment: Rorty knew the American pragmatic tradition well—he had read Peirce, James, and Dewey—but out of all of them, his preferred pragmatist was James, because it was James who seemed to respond to the philosophical demand that we need a theory of truth most like Rorty himself wanted to respond to it. In other words, James—as we saw in an earlier lecture—was wont to say things like "Truth is what works" and "Truth is what is successful"; these are the kinds of terms that drove his older friend Charles Peirce crazy because he thought they were far-too-sloppy descriptions of what pragmatist theory of truth is all about (that may be true or that may not be true). However, from Rorty's point of view, he would say James is being very shrewd. What Rorty would claim is when James says things like "Truth is what works," what James is really doing is simply denying the need or the usefulness of any theory of truth. Rorty wanted to interpret James even more radically, not as offering a different account of truth—remember I said before in an earlier lecture that most philosophers would say there are three different canonical theories of truth: the pragmatic theory, the correspondence theory, the coherence theory—Rorty is saying that's a mistake; if it's properly understood, the pragmatic theory of truth isn't the theory of truth. Pragmatism for Rorty is the denial of the need for any account of truth at all. In Rorty's version, Jamesian pragmatism is not a theory of truth; it's simply a denial of the need or usefulness for any theory of truth.

By rejecting the whole idea of a theory of truth, Rorty's version of pragmatism simply leaves us with the verification procedures of our culture. Thus, as he put it in one of his later books, "solidarity" not objectivity is the desideratum of truth. This is an important point, because to say such a thing looks very much like conventionalist relativism. There are many kinds of relativism in the world; whenever we say that something is not just true but true for or true with respect to or true relative to, we're adopting some limited type of relativism. In the case of conventionalism, conventionalism is the claim that what truth is relative to is a social agreement, the conventions of society. To refer to solidarity or social convention as the desideratum of truth seems like a conventionalist form of relativism. For Rorty, truth can only mean the compliment we pay to claims that satisfy our community's verification procedures, whatever they happen to be.

Asked on one occasion—actually I should say he was asked on all occasions, but on one particular occasion—the question about whether he was a nihilist or a relativist, Rorty responded by claiming we in the West should be "frankly ethnocentric," endorsing those verification procedures that have led to the greater happiness, liberty, and progress of modern Western society. The value of those procedures is their contribution to our form of life, in the modern Western case of progressively liberal societies. Let's pause again for a moment here: This can be seen in various ways; you might even say this is a rather politically conservative thing to say, for Rorty to say that we in the West should be "frankly ethnocentric." What's happening here really is this: Whatever his political notions, Rorty is saying there is no philosophical foundation or philosophical bottom floor that can tell us which ultimate values and commitments are the right ones in human life or in science. We in the West developed certain procedures for seeking truth, like modern science. Why is that good? Why is that valid? Not because it's more true than every other method of truth, but because we happen to notice that, in the long run, as we have used modern science in society and enlightenment methods in society, we've wound up with better social conditions; so that's good enough for me, Rorty says. From his point of view, we ought to be simply "frankly ethnocentric"; we in the West are going to follow a particular tradition of understanding truth in a certain way as connected with individualism and science because things have worked out pretty well following that program.

The picture of the world we are left with, according to Rorty, is essentially a nonphilosophical naturalism. Rorty didn't say a lot about metaphysics, but when he did he implied that he was a naturalist. He followed Arthur Fine, another philosopher, who suggested what Fine called a "natural ontological attitude"; something that needs no philosophical justification. It can't, by the way, for Rorty, because if Rorty were to try to give a philosophical justification of naturalism, he'd be doing the kind of metaphysical Philosophy that he's criticizing. What he wants to say, though, with Fine is that our naive, everyday, natural approach to the world is a kind of naturalism, it needs no philosophical justification, and in this context the function of philosophy should just be a generalized cultural criticism that opens up new ways to conceive society.

In this way, he thinks he's bringing together Dewey and Foucault. Just as Foucault (postmodernist) thought that in the end all truth is power and all claims to truth are claims to power, so we can't get outside that to create a social theory or social norms that escape his criticism (Foucault would say); nevertheless—still within this realm where everything we say is a discourse about power one way or another; even when we're trying not to use power, we're using it—Foucault would say, we can find ways within that to improve society, to create more freedom. At the same time, Dewey—who made this much more explicit—as we saw in an earlier lecture, thought philosophy itself is ultimately concerned with the improvement of society; indeed, arguably, for Dewey, the ultimate goal of philosophy isn't truth; or rather it's truth, but truth is only evident in the ongoing improvement of social conditions. In this sense, too, Rorty feels like he's part of the pragmatic tradition. For him, philosophy has a role in supporting progressive society and freedom, and by critiquing society to exhibit new options for the future. What it can't do is prove that one of them is right; it can't give an underlying justification of its own recommendations, because to do that, at a philosophical level, would be to sin against the every things that Rorty has been criticizing all along.

Rorty extended this view over a slew of later books, most prominently *Consequences of Pragmatism*; a book called *Objectivity, Relativism, and Truth*; another one called *Contingency, Irony, and Solidarity*; and many others. Rorty's impact was enormous, and extremely controversial. He was widely interpreted as saying that philosophy as traditionally understood is simply at an end, and aligning himself with the similar view of the later Heidegger and perhaps the later Wittgenstein, with the exception that Rorty always eschewed the Germanic drama with which Heidegger expressed it. In other words, Rorty's way of saying this was something like, "Let's just give up Philosophy. It's not useful, it doesn't do anything for us, it accomplishes nothing, it can't be shown to be valid, and in a sense it's boring. Let's turn to something else"; not a claim like Heidegger that philosophy is involved with the degeneration of the world or may generate some kind of apocalypse. In other words, an emotionally toned down version of the Heideggerian critique of philosophy. The result was to create a minority of converts to Rorty's views—not that many, because his views seemed too radical—but a much larger industry of philosophers who disliked his view and tried to prove it wrong; and that was very common.

In some of his last works—like the book, for example, *Truth and Progress*—it became clearer that for Rorty, all of this did serve a political aim of extending and supporting a progressive liberal politics; an American-style politics, not linked at all to Marxism and less, shall we say, extreme or at least rhetorically shrill than the politics of some of the French poststructuralists. The ongoing self-critique of inquiry, for Rorty, by which it undermines potential foundations, leaves us with an ironic defense of liberty and human welfare. I say "ironic" because, again, whenever we argue for a political or social end, we have to recognize that we cannot give a foundational argument for it. At some point when someone asks, "Why should you value freedom understood this way, or individuality understood this way, or equality understood this way?" Rorty is going to say, "The only reason I can give you is that it's my culture, it's my tradition, and I think it's worked out pretty well." He cannot give a philosophical argument that goes any further.

In fact, if I may add a brief story at this point, at one point, Rorty traveled to an inter-American conference of philosophers in Guadalajara, Mexico. This was a marvelous occasion when philosophers from South America, Central

America, and North America got together; and clearly at many of these conferences there was some concern that a great philosopher from the north, North America, would not speak down to philosophers from Latin America, and that was some concern. Rorty gave a speech that rather raised hackles; and you may regard it well or ill, but whatever you say, it was certainly honest. What Rorty essentially said to this group—this talk was given 20 years ago when there were far more military juntas and authoritarian societies in Latin America, less democracy than there is today—to the gathered philosophers was, "I'm sorry. We in the West, following the foundationalist tradition of philosophy had John Locke, Jean-Jacques Rousseau, and all these philosophers, and Thomas Jefferson who gave us philosophical foundational reasons for thinking God wants us all to be free individuals living in a democracy. Now it's the 20th century and we have a pretty well-functioning democracy; we have our problems, but we have a society that's on the way toward equality and freedom for all.

"You people in Latin America who live inside military dictatorships, I understand that you may want to avoid yourself of a foundationalist philosophy that can prove that freedom is better than tyranny, and can prove that liberal republics or democracies in your society would be much better. You want foundational philosophies you can use in weapons in your fight against the tyrants who control you. Unfortunately, I am here to say," Rorty said, "as a late 20th century American philosopher, you can't do that anymore because foundationalism is dead. The only reasons you can ultimately give for wanting to increase freedom in your societies is ethnocentrism; there is no foundationalist option, that's all over." This was not a very popular speech.

Whatever one's view of Rorty's conclusions, Rorty clearly performed a remarkable feat that deserves some credit: Leading philosophers to read widely across all three philosophical dialects, the analytic, continental, and pragmatic. This was actually a novelty; Rorty's *Philosophy and the Mirror of Nature* was really the first book that seriously tried to discuss pragmatism, continental philosophy, and analytic philosophy within the same pages. Rorty was a philosopher for whom Nietzsche, Carnap, Heidegger, Wittgenstein, Quine, Davidson, and Derrida were all part of the same discussion. He thereby helped to thaw the atmosphere of rigidly distinguished and frozen philosophical subcultures that preceded him.

In closing, Rorty remains deeply controversial; loved by some, disliked by most perhaps. At the very least, we can say that Rorty really did announce more clearly than any other philosopher of the mid- to late-20th century the end of foundationalism; the end of the task to justify epistemic realism—the notion that our knowledge is true of things as they really are independent of our mind—and that project of philosophy trying to prove that we have such knowledge; that's over. The deeper question we're left with is: Is philosophy wedded to that foundationalist project? If it is—and essentially Rorty thought it was; Rorty said philosophy is wedded to the foundationalist project—if that's true, then philosophy as we understood it is at an end; it has to be essentially abandoned, or at least philosophy that tries to figure out the answers to big questions. Perhaps we're left with a philosophy that's just a form of social criticism or literature; and that's how Rorty thought of philosophy at the end.

But what if philosophy is not wedded to foundationalism; what if you can do a nonfoundationalist philosophy? That's the question. The next two lectures, we will see, will show different ways of avoiding the postmodern judgment on philosophy by separating foundationalism from the philosophical quest.

Rediscovering the Premodern
Lecture 33

> For Hannah Arendt, the meaning of human existence cannot lie in nature, or biological needs, or ecology, but in two things: the free action of human agents in politics (their deeds and speeches in front of others) and the construction of durable cultural objects that provide us with a meaningful artifactual environment. From her point of view, nature by itself is meaningless; only human creation or creative activity gives life meaning.

If modern philosophy has reached a dead end, then perhaps it was its departure from premodern thought that created the problem in the first place. A series of 20th-century philosophers, some inspired by Martin Heidegger, have called for reincorporation of premodern notions to supplement modernity. The most notable of these thinkers in political theory are **Leo Strauss** and **Hannah Arendt**.

In ethics, **Alasdair MacIntyre** produced the most comprehensive account of a premodern epistemology for a modern age. The kind of intelligibility a human life can aspire to is narrative, the intelligibility of a story. Individual stories gain their sense from traditions. MacIntyre claims that rationality only operates in a tradition. He forges a sophisticated notion of living traditions and their prerequisites. But mustn't this lead to relativism? MacIntyre argues that it does not. ∎

> **Alasdair MacIntyre produced the most comprehensive account of a premodern epistemology for a modern age.**

Names to Know

Arendt, Hannah (1906–1975): A student of Martin Heidegger, she was one of the great political philosophers of the 20th century. Politically a representative of civic republicanism.

MacIntyre, Alasdair (b. 1929): This American philosopher was one of the most prominent ethicists of the second half of the 20th century. Early in his career, he participated in the rationality debate with Peter Winch and Ernest Gellner. Late in his career, he formulated a neo-Aristotelian notion of ethics and rationality itself in the books *After Virtue* and *Whose Justice? Which Rationality?*

Strauss, Leo (1899–1973): A controversial historian of political philosophy who had a significant impact on political theory and even American politics in the second half of the 20th century.

Suggested Reading

Arendt, *The Human Condition.*
MacIntyre, *Whose Justice? Which Rationality?*
Strauss, *Natural Right and History.*

Questions to Consider

1. Can the concept of rationality-in-a-tradition avoid relativism?

2. Has modernity made rationality empty, leaving us only with political power to decide our questions?

Rediscovering the Premodern
Lecture 33—Transcript

There are always historians of philosophy who remind us that past thinkers may well have resources that most contemporary philosophers, in a rush to create or respond to the latest theory, sometimes ignore. In the second half of the 20th century, a number of philosophers came to believe that the antirealism, relativism, and "end of philosophy" that some contemporaries were announcing were actually the result of a wrong road having been taken in the 18th century. The question is: Do the problems of relativism and postmodernism, or the problems that postmodernism point to, do they indicate that modernity or the Enlightenment was already a wrong turn? People who make this claim, we might call them premodernists.

Some philosophers, like Hannah Arendt and Martha Nussbaum, simply sought in the politics and ethics of ancient Greece, particularly Aristotle's ethics of virtue, a needed alternative to contemporary thought. Others were more radical, like Leo Strauss and Eric Voegelin, who argued that the "classical rationalism" of the Greeks and the medievals recognized the proper bargain between philosophy and politics that modern thinkers have forgotten at their peril. Among this group of thinkers, Strauss is the most controversial. Leo Strauss gave a critique of what he called the modern rationalist tradition of political philosophy in favor of an older rationalism, which he found to span from Plato to just about or before Machiavelli. The modern political thinkers, like John Locke, according to Strauss, rested their views on a totally different basis than the ancients: reality, rather than moral ideals. Modern political philosophy, Strauss said, following Machiavelli, tried to design procedures that would lead to a more or less just social outcome without presuming virtue on the part of officials or citizens. The strategy of Plato, Aristotle, and the medieval thinkers was very different: When they asked what would make a just society, their answer was always you can only have a just society if you have virtuous citizens or rulers; that's a necessary condition for a just society. Strauss pointed out that modern political philosophers asked the question: Even with mere self-interest, rational self-interest not virtue, on the part of citizens and rulers, can we nevertheless design a system that will result in justice or a good society?

Strauss was particularly upset by the modern fact-value distinction—which we've talked about in some earlier philosophers—naturalism, relativism, historicism; he saw these all connected. That is, Strauss believed that once a certain premodern, idealistic view of politics and philosophy was lost, then essentially the notion of ideals and the notion of the real tended to collapse into each other.

Another difference between modern and premodern political philosophy, according to Strauss, was controversially described in his famous *Persecution and the Art of Writing*. The great tradition of ancient and medieval philosophers, he said, could not be honest; that is, when we read ancient and medieval, and even some early modern, political philosophers, the philosopher had to protect him or herself from political authorities. That meant they actually had to lie in their political philosophy. Furthermore, philosophy is, in fact, dangerous to the polity, because, Strauss admitted, philosophical investigation can lead to skepticism regarding those very beliefs that keep citizens obedient to moral and civil rule. Politics, in a sense, has to lie; or, if one wants to put it a little more gently, politicians and political life have to affirm the crucial and basic validity of values and rules that philosophers cannot justify, because philosophers, when they try to justify them, run into the kind of interminable philosophical problems that we have at many points in this course.

One might notice, if you're familiar with Plato, that this notion of Strauss's is very similar to Plato's notion of the noble lie; that is, Plato in the *Republic*—if we can pause to remember this—argued that the artists and those who are responsible for promoting the culture of the political society must be censored and kept under control, and we must tell those people who are going to be the virtuous leaders of our societies noble lies that will make them act justly and virtuously in all situations. This meant, for Strauss, that political philosophy faces a dilemma, because political philosophy sits at the intersection of the conflict of philosophy and the polis; what philosophy does to our beliefs, which is many times to undermine them, and the polis, which needs a reliable set of beliefs to have a virtuous and just society.

At any rate, Strauss's views—which were very intriguing and mostly came out of his studies of historical figures—oddly enough moved far outside the academy, because many Straussian students, and students of students of Strauss, have, it turns out, played a significant political role in conservative administrations in the United States in the last 20 years, often called "neoconservatives."

Turning to another one of our premodernists, Hannah Arendt was one of the great political philosophers of the 20th century. Her range was remarkable: She wrote deep analyses of the very nature of the political—what makes politics and the political dimension of social life different from the social, economic, cultural, etc.—she wrote deep analyses of political history, works on the nature of human activity and contemplation, and, most famously, she's the author of the three-volume work *The Origins of Totalitarianism*, and a smaller book called *Eichmann in Jerusalem*, which was actually a series of reports on the trial of the Nazi Eichmann by the Israelis. In that report, she famously invented the concept "the banality of evil" to try to describe Eichmann and his fellow Nazis. At any rate, Hannah Arendt is philosopher, historian, journalist all rolled into one.

In perhaps her most interesting book, *The Human Condition*, she argues that modern politics has forgotten the lessons of Aristotle. In the ancient Greek world, the word *oikos* meant "household." Interestingly, it's from the word *oikos* that we get our word "economy." *Oikos* or household for Aristotle was understood to be private, literally, the home; the arena were individuals have their biological needs satisfied. The public realm, in contrast—according to Arendt's description of Aristotle—is the political realm. The political realm and the realm for the fulfillment of biological needs are, in Aristotle's view, to be kept quite separate from each other. Hannah Arendt distinguishes three different forms of the vita active, or what she called the active life; this is in distinction from the contemplative life of humanity. But regarding our active life, she distinguished three different features or domains: labor, work, and action. Let's pause for a moment and explain these.

By labor, Hannah Arendt meant the cyclic—in fact you could almost say metabolic—activities that human beings engage in order to produce the biological necessities of life. The perfect examples would be on the one hand raising food: We labor to create food; once we've created it, what do we do with the food? We eat it and destroy it, and it's gone. In other words, labor leaves nothing behind it. Labor's absolutely necessary, but it is for her the lowest and least meaningful form of human activity. In other words, what Arendt is doing is she's presenting this theory as a way of explicating the ancient view of Aristotle; she's saying this is what Aristotle would have said. Then we move to work: Work is the construction of artifacts; it's the activity in which we make things.

In this kind of activity, which is quite different from labor, there are a couple of key considerations. One is in work we always have a distinction between means and ends; there are my tools and methods and procedures by which we produce the finished object. The finished object is the goal and has a special value; the procedure has a value because it leads to the goal. Work is supposed to create durable objects; doesn't mean they have to last forever, because if that were true there wouldn't be any, but in other words she's referring here not only to all art, fine art, but also building, engineering, architecture, the painting and the sculpting and the care for a home; all the activities that make something durable that's supposed to last or create the artifacts of culture. Last is action: Action for Hannah Arendt specifically means politics; action is the deeds and speeches that human beings engage in, in public, in front of a forum of their equals and peers. Politics means me, or any of you, entering into the forum. Some context: In my life, we could say the New England town meeting; someone who steps up and speaks up at the town meeting, takes a position, gives their view, and sits down. Those deeds and speeches that take place in the public realm, that's the real of action; and the realm of action is very, very different for Hannah Arendt than labor and work, as we'll see.

From this distinction, she gets her critique of the modern age. Writing in the 1950s, Hannah Arendt argued that both the liberal capitalism of the West and the Marxism of the East had something in common, something bad in common: They both made politics the servant of economics; that is, they both regarded public life as nothing but the public organization of a massive collective household or collective economy. In other words, on the one hand in the East, the Marxist view made the sole collective business of society the state organization of the economy. On the other hand, in the West, government was, of course, kept separate from the economic life under capitalism, separate to some degree; nevertheless, the sole business of politics was how do we tinker with the economy in order to make it run right? In each case, politics is being put in the service of economics; something that, if we were looking at this from the point of view of Aristotle, we would say, precisely puts the cart before the horse. For Aristotle, economics is the care for those private, biological necessities that we want to get taken care of so we can then go out in the public realm and do what really gives life meaning: participate in political activity. For Aristotle, politics is intrinsically good; political activity is of much higher value than economic activity. Economic activity is a need; political activity is the expression of one's self, the creation of a persona, in an appearance before one's peers. The results of political action, while effervescent—that is, they just take a moment; you give your speech, it's over—but it becomes recorded and remembered through acts of work; that is, the artists and artisans record, if you will, the great acts of the great political actors.

This may sound like politics at a very abstract level, but it does have some rather concrete political implications. Arendt endorses what we call civic republicanism; civic republicanism, which was one of the two major traditions in the modern Western world for how to conceive a free society. One way is the typical liberal conception—I mean liberal in the classical sense, it has nothing to do with the American Democratic Party—the classical liberal sense that a free society means one in which government gets out of the way of the individual and the individual is free to avoid politics or government. Civic republicanism says that a free society is the one in which the citizens actively participate in political activity; they participate in their own governance. That's the form of a free society that she tried to promote with this theory.

But this is more than just a political theory, the view of Hannah Arendt. For her, the modern world uses a set of categories that fail to grasp the human condition. For Hannah Arendt, the meaning of human existence cannot lie in nature, or biological needs, or ecology, but in two things: the free action of human agents in politics, their deeds and speeches in front of others; and the construction of durable cultural objects that provide us with a meaningful artifactual environment. From her point of view, nature by itself is meaningless; only human creation or creative activity gives life meaning.

Now we're going to move to a third thinker, the most recent of the three, the American philosopher and most famously an ethicist Alasdair MacIntyre, and see how he tries to embed rationality into historical tradition. If the modern project of the Enlightenment sought to justify realism from purely rational grounds that abstracted from all cultural and traditional resources, and if that has failed—in other words, if Descartes, Locke, Kant and others tried to ground and prove the existence of knowledge independent of accidental factors like where you were born, what your cultural tradition is; if that Enlightenment project has now failed—then we must either accept (this is what MacIntyre says) that power, not truth, should adjudicate our value questions, and he labels that with the name of Nietzsche (Nietzsche's notion of the will to power), or we have to go back to a different kind of rationality, the rationality of the ancients and the medievals. In other words, what MacIntyre says very straightforwardly is: If the Enlightenment project of modernity has run into a dead end, then the only options are Nietzsche or Aristotle.

MacIntyre's own claim, which is to return to the ancients, is quite radical: MacIntyre expressly admits that rationality itself only operates within a tradition. That is, rationality is not structured not structured to achieve reasonable solutions to philosophical or ethical problems without being contextualized in a tradition. This is a basic blow against certain parts of the Enlightenment tradition, because part of the Enlightenment was all about telling us that we must leave behind superstition, tradition, custom, culture; there are the things that hold us back. What we should trust to is reason, experience, and nature; and these things will tell us the truth about the world and become the basis for which we can rationally organize society so that it best serves human beings. MacIntyre is claiming there is no such reason or rationality outside the workings of a cultural customary tradition.

This coheres with MacIntyre's basic anthropological point that humans achieve intelligibility in their lives through narratives. The characteristic form, he claims, of intelligibility for a human agent is the story. Traditions are organized around such stories, from whose elements individuals in the tradition fashion the meanings of their lives. In other words, how do I, Cahoone, understand myself? Through continually rewriting in my own mind my own autobiography; where I have been, what I have done, what has happened to me, and what it means. When I do that—that is, write my autobiography in my head, if I don't write it down on paper—I take figures, tropes, ideas, dramatic elements from my cultural tradition, which is like the autobiography of the whole society that I'm a part of, and I take elements from it and incorporate it in my own self-story.

MacIntyre emphasizes that "living" traditions—that is, living cultural traditions—are not monolithic. This is very important, because if you're going to base everything on cultural tradition, you have to have a sensible account of what cultures are like. The first thing he wants to tell us is: Cultures are not monoliths; they are full of disagreement and debate. Nevertheless, they do structure and constrain debate. Rational discourse within a tradition makes use of the available resources within that tradition. His point is that for reason to be effective, there must be a fund of plausible reasons people can give for what they do and what they value, and a set of constraints, as provided by a living tradition. There are several ways that a tradition typically gives such constraints: The first is through a set of canonical texts. Cultures have books that stand behind them that everybody reads. These texts—you take the Bible, the Declaration of Independence, the Koran—form a fixed set of nodes. But they can be interpreted various ways; so in a tradition, let's say in the Muslim tradition, one can hold many different views, but they will be different views about the Koran, the sayings, or the Prophet; and rational arguments will take place between those who disagree. The same is true in the Christian tradition, the same is true when interpreting the Constitution of the United States in the last 200 or so years; they can be interpreted, these canonical tests are interpreted in various ways, and the living tradition is the ongoing debate among these alternate interpretations of the canonical texts.

But along with the set of canonical texts goes canonical practices that contain their own goods. What he means by "practices" is not just behavior or even just human action, but complex series of actions that are relatively self-contained that many different people can participate in at any given time. Marriage is a practice; it's an institutional set of activities that lots of people engage in. Practices are good-containing; that is, you could define goods within practices, and with them, many of the devices or artifacts used in them. MacIntyre is a very interesting ethicist, and he would point out that while philosophers have traditionally worried, "Can we prove that anything is good because of the distinction between fact and values; maybe there's no rational way to adjudicate values," MacIntyre points out within practical contexts of activity, it's quite possible to show that every rational person will accept the same set of values or goods. As he liked to quip, the knife is supposed to be sharp; that's what it's for. It's difficult to say maybe what you should do with the knife, but if the knife's supposed to be used, it's supposed to be in a certain condition to accomplish a certain purpose. Likewise, we can't describe making babies, or searching for food, or resolving a conflict, or building as if they are value-neutral activities. Each of those practices or activities, once you engage in them, contain their own goals, hence goods or values. The practices are a second part of the tradition.

Then there is an ultimate good: Any living tradition posits some ultimate good; however, the members of the tradition disagree about how to interpret it. That one ultimate good doesn't by itself logically dictate a whole set of activities or practices. For example, one might say love is an ultimate good in the Christian tradition; and then there are Christians who very differently interpret what love means and what it entails. Thus the tradition is an ongoing debate about the meaning of its ultimate good, its canonical practices, and its canonical texts.

Without tradition, according to MacIntyre, we are left with what he calls "bureaucratic liberalism"; and, in fact, this gets into his diagnoses of our current predicament. In MacIntyre's point of view, our modern post-Enlightenment languages— in other words, French, English, German, Spanish, the languages of the most economically advanced countries on earth; he should include Japanese—have become "decontextualized" from any ethical tradition. They are "context-less" modes of communication. They are thereby more universals, but at the same time they don't involve a commitment to a tradition. In other words, historically, to speak a language was also to be a member of a tradition; but today in the modern age, that's no longer the case. Consequently, when we talk in English—this is a little bit more technical part of his discussion—he would say when you get a bunch of American students in a philosophy class and you have them speak in English and argue about ethical problem, the English language he thinks, actually, at this point lacks resources for resolving ethical questions. It's in such languages that the "fact-value dichotomy," or the claim that value judgments have no rational justification, can make sense. Have you ever sat in a class or a discussion where somebody says something and someone else says, "Oh, that's a value judgment." From MacIntyre's point of view, every legitimate or interesting judgment that a human being has to say probably is a value judgment or has value implications; and he wants to claim traditions are themselves value-imbedded. You might put it simply this way: You can't make ethical or philosophical conclusions without premises; and it's the traditions that provide us with a set of premises, or rather they provide us with a thick language that is not a value-neutral means of communication, it's a value-full means of communication.

Modernity, on the other hand, has invented a tradition-less, hence rootless and value-less method of communication. In such a mode of communication, it's never "rational" to assert a substantive Good; there are no justificatory values or reasons embedded in the discourse itself. Understand what this means: It doesn't mean that there's something immoral about speaking English; it means that the modern conception of rationality applies independent of any particular forms of value. In other words, when two Nazis at a concentration camp were having a discussion and one said, "I really think we can't kill more than 3,000 Jews today," and another says, "No, no, no, I think we can push production up to about 4,000," they're having a perfectly rational discussion. It's an evil discussion, but it's rational. Rationality has become separate from moral standards.

The claim of "rationality-in-a-tradition" that MacIntyre is making might seem to lead to relativism. As we saw in our very first lecture, relativism, or at least the most disturbing kind of relativism, identifies "true" with "seems true to us," or defines "true" as "true-in-a-perspective" or "true-in-a-particular-language." That kind of relativism would make contrary claims of differing traditions or cultures equally valid. For example: If someone claims the Holocaust never happened, the relativists would have to say that is true for them, while for the rest of us the Holocaust did happen. Relativism would say each claim is true, because the truth of a claim is now relative to the people or culture who assert it; and there's no universal, or perspective- or culture-independent truth to serve as the standard from which any culture-dependent claim can be criticized. Not only would this throw realism out,

MacIntyre fears, it would also mean anyone or any group with power can claim that their view is as true as any other; in effect, anything goes.

Notice, just something to remember: When someone says (as one often hears), "Nobody has the right to impose their view or truth on anyone else," they are not a relativist; someone who says that is making a claim of universal tolerant morality. A relativism of the above kind that we've been describing would say instead, "If your culture says it is right to impose your view on others, then it is right-for-you, even if it's wrong for the culture you're imposing on." At any rate, MacIntyre argues that such relativism is avoided as long as tradition retains criteria for rational progress that can judge particular ideas and practices from another tradition to be superior to its own. Living traditions can do just that. When a living tradition faces problems it can't solve by its own criteria, it's perfectly capable of importing foreign ideas that it judges superior by its own criteria; which, from a relativist standpoint, could not happen. This means it always has a standard of rational progress independent of its own beliefs of the moment. A tradition that can do this never faces the position of saying that whatever seems true to us must really be true.

Moving on, we can see that one option for avoiding postmodernism is to recapture a notion of rationality that is, unlike the modern Enlightenment notion, traditional; that incorporates traditional ancient elements; to turn, as MacIntyre put it, to Aristotle instead of Nietzsche, or postmodernism. That's how MacIntyre thought of postmodernism: as essentially the Nietzschean will to power. But as we'll see in the next lecture, there are other philosophers who believed the Enlightenment conception can be retained if reconceived, and without falling into postmodernism.

Pragmatic Realism—Reforming the Modern
Lecture 34

For Campbell, all cognition is to be understood pragmatically, and in several senses. The most basic method of cognition in any species is the selective retention of action patterns that work, that are successful; in other words, knowledge comes by trial and error.

The attempt to preserve the philosophical search for realist truth in the absence of foundationalism led to the resurgence of pragmatism, the view that knowledge arises in the context of action. **Jürgen Habermas**, a major German philosopher, argues that Reason is a kind of social practice of communication, not the possession of a private mental capacity, and as such, democratic institutions and science can be justified as the necessary conditions for such communication. Hilary Putnam, a prominent American analytic philosopher, argues that while there is no "God's Eye view" available to us, none is required to account for objectivity in a pragmatic realism. Joseph Margolis presses the symbiotic relation of thought and thing in a relativist direction, but he nevertheless accepts that pragmatism justifies a realist view of the whole of our knowledge. In a related development, Konrad Lorenz and **Donald T. Campbell** argued for an **evolutionary epistemology**, that our cognitive capacities do actively project a perspective on the world, but one pragmatically shaped by survival in the environment. It is striking that many of the battles of contemporary theory of knowledge are being fought on pragmatist turf. ∎

Name to Know

Habermas, Jürgen (b. 1929): The last representative of the Frankfurt School, a former assistant to Theodor Adorno, and the most prominent German social philosopher of the late 20th century. He combined American pragmatism with German thought into a theory of modern democracy. Author of *The Theory of Communicative Action*.

Important Term

evolutionary epistemology: A theory that tries to account for the nature of human cognition through natural selection, as a result of our biological evolution. The most famous expositors were Donald T. Campbell and Konrad Lorenz.

Suggested Reading

Campbell, "Evolutionary Epistemology."

Habermas, *The Theory of Communicative Action.*

Lorenz, "Kant's Doctrine of the A Priori."

Margolis, *Pragmatism without Foundations.*

Putnam, *Reason, Truth, and History.*

Questions to Consider

1. How can pragmatism, placing cognition in the context of action, avoid relativism?

2. Can naturalistic epistemology be combined with the fact of historical and cultural constitution of our cognition?

Pragmatic Realism—Reforming the Modern
Lecture 34—Transcript

If some thinkers, as we've seen, see in modern thought since the Enlightenment a mistaken departure from older, necessary patterns of thought, and others find a slippery slope leading all the way to postmodernism, most philosophers to be sure remain convinced that modern thought is unavoidable and not doomed; so somewhere in the middle. They seek ways of avoiding foundationalism, hence the postmodern critique, while retaining the modern norms of science, rationality, and cognitive progress, and the philosophical inquiry into them. They seek to reform and reinterpret the modern rather than abandon it. We could call them if we wanted "promodernists"; and in this lecture, we'll trace several of those promodernists options: the theory of communicative rationality from Jürgen Habermas, the internal realism of Hilary Putnam, the pragmatic relativism of Joseph Margolis, and finally, the naturalistic epistemology of Donald Campbell and others.

Strikingly, while coming from four very different directions—analytic philosophy of language and mind in the case of Putnam, European social philosophy in the case of Habermas, analytic aesthetics and philosophy of culture is really Margolis's background, and finally biology and psychology in the work of Campbell—nevertheless, from these different perspectives, it's interesting that these thinkers converge on pragmatism; that is, they all use pragmatic resources. We've already seen Rorty take pragmatism as the ultimate form of postmodernism, really an end to philosophy's search for truth altogether; that's how Rorty interprets it. But a number of thinkers have found in pragmatism and its attendant naturalism a means of justifying a chastened, pragmatic realism; a realism that holds that our knowledge is perspectival and dependent on human activity (hence pragmatic), yet nevertheless grasps realities that obtain independent of the mind, and do this all without foundationalism. That's what we're going to examine.

Let's begin with the thinker Jürgen Habermas, perhaps the most important German philosopher of the second half of the 20th century; and he had been as a young man an assistant to Theodor Adorno of the Frankfurt School. Nevertheless, Habermas argues against Adorno's and Horkheimer's pessimistic conclusions in the book *Dialectic of Enlightenment* that we saw in an earlier lecture. Their mistake, he claims, was that they thought of reason or rationality in only two ways: on the one hand, as a value neutral inferential power; and on the other hand, as instrumental, discovering the most efficient means of accomplishing a goal; but in either case, value-neutral. In short, they stayed too close to Max Weber's account of the instrumental rationality of distinctive value spheres. Just to clarify what this means: For Adorno and Horkheimer, they understood reason not because they wanted to think of it this way, but they thought, in fact, this is what rationality had come to mean, at least in the 20th century; that rationality is simply the ability to fit means to ends. If I'm trying to decide how many people to kill in the house next door or how many houses in my neighborhood to burn down and I calculate how much gasoline I'm going to need, etc., that's perfectly rational. My goal may be insane, but if reason is just the instrumental process that gets me from where I am now to whatever goal I've chosen in steps that make sense, if that's all reason is, then what I'm doing is rational even if my ultimate goal is crazy.

Habermas thought that the Frankfurt School thinkers Adorno and Horkheimer had basically adopted a sufficiently cramped notion of reason or rationality that it led them into a blind alley. Habermas turned to supplement Weber's account of instrumental rationality—which was used by the Frankfurt School—with the Americanist philosophers, especially George Herbert Mead. For Mead, rationality was understood as based in communication, which is in turn based in the ability to take the perspective of the other. Consequently rationality has ethical implications. That means literally for Mead that reason or rationality is a certain way of communicating with other people; it's not primarily instrumental at all.

On the basis of this, Habermas defined "communicative rationality," his own concept, as the rationality oriented to achieving agreement among speakers. When we engage in communicative rationality, as opposed to instrumental or strategic communication—to explain instrumental or strategic communication means when I'm talking to you and all I want to do is get something out of you, I want to convince you of something but I don't care what you say, that's strategic communication—but in communicative rationality, we actually embody and presuppose moral norms: sincerity, belief in the truth of what we're saying, belief in the validity of the reasons we offer, and in the moral appropriateness of what we say. We have to presume these norms, or else become trapped in what Habermas calls "performative self-contradiction." When I talk to you and you talk to me when we're trying to decide where I left my keys, or what candidate to vote for, or should we allow our kids to get Facebook accounts; when we're arguing about this with each other, we're trying to convince each other to be sure, but we're taking moral stances not just about the subject we're discussing, but the discussing itself is moralized.

From Habermas's point of view, this is also true of democracy and science; democracy and science—and this is something Dewey and Mill believed before Habermas—are based in communicative rationality. In science and democracy, we allow the other to speak their mind as long as they're sincere and they try to give reasons, and then we try to evaluate their reasons. For Habermas, our social world—this is part of his critique of life in the 20th century—is divided between the instrumental governmental and economic system (he called it "the system") in which agents' actions and statements are coordinated by instrumental outcomes. He distinguished that range of action that is, in effect, what we do in many of our jobs and what we do when confronted with government edicts; in the world of money and power we do what we do because the consequence is dictated to us in some way, or is dictated simply by the flow of money, in other words, profit. That's the system. Part of our life is in the system; but the other art is what he calls the communicative lifeworld, in which our actions and statements are coordinated by communicative rationality. The political task, from Habermas's point of view, is to expand the control of the system by the lifeworld. What does democracy mean? Democracy means when the lifeworld, that kind of communicative rationality between the citizens controls the system rather than the other way around.

To Hilary Putnam: Putnam is one the most prominent American philosophers of the second half of the 20th century, an emeritus professor from Harvard. He's most famous for promoting functionalism in the philosophy of mind, which had to do with the use of computers to artificial intelligence programs to at least using their logic to understand which processes must be taking place in the mind. He was also well known for what's called externalism in philosophy of language; that is: the view that the meanings of our terms are not ideas in our head but are rather dependent on things external to the mind of the speaker. But we're more interested in his theory of knowledge today. Putnam, in his theory of knowledge, accepts with others that we've already seen that there can be no (to use his phrase) "God's Eye view" of the universe or of reality; in other words, we cannot aspire to a "God's Eye view," meaning the one true view of reality independent of our thoughts, hopes, cultures, fears, and projections. There is no such view and it's impossible. Neither do we have available to us what Thomas Nagel called a "view from nowhere," that would mean a perspective devoid of background assumptions, perspectives, biases, and presuppositions. We cannot even describe an environment in the world without having a background conceptual scheme. We cannot say what there is independent of all conceptual schemes. Putnam accepts that as given. Furthermore, there's no ontology of the world that is uniquely "right." For various other reasons, partly having to do with his work in logic, Putnam would say essentially we cannot believe that there is in the end one unique, true description of all of reality; there have to be multiple possible descriptions that are equally true, that has to be the case.

It's true that our true statements are, for Putnam, relative to conceptual scheme. This sounds like relativism; but his point is that it doesn't have to. Dependence on a conceptual scheme is compatible with what Putnam long called an "internal" or "pragmatic" realism; he's taking that notion of realism, which is that or true knowledge is really true of things in the world independent of our judgments of them—true of the way they are really independent of us—and he's modifying a bit with a prefix in a sense, internal or pragmatic realism. More recently, he's come to call it "common sense" or "natural" realism; for, Putnam's point is, even within a conceptual scheme, reality still imposes constraints on us. When we bring a conceptual scheme to any moment of experience—and we always do that, we can't operate without one—reality puts constraints on us, and then our conceptual scheme gets disciplined, so to speak by real experience. There is realist truth in a conceptual scheme, meaning that our understanding of truth is always dependent on our framework or our cognitive activities. We cannot achieve the sole approximately true picture or reality; there's not just one. Reality is not compatible with just one; there's no "God's Eye view" of reality. But as that does not destroy the possibility of cognitive progress—and it doesn't—the dependence of our claims, even our true claims, on conceptual schemes is not required, this doesn't render our knowledge un-useful or unreasonable. There can be cognitive reasons indeed still for preferring one conceptual scheme over another. We simultaneously have the notion that reality is still, though interpreted within conceptual schemes, constraining us; in other words, it's not the case that anything goes. Second, there are real cognitive rational reasons for preferring one conceptual scheme over another; as long as we have those two things, we still have realism as far as Putnam is concerned.

On the other hand, we can turn to Joseph Margolis, a philosopher at Temple University, who also happened to fight in the Battle of the Bulge in the Second World War. His thought ranges across analytic, continental, and American sources with ease, and he uses pragmatism to justify relativism. This sounds like this would be a problem, it sounds like he would be on the side of Rorty and other postmodernists. However, Margolis claims he can justify a minimal kind of relativism that doesn't disturb realism; so we can still get the claim that when our beliefs are true, they are made true by, they are true of, the world independent of the judgments themselves. Let's see how he tries to do that.

Margolis argues that realism requires that there be one real universe, independent of mind; no problem, he says, we assume this. Truth, he also assumes, is correspondence of our utterances to that universe in at least a nominal sense; in other words, whatever more complicated notion of truth or knowledge you want, there is some kind of correspondence, some kind of fit or adequacy between our claims and the world. Our informed cognitions, here understood now as—and this is important term of art for Margolis—adverbial modes of constructive handling can and do judge their objects, albeit never in a final or universally valid way. Just briefly to clarify that notion of our cognitive medium being adverbial: Again, my background language, my conceptual scheme, my culture, my presuppositions, all this stuff that I bring to experience—with which, as Dewey once said, we fund our experience with these things, whether we want to or not—Margolis said these are not to be understood as some kind of container that blocks my access to the world; on the contrary, these are the things that give me access to the world. They are features of the way I grasp the world; so I grasp the world with that medium if you will. They're adverbial; they're part of a dependent on an action.

But Margolis goes on to accept as the up-shot of the multiple 20th century critiques of cognition that cognition and world are, in his word, symbiotic. That is, he accepts we never face, whatever kind of scientific or philosophical analysis we go through looking at the act of knowledge, we never get down to face naked world without our own linguistic/cultural/historical means of access to it—or what Kant called the thing in itself—and, he points out, we also can never pare down the experience of knowledge to the point where our language or cognitive faculty, our medium, is also known negatively without reference to the world. In other words, our knowing and the known are symbiotic, they're tied together, they're interwoven; or, in his phrase, we have a "worlded" language and we have a "languaged" world, and we can't get beyond that.

Margolis discards the famous logical notion of bivalence; and here we have to go back with a bit of a little logic lesson. Bivalence holds—this goes way back to Aristotle's logic—that every well-formed proposition (in other words, every statement that's in the right condition) must be either true or false; that's all it claims. Margolis holds that that is a perfectly reasonable claim in certain fields like mathematics and the natural sciences, but not in some other areas of our cognitive life. He holds that it's perfectly reasonable to relax this requirement: In some subject matter areas, our cognitive values may not be bivalent, they may include not just true/false as the only two options, but rather "apt," "reasonable," "valid," or "weakened"; truth-like values, because our judgments are nondetachable from evidence. That is to say, because of symbiosis, my judgment of a particular part of the world is not independent of that part of the world, our judgment is relative to evidence; consequently the norms I use to decide how good my judgment is—is it true, is it false?—don't fit the old bivalent model. This then permits what he calls incongruent valid claims in differing subject matters.

This seems rather complicated, but what's behind it is something rather simple: Literally, the truth of particular claims is relative, but it's relative to fields of evidence, not relative to my culture or what's in my head or anything personal about me. This he calls a "robust" relativism, in contrast to any relativism that defines truth as identical to "true-in-some-language" or "true-for-this-culture." The reason Margolis does this is that he's keenly aware that our natural scientific knowledge is very different from our knowledge of the human domain. What he means is knowledge of the so-called human sciences; our historical knowledge, for example; our judgments of human actions and motivations in everyday life, hence our psychological knowledge of other people; and our aesthetic judgment of cultural objects, like objects of art or literature. In these areas, and here he's speaking somewhat like Gadamer, who we saw earlier, if all these are to be capable of truth—in other words, if we're going to have a theory of truth and knowledge that allows the fact that we know some things about other people, psychology, history, aesthetics, works of art; if we know something and say some valid statements in those areas—we have to open our theory of knowledge to the possibility that our truth-claims are relative to evidence, so relevant to the kind of subject matter we're dealing with (aesthetics, art objects, versus let's say corks and electrons), and in some of these evidence domains (like art), we will not be able to achieve bivalent claims as we do in logic, math, or science.

What he means is: If I'm trying to explain why I love Betsy, if I talk about or we talk about neurological claims about my brain function, that's one thing; we might need a theory and a set of claims that can only be true or false about my brain function. But what about my practical claims about my reasons for loving her, my goals, what about my aesthetic appreciation of Betsy, or of a love poem that I've written her; these are cultural realities, human things that have meanings, and need to be open to different yet valid interpretations. The interpretation of cultural things can yield objective yet incompatible interpretations, for example in art criticism, but also in history and the interpretation of human behavior generally. He's accepting that of the love poem I write to Betsy, you could have two different interpretations, very different, say different things about it, and we might have to accept, nevertheless, that each one's true in some way. Now we have to have more values, cognitive values, to describe the usefulness or validity of these interpretations than just saying, "One's true and one's false"; that is ok for mathematics and the sciences, but it's not ok for art, culture, or even interpreting human history and human beings.

Nevertheless, outside this, if we take all our judgments and utterances and beliefs and ideas about the world together, the whole of our view of the world has, according to Margolis, an en bloc correspondence to the world. At that level, the total human judgment of the world must be more or less valid or true. Why? What justification could there be for that? It has to be justified, he says, pragmatically, by the success of our cognitive practices in the survival of our species. Once foundationalism is done for, Margolis writes, "we can remain realists, but the only defense possible pretty well requires that we turn to pragmatist or biological grounds," hence "that human inquiry is continuous with, and develops out of, the biological and precognitive interaction between organism and environment."

This idea connects us to the fourth and last of our pragmatic realisms for the day, and that is to the naturalism that was originally formulated by people like Peirce, Dewey, and Meade, but a particular effect or a particular subtopic within naturalism that is called evolutionary epistemology. From a psychological and a biological perspective, human perception and cognition are, after all, processes that can be studied scientifically. We do study them scientifically; indeed, given Darwinian evolution, it seems that our knowing apparatus—whatever you want to call it; all the various cognitive structures that combine to create knowledge—is a unique product of natural selection. If one abandons the goal of justifying knowledge per se to the skeptic as impossibly circular—and you remember Quine did that in an earlier lecture—then the way is clear to form a naturalistic and evolutionary account of human knowledge. Instead of trying to form a philosophically nonscientific justification of the knowledge that's used in science, we now use science to try to give a description of how human beings come to know things.

The philosopher Karl Popper; the ethologist, or student of animal behavior and animal psychology, Konrad Lorenz; and the psychologist Donald Campbell, one of the premier American interdisciplinary theorists of the 20th century, all contributed to a new, naturalistic theory of knowledge called evolutionary epistemology. There's a remarkable 1941 essay by Lorenz called "Kant's Doctrine of the A Priori in the Light of Contemporary Biology," and Lorenz argues there that Kant's synthetic a priori—remember, which organizes our experience—is true in the light of Darwinian biology; the human perceptual cognitive apparatus does construct its environment as Kant held, but it has evolved to construct an environment that matches in key ways the reality to which humans had to adapt in the course of evolution. In other words, what Lorenz is saying is evolution provides the link between the things in themselves in Kant and our cognitive organization of appearances. Our synthetic a priori evolved under the pressure of real things in themselves; that is, a real environment that would have killed us if didn't learn to know it pretty well.

For Campbell, all cognition is to be understood pragmatically, and in several senses. The most basic method of cognition in any species is the selective retention of action patterns that work, that are successful; in other words, knowledge comes by trial and error. The organism does something, does something, does something; it hits, it gets the food, it avoids being eaten, something good happens, and if it can learn it has the ability to retain that information. Higher organisms then construct much more complicated action patterns, but also at very high levels an internal mental representation of the world; they can imagine or think their way through possible actions. As Popper once put it, this allows "our hypotheses to die in our stead." In short, the Kantian notion that knowing is an active imposition on the world is here being naturalized and pragmaticized; the organism must gain knowledge by acting in the world.

These views of Putnam, Habermas, Margolis, and Campbell are much more complex than what I have allowed here in these four brief presentations. I don't even argue here that they are right. My point is to show there are ways that philosophers in the last 20 or 30 years have tried to adapt realism to the critiques postmodernists and others make; to try to formulate a nonfoundational realism. It's rather striking, again, to note that they tend to employ pragmatist resources. In fact, from the 1980s until Rorty's death in 2007, Putnam, Habermas, and Margolis carried on a sort of ongoing debate with Rorty, their forms of pragmatic realism bumping up against his neopragmatic postmodernism, if you want to call it that.

In our remaining two lectures, we'll try to suggest just what all these disagreements between analytic, continental, and pragmatic philosophers and between the post-, pre-, and promodernist philosophers that emerged from the kind of philosophical crises of the middle of the 20th century, to see just what this all amounts to.

The Reemergence of Emergence
Lecture 35

One of the enduring themes of modern thought has certainly been the need to understand reality systematically in light of the achievements of modern science, yet still leaving room for the human mind, meaning, and hope.

The decline of positivism took some of the wind from the sails of the physical reductionists, who wanted to claim that ultimately, if we knew enough, physics would explain everything. But more important in the late 20th century were the rise of the philosophy of biology as a field and a new set of scientific concerns about complexity. It became evident that in chemistry, solid-state physics, and biology, there is more to be learned, more unexpected phenomena—chaos, nonlinear systems, self-organizing and hierarchical systems, critical-point phenomena—than reducing systems to their smallest components could account for. This helped to inspire some philosophers to think differently about reduction and **emergence**, perhaps the most important being **William C. Wimsatt**. In all this, the old metaphysical doctrine of emergence seems to be making a comeback, or a reemergence. And with that, the options for a complex, nonreductionist naturalism seem better than ever. ■

> In chemistry, solid-state physics, and biology, there is more to be learned ... than reducing systems to their smallest components could account for.

Name to Know

Wimsatt, William C. (b. 1941): A philosopher of biology at the University of Chicago, he has done the most sophisticated recent work on emergence and reductive explanation in the context of actual scientific practice.

Important Term

emergence: The claim that some natural systems exhibit properties that are not exhibited by the components of the system. Hence the novel, or emergent, property is irreducible to properties of the components.

Suggested Reading

Clayton and Davies, *The Re-Emergence of Emergence*.

Wimsatt, *Re-Engineering Philosophy for Limited Beings*.

Questions to Consider

1. How should emergence and reduction be defined?

2. Can the notion of levels of reality be objectively applied?

The Reemergence of Emergence
Lecture 35—Transcript

It's been quite a journey through 34 lectures of modern thought. You should pat yourself on the back for a job well done. In these final two lectures, I'll try to show that the radical criticisms of first philosophy, of metaphysics and the theory of knowledge that we've seen in the 20th century, do not end the story of philosophy. Now it certainly seems to some philosophers that systematic metaphysics, trying to come up with a metaphysical theory of reality in general, is a dead letter, a dead field. But in today's lecture I want to show that it's still possible to respond to some of these many criticisms we've seen constructively, to give a constructive response to them. Today I'll feel free to express my own views, not because they are so important, but to try to show how one working philosopher can still try to come to metaphysical conclusions in light of all the radical 20th century criticisms of metaphysics that we've reviewed, as to do this as an example to show how you yourself might find your own way forward with respect to these questions.

You may remember a quotation from Bertrand Russell in our first lecture, saying that modern science presents a purposeless world void of meaning, all our lives being just "accidental collocations of atoms." We could add to this a more recent statement from the Nobel Prize–winning physicist Steven Weinberg's excellent book on the big bang called *The First Three Minutes*. He concluded his book by writing, "The more the universe seems comprehensible, the more it also seems pointless." Is this true? Is this what science tells us? Or do the promodernist views of the preceding lecture, the pragmatic realist views, combined with a more complex, nonreductive view of nature, might these show us an alternative? Let's see.

One of the enduring themes of modern thought has certainly been the need to understand reality systematically in light of the achievements of modern science, yet still leaving room for the human mind, meaning, and hope. Can metaphysics still hope to do these things? First of all, the form or method of metaphysics can be clarified: Metaphysics doesn't have to claim, as it did for Descartes, Spinoza, and Hegel, certainty, or finality, or necessity. It can just claim to be the best hypothesis about what everything is and how it all fits together. This was indeed the view of Peirce and Whitehead about their own efforts: Metaphysics is a hypothetical, fallible, partly empirical, contingent discipline.

Now to the content of such a theory. One simple way to understand metaphysics since the 17th century is to ask: What is inside, or what is based on, what: Mind or Nature; that is, is Nature based on mind, mind based on Nature, or what? There have been many ways of understanding mind and nature, of course, and many ways of presenting what might be called substitutes for them; for example, proponents of mind might talk instead of experience, or spirit, or representation, or signs, or practical human activity, or culture itself, and the representatives of the priority of Nature sometimes speak of just the material or the physical. Some alternatives make the two sides more different, some closer together; Descartes, of course, made mind and nature, understood as mind and matter, totally different, so it was hard to imagine how they could possibly interact. Spinoza's philosophy brings them a little closer together; makes them both attributes of a single substance related by what he called psychophysical parallelism, as you may remember. Some philosophers have tried to merge the two, or get beneath the distinction between them, like Hegel, Dewey, and Heidegger, each in different ways.

But these attempts, mostly I would argue, end up putting one or the other, mind or Nature, first, so don't actually escape the dichotomy. For example, Heidegger's notion of "worldhood," as opposed to mind, is actually a dimension of *Dasein*'s experience, a part of *Dasein*. That's why the early Heidegger said that the question, "Would there be being without *Dasein*," makes no sense. James and Dewey both say that everything starts with something called "experience" understood as prior to the distinction we make between the objects of experience on the one hand and the process of experiencing on the other. But if that's true, then you have to say before there was any living organism in the universe, there still was "experience."

A different approach would be to accept, as modern science tells us, that Nature comes before and is the basis for mind or experience; yet, but make Nature pluralistic, not identical to the physical or the material. Doing this would mean dropping what I would call the dominant bipolar disorder of modern metaphysics: thinking that matter, or mind, or both, exhaust reality; reality has to be one or the other, or both, and there's nothing left. What if, instead, reality is pluralistic; what if matter and mind are only two kinds of things and there might be many more? Living organisms, life, might be another kind of thing that's quite distinct; cultural signs, culture, might be distinct again and different from mind and matter, or Nature understood as matter.

Most philosophers who consider themselves naturalists are actually physicalists. We dealt earlier with the problem of reduction and with that idea. Both ontological and explanatory reduction was common in the mid-20th century. Watson's and Crick's discovery of the structure of the DNA molecule in 1953 seemed to promise that biology could be reduced to chemistry, just as quantum mechanics in the late 1920s seemed to show that chemistry could be reduced to physics. This physical reductivist attitude was epitomized in a lovely cartoon by Sidney Harris that shows an older male physicist and his new, younger female colleague chatting outside an observatory. He explains to her: "I'll be working on the largest and smallest objects in the universe—superclusters and neutrinos [superclusters means superclusters of galaxies]." He continues, "I'd like you to handle everything in between." Is this really an accurate depiction of Nature? Is it really the case that the smallest and biggest provide the essential laws and rules that govern everything in between? Is there nothing really novel in the rest of the universe?

Since the 1970s, however, there has arisen, first of all, the field of philosophy of biology, which, as I told you once before, throughout the early and mid-20th century, philosophy of science was dominated by philosophy of physics; but in the 1970s, starting then, philosophy of biology became more and more prominent. Many of its practitioners specifically denied that biology can be reduced to physics or chemistry. To take a quip from Jack Cowan, who tried to distinguish the biophysicist from the biologist—the biophysicist is essentially a physicist who studies biological phenomena—Cowan says the way to distinguish the two is: "Take an organism and homogenize it in a Waring blender. The biophysicist is interested in those properties which are invariant under that transformation." One of the properties that isn't invariant under that transformation is life, which is, of course, what the biologist is interested in in the first place.

Even more important, also starting in the 1970s, a new set of scientific concerns arose under the name of "complexity." Their consideration was led most famously by a Belgian chemist, Ilya Prigogine, a Nobel Prize winner; and the study of complexity essentially showed that in chemistry, solid state physics, and biology, there is far more to be learned about unexpected phenomena that cannot be deduced from the laws of physics. Some of these phenomena go under the names of chaos, nonlinear systems, self-organizing systems, critical point phenomena, complexities in turning genes on and off; and as Philip Anderson famously wrote in his 1972 essay entitled "More is Different," processes above the atomic and sub-atomic levels, hence with larger and more complex entities than the relatively simple particles dealt with by quantum mechanics and at the atomic level, often do not follow the same rules as their subatomic components. That is, more in the sense of greater size almost always means more complex, and more complex is indeed different.

As a result, today many philosophers reject explanatory or theoretical reductionism, admitting that there's no hope of ever reducing psychology or biology to physics, so we just have to accept multiple sciences at different scales—different sizes of phenomena—to give irreducible explanations. But many of these same philosophers still accept ontological reductionism, meaning that every being is in fact nothing but the smallest components of matter that compose it; quarks and leptons, the most famous example of a lepton would be an electron, so let's say quarks and electrons. Am I nothing but quarks and electrons? The explanatory reductionist certainly says yes; the ontological reductionist says yes; but many contemporary philosophers accept ontological reduction but not explanatory, they're chastened about that.

But if the only reason to posit an ontology is that it's explanatory, why should ontological reduction be accepted, if in an explanatory way reduction is unacceptable? Why should our ontology of nature be physicalist at all? Why should one feature or level of natural phenomena provide our ontology? Why follow Willard Van Quine's famous quip that he wanted a minimal ontology, one suited, he said, to "desert landscapes." One of the most interesting analysts of these issues currently is the philosopher of biology William Wimsatt, himself inspired by Campbell's evolutionary epistemology, among other things. Wimsatt distinguishes three types of explanations in science: the reductive, the phenomenological, and the functional. The reductive explains a system's properties or behavior by "reducing" it, or reducing the system, to its components, and discovering among their properties or behavior and the interaction rules that govern them what explains the properties of the system. A phenomenological explanation—and this use of the word "phenomenological" now has nothing to do with Husserlian phenomenology or its derivatives—explains a system's behavior or properties by reference to another system at approximately the same scale; in other words, you explain the dent in the fender by the impact of the other car. Lastly, a functional explanation finds the explanation of the system's properties or performances in a more encompassing system, which selects the system in question or some state of it. In other words, when in a biological organism our DNA molecules have to be manufactured by cells; the processes and the structure of the cell have to play a role in the explanation of how particular atoms, different chemicals, associate themselves into the strand of DNA. To explain how they come together, you have to refer to the cell or structures of the cell that are busy manufacturing that DNA molecule; that's a functional explanation to a higher level of scale.

Wimsatt shows that reductive explanation is complex, it's dependent on decompositions of the system that it's reducing; that is, it has to determine what the parts of a system are. This may not be apparent to many, but, in fact, there are lots of different ways to pick "parts" or map the parts of many natural systems. This is especially true once you get to biology. For example, parts can be understood as organs, as the density or amount of different chemicals, as charts of electrical conductivity, as cybernetic or information channels; all these are different ways to divide up an organism into parts. For example, take me: On the one hand, you could say that my parts are, let's say, my major organ systems, heart, lungs, etc., and we could imagine taking them apart and putting them on a table. But that's not the only way to divide me up into parts; we could go through my body and look for the concentrations of different kinds of chemicals, which would be quite a different map. Or we could look at the movement of nutrients around the body, the circulatory system. Or we could look at the command system of my organism; that is, my central nervous system and the flow of electrical information. These are all different maps; so there's not just one list of parts, there are many. Furthermore, when parts interact complexly, reduction explains less and less.

The point of a reduction is, after all, to substitute a simpler problem for a more complex one. If the components have fantastically complex interactions that cannot be simplified, then that probably means the whole system has some inner structure or process that we must refer to in explaining why the parts are doing what they're doing. But if we do that, we are no longer producing a reductive explanation; we are now using the whole to explain the parts to explain the whole. That is, if someone tries to say, "The whole has certain properties because the parts do," but then we find we can only explain the relevant properties of the parts by referring back to the whole, we have an explanation that's fine, but it's no longer a reductive explanation.

For Wimsatt, "emergence" is simply "non-aggregativity," that's what he calls it; but we can just say what this means is an "emergent" property of the systems that can't be explained reductively as an aggregation of component parts and their interaction rules. Whenever we try to explain a whole by its parts, but then find that the parts have complex relational properties that themselves can only be explained by the parts' positions in the whole; because of the whole system's structure or processes, we're admitting the whole has irreducible properties. This doesn't mean the properties of the whole are mystical or inexplicable; it just means we have to return to a phenomenological explanation or a functional explanation, and we do this in signs all the time. That's all emergence is, according to Wimsatt.

The rise of the sciences of complexity since 1970, coupled with the demise of positivism, has suddenly breathed life into the old ideas of the British emergentists, which we can now state with greater precision; thus the title of a recent book by Philip Clayton and Paul Davies, *The Re-Emergence of Emergence*. There are many ways to view this reemergence, but the point is the idea of emergence has come back; it no longer looks as moribund as it once was.

Wimsatt has no reluctance to draw the ontological conclusion from this; unlike Quine, he endorses what he calls a tropical rainforest ontology. That is, there are innumerable metaphysical kinds of entities and properties; not all entities and properties are physical. Nor are they either physical or mental. There are levels of scale in the universe; a hierarchy of levels. Each of these levels have real metaphysical distinctiveness, there are novel properties in the world; in other words, our picture of nature can't be so simple anymore. Cosmic, chemical, and biological evolution have been such as to produce causal entities at particular scales or sizes, constituting layers of causal interaction, or, as Wimsatt puts it, "peaks of regularity and entification." Societies and ecosystems are as real as individual organisms; organisms as real as their macromolecules, the biomolecules; which are as real as their molecules, atoms, and subatomic particles. These vast kinds of things are arranged in a hierarchy of levels of complexity.

The point here is that if some version of emergence is not only epistemically but ontologically true, then we have a pluralistic universe of many kinds of entities at different stratified levels. What these levels are is a matter of disagreement; but to start with, we can at least distinguish the physical, the chemical, the biological, the mental, and I would say the cultural. This would, surprisingly enough, be a metaphysical picture uncongenial to foundationalism; for if ontology is emergent, we cannot say that the simplest or the largest determines the nature of what is in between, unlike the cartoon we discussed earlier. We have multiple orders of nature, interacting and connected, but which are build up over time. It would then be possible, in an updated form of British emergentism, to understand the physical, the chemical, the biological, and yes, the mental and the cultural as different metaphysical kinds of natural entities and properties arranged in a hierarchy of dependence. In other words, it would be granted by this view that the mental cannot exist without the biological, or the chemical, or the physical; but nevertheless, the mental does exhibit properties and entities that do not obtain in the merely biological or chemical or physical scales or orders of nature. We have metaphysical novelty; in other words, different kinds of things that are not reducible, even though we have dependence on all the less complex orders.

Mind and culture are dimensions of reality that many have claimed cannot be understood within nature. But if nature is no longer solely physical or material, but now it's understood to be pluralistic and hierarchical, then it may well be possible to include the mental and the cultural in nature. For example, following philosophers like George Herbert Mead and some of the American pragmatists, mind could be conceived not as a substance but as the novel intentional activities of higher organisms with complex nervous systems. At the same time, language, meanings, history, in effect, culture—which to many thinkers could not be included in nature—perhaps could be if nature is not just physical or material. Within a pluralist, rainforest ontology of nature, it may be possible to think of culture not as the opposite of nature, as in the old mind-nature bipolar disorder, but to think of culture as a zone or dimension or part of nature. For it is true, after all, we humans are the cultural animals; we evolved to be able to make signs; this enabled us to manipulate meanings or ideas as objects; and this allows us to be uniquely creative animals who live by making things and making things that mean, something that can't be said in anything like the human kind of scale of any other creature.

My suggestion is that the solution to the bipolar disorder of mind and matter is not to choose one over the other, but to demote each to membership in a pluralistic nature; for there are three interesting facts about nature that reinforce each other and reinforce this hypothesis: First, it's a fact that the physical, chemical, biological, mental, and cultural orders do exhibit a hierarchy of increasing complexity. Second, as such, nature has forced us to construct different sciences for these orders. It's not for no reason that we have more than one science; we have a bunch of sciences, and that seems to be forced on us by the natural world. That itself is an informative fact. But third, and most remarkable, the levels of complexity in nature in fact match what science tells us is the actual development of the universe; that is, generally speaking, the complex has come later. For as far as we can tell, the physical universe began about 14 billion years ago with the big bang, an explosion of energy and hydrogen and helium, the lightest elements; it took billions of years for stars to form, and in their nuclear furnaces to fuse nuclei together to form heavier elements, and hence chemical complexity. Without that, there would hardly be a science of chemistry at all.

Only eventually did the death and explosion of stars generate the heaviest elements and spread all other stellar elements across the universe, eventually leading to the formation of more stars and stellar systems, some with terrestrial planets. This all took about 10 billion years. Then at least in one case—we don't know how many others there are, if there are—a planet formed with the ability to house life, which has then taken its own 4 billion year history of creating myriad forms, societies, and ecosystems. The most developed animals, the most complex animals, gradually evolved a central nervous system necessary and able to support the intentional activities, like experience, which we call mind; and out of these creatures, one developed language and culture, and therefore history, able to accumulate knowledge and pass it across generations.

One might wonder, one might ask, can there be a religious feature to such a view? This is, of course, very controversial. Today there's great hostility between the forces of religion and science; but some thinkers remember a time when the conflict was not so strident. For example, back in the day of Einstein and Schrodinger, there was no notion that somehow to pursue science meant to leave religion behind entirely; these were seem as compatible. Karl Popper himself pointed out that Darwin's discovery that the fitness of an organism for its environment can be the result of natural selection and not divine design does not rule purpose or design out of the natural world. Popper actually quotes Darwin; Darwin was responding to William Paley's famous old argument for the existence of a designer of the universe, and Darwin wrote, "I cannot think that the world, as we see it, is the result of chance; and yet I cannot look at each separate thing as the result of Design." He concluded, "With respect to Design, I feel more inclined to show a white flag than to fire … [a] shot."

Popper continues to say in the light of late 20th-century science, then:

> I do think that science has taught us a lot about the evolving universe that bears in an interesting way on Paley's and Darwin's problem of creative design.
>
> I think that science suggests to us (tentatively of course) a picture of a universe that is inventive or even creative; of a universe in which *new things* emerge, on *new levels*.

None of this creativity has to be understood as deterministic, I should point out, or certain, or inevitable. The physical constants of the universe—the basic constants that are studied by physics—many have noticed occupy very narrow, improbable values. It may be the case that these simply make the creation of higher levels of complexity likely, not inevitable. There is no contradiction between a universe of chance and a universe structured so that chance is likely to lead to increased structure. There's also no contradiction between recognizing that in our universe because of the second law of thermodynamics, entropy—or you could say disorder, or better lack of structure, movement toward equilibrium—is constantly spreading and increasing. That's simply the price that must be paid by locally increasing complex structure. Whenever structure increases in one place, disorder, you might say, increases elsewhere. That doesn't conflict with this underlying view.

My point is: Nature seems to be in the business of making ever new and more complex kinds of things. It may well be that nature has a point. What that point is, I don't know; but my guess is at least that whatever it is requires a universe that is creative and generates more complex systems. At least, that's how one philosopher would begin to pursue metaphysical questions in the light of all the attacks on metaphysics in the 20th century. It seems to me such questions are not over, and perhaps they're just beginning.

Philosophy's Death Greatly Exaggerated
Lecture 36

> Philosophy is just the name we give to our trying to figure out what the world and life are like in the widest possible sense, by using the method of inquiry; that is, the method of saying what we think is true and giving reasons and evidence for and against.

Philosophy moves forward in a spiral, rendering some theories unsupportable, pressing forward with others, and recycling parts of older theories in new projects. Today we cannot but accept many of the criticisms of traditional philosophy raised in the radical 20th century. Foundationalism is dead, and with it any notions of incorrigible, immediate, uninterpreted access to reality.

But that does not have to mean philosophy is dead. Even if knowledge is fallible, funded, thickly laden, mediated, constructed, and symbiotic, it can still be approximately true. We have an adverbially thick cognitive apparatus, partly biological and naturally selected, partly historical and cultural, and certainly social, which grasps approximate truths about its objects. These are not all of, or the only such, truths.

> **Foundationalism is dead, and with it any notions of incorrigible, immediate, uninterpreted access to reality.**

Metaphysically, if emergence is accepted against a narrow reductionism, then the unique functions of humanity—cognitive, ethical, aesthetic, even spiritual—can be entirely compatible with a naturalistic account of reality. Such, at any rate, is one philosopher's opinion, but there are many more, and the supply shows no sign of diminishing. ■

Philosophy Alive and Kicking

Today, in the early 21st century, philosophy is still in business. In fact, the philosopher's job may be more central than ever. Although over the centuries philosophy has been diminished as more and more fields—first the physical sciences, then the social sciences—have gradually split off from philosophy to pursue their own methods, the problem of integrating the knowledge of those fields and of the fields of everyday life is greater than ever. The attempt to know the world and ourselves, to know what is true, good, and beautiful, remains a philosophical job.

The alternative to philosophy would be essentially to stop wondering, to stop asking questions that go beyond the methods and intellectual boundaries of the many contexts of our lives. The choice is either, as Aristotle knew long ago, to accept our unreflective, uncoordinated, often contrary beliefs, or to ask ourselves if they are true and how they hang together. If you ask those questions and try to answer them, you are doing philosophy. It may be that we are just not built for cognitive rest: Human beings are condemned to ask questions beyond and about what they do and what they experience. So the journey of modern thought is not over; perhaps it is just beginning.

Suggested Reading

Cahoone, *Cultural Revolutions*, chap. 7, conclusion.

———, *The Ends of Philosophy*.

Questions to Consider

1. Do the many critiques of philosophical knowing in the 20th century—from Quine to Kuhn to Derrida to Rorty—mean that philosophy can no longer seek the kind of comprehensive knowledge that has always defined it as distinctive?

2. What kind of philosophy, then, will the future bring?

Philosophy's Death Greatly Exaggerated
Lecture 36—Transcript

Many students of philosophy understandably suffer from a kind of exhaustion due to vertigo; perhaps you feel like one of them. All these disagreements, every philosopher rejects the one before, it seems nothing reliable is gained in the process; and the last hundred years of philosophy seem more subject to that charge than any other. To some extent though, I must say, how could we expect otherwise? Philosophy is the most comprehensive, most open-ended kind of rational inquiry. Nothing—no cultural change, no new scientific discovery, no new kind of ethical demands made by a changing society—none of these can be ignored by philosophy. Philosophy is just the name we give to our trying to figure out what the world and life are like in the widest possible sense, by using the method of inquiry; that is, the method of saying what we think is true and giving reasons and evidence for and against.

John Herman Randall, a Columbia professor of mid-20th century and, in fact, one of the greatest writers on the history of philosophy in the English language, once said that no great philosophy is ever proved wrong, it's just shown to be irrelevant to a new kind of experience. I don't agree with him that no great philosophy is ever proved wrong; but his point is still well taken: Human beings, especially in the modern world, face many different "spheres" of experience—personal, private feelings; the demands of family life; economic reality; the natural, ecological world; the discoveries of science; the development of new technologies; civic responsibilities; aesthetic value; the engineering of own physical environment; the demands of a decent ethical life; the question of religion and spiritual growth—all of these things change over time independently of each other. It's is increasingly difficult to forge a philosophical view that can adequately address more than one or two of these spheres, not to mention all of them. The point is: Things are complex and getting even more so, and harder to comprehend in one philosophical view. There is one fact, or one criterion, or one pressure on philosophy that simply comes from the nature of the times that we live in: Philosophy has a more complex subject matter to deal with. Some of its subject matters haven't changed, of course; but it still has more and more complications to deal with, and it's not so surprising if it's difficult to forge overall views that can seem to be adequate or valid.

The most radical blows to traditional philosophy in the 20th century mostly concerned epistemology—that is, the theory of knowledge, what is knowledge—and related fields like philosophy of language, associated with names like Wittgenstein, Quine, Heidegger, Derrida, and Rorty. In today's lecture, I'll try to respond to some of these charges; and I will suggest that rumors of philosophy's death are greatly exaggerated.

Certainly, the criticisms of the history of philosophy presented by the 20th century have taught us something. We have learned a few things. First, we've learned that we cannot find human judgments or perceptions that give us incorrigible information about what exists independent of our judgment or perception. That is to say, our judgments are always fallible. The old notion that we could isolate some strand, some dimension, some part of the cognitive process—call it sense data, call it perception, call it whatever you like—that we could isolate some layer of our cognition that had contact, that wasn't purely analytic, but nevertheless was certain, and indubitable, and immediately contacted the presence of the world; that view is pretty well discredited. We seem to have learned that. On the other hand, our contact with the objects of knowledge is always mediated by our means of knowing, which is biological, historical, and cultural. You can look at many of the critiques that we've learned in the past 35 lectures; many of these criticisms have explored a different respect with which knowledge is funded. In other words, those who've pointed out that signs, the use of linguistic signs, bring their own kind of complexity to our understanding of experience; that we bring our theories with us; that we bring conceptual frameworks; that we bring cultures. We've come to understand, as we hadn't so much before the 20th century, just how complex is the funding that we bring as cognizers to our experience, and it includes biological funding—the types of perceptual systems and the types of organisms in our evolutionary history are all relevant—and it includes history and culture, things studied by the human sciences and the humanities.

Furthermore, we cannot provide a logical inventory of assumptions and perspectives that can fix the most fundamental features of the way we know. This is to say, as I just mentioned, our knowing is biologically, socially, culturally, and historically laden; just as Quine and others discovered that our statements of sense data or of observations are laden with theory, theoretically laden, we've learned that our knowing is biologically, socially, culturally, and historically laden. It is thickly determined, but the point here is also that determination changes, because some of those things change; society, culture, and history change. With the preceding point, this means we can't analyze out of either the experience or the event of knowing something—experiencing something or knowing something—the contribution of the things themselves and our contribution to knowing fully. As Margolis said, we never get to the naked word or things in themselves and a complete description of our contribution, which doesn't itself involve referring to the world.

Furthermore, we cannot know that any theory of the world we have, even if it is true, is the one true theory; this is one of Putnam's points, and it's hard to refute. It may very well be that a different kind of being, a different kind of rational creature from a different planet, would have a very different theory of reality than we would, even their best possible theory; we can never assume that our view of the world is the one true view. Again, we can't give a noncircular argument to prove that we have knowledge at all; this is the kind of project that Quine gave up when he said I'm not even going to bother trying to prove we have knowledge, it can't be done. He's almost certainly right; that is, any time I try to prove to the skeptic, the absolute skeptic, that we have knowledge at all, the only way I can do it will be to use knowledge in the proving. I have no noncircular argument against the skeptic on that score.

What does this mean taken all together, all these have-nots I've just been describing; all these things we learned we can't do. In short, it means the foundationalist approach to philosophy that was enshrined by Descartes; but also used in a different form, an empiricist form by Locke; used in another kind of rationalist form by Descartes; and then in various ways informed much of the development of modern philosophy, even among philosophers that objected to Descartes. This is, of course, one of the great secrets—or it's not much of a secret anymore, it has something to do with what some call the anxiety of influence—even that thinker you are rebelling against, you probably have adopted some of their habits yourself; that's part of what's so frustrating and why you want to rebel. Descartes has certainly influenced modern philosophy right through the 20th century, even though in his lifetime many were objectioning to his mind/body dualism, as we saw.

The foundationalist approach to philosophy seems to be dead. The real question is: Now what, or so what? None of this has to mean that we don't know or can't know anything, or can't know anything important, or that realism is dead. Remember that epistemic realism—which we talked about from the beginning of the course—is the view that our knowledge is true of its objects independent of our ideas, theories, and cultures. In other words, when we judge something and we're right—we're often wrong, but when we're right, when what we say is true when we have true knowledge—it's knowledge that's true of things insofar as they exist and obtain and have characters independent of the judgment we're making; we don't make the judgments true, the object plays a role in making them true. Do we have such knowledge? Antirealism—or its most famous form, relativism—holds that our true knowledge is made true not by its objects independent of us, but by our own experience, ideas, perspectives, theories, and cultures. Rorty and the postmodernists either accept antirealism—some postmodernists accept antirealism—or they simply deny realism. Rorty, as we saw, is much more careful; he wants to say the whole question between realism and antirealism is a senseless question, impossible to address. What that means in practice is, of course, he leaves realism behind.

But what does realism really require? One way of looking at it is a minimal realism only requires a few things: that our true judgments are true of what they judge, and true of the character of those objects independent of the judgment or judgments. What's being judged, what our statements are true of, is a truth about something whose character, insofar as it's being judged, is independent of the judgment I'm making; so the judgment isn't making the thing true. Some of those independent features of the object are part of what makes the judgment true. Notice not all; certainly, without question, some features of my judgment also play a role in making it true. It has to be grammatical, it has to be what logicians would call a well-formed formula, in other words the statement has to make sense and be put in the right way; there are a bunch of rules for the language that I use to describe reality, that it must satisfy. But the point of realism is that realism only requires that such rules do not decide the validity of the statement by itself.

Likewise, what is known only needs to be partly determinate, not wholly determinate. What I mean by that is the objects of our knowledge don't need to definitely have or not have every possible property that we could list; the object merely has to have some properties. Without any properties, we have nothing to say about it. The point is: A realist account of knowledge doesn't require that the world be completely determinate in every detail; it's perfectly compatible with a world in which there's, for example, causal indeterminacy, as we see in quantum mechanics, it's perfectly compatible with a world where some things are vague and indeterminate and unknowable, or only knowable in a vague or general way. The doctrine of realism doesn't have to oppose any of that.

The pragmatic and aesthetic recognition that our cognition is active does not amount, I suggest, to what is called constructivism. The notion of constructivism, which ultimately is ascribed to Kant—Kant never used that term, but other people have used it of his view; and other people have said we construct our knowledge, we construct our world even by the active funding of our experience in cognition, we're constructing the world—construction is building, which implies making and control. If it were true that we cognitively make the world, we would presumably have done a better job, like left out pain, misery, and death. Our knowing doesn't construct the world, it selects, modifies, strains, construes, always with constraints imposed by the environment it's trying to know. If I can stop for a moment and bring in a lovely remark by the ethologist and evolutionary epistemologist Konrad Lorenz, Lorenz asked himself: "Does the hoof of the horse construct the ground?" Of course not; it deals with the ground, it senses some things in the ground, it stumbles, it doesn't always fit, and it doesn't always fit the ground properly. Lorenz says in the same way, the human nervous system, which underlies our cognitive abilities, doesn't construct the world or its environment; it, like the hoof, deals with the environment in its way, sometimes successfully, sometimes not so successfully. But it's not a matter of making or constructing a world out of some kind of raw data.

Our knowledge, our cognition, doubtless has parameters dictated by the perceptual and affective and cognitive motor capacities liberally distributed among modern *Homo sapiens*; that's all the biological stuff that we've gotten from our evolution. Add to this language, something we have that essentially no other creature on earth has, or sign-use generally, our ability to create things that mean and use them as signs. Add to this culture, which really is the creation of a world of artifacts that mean; and then history, which only beings that have cultures have histories. Add all this together and human knowing brings an enormous fund, biological, psychological, and cultural, to each thing to be known. Of course, this fact, the funding of experience by our biology, culture, and history is often taken by antirealists as a reason to say, "Well, we never confront the things in themselves because we're acting through a sort of a big gauze or haze, we never contact things, we only contact things as we construe them through the media we've inherited through which we know"; but not if we don't think of all this funding as a container, or an obstacle to knowing reality. The biological, historical, and cultural constituents of the way we know, this is the means by which our species grasps the world. These perspectives, schemes, theories, are "adverbial," to use a word that appeared in an earlier lecture; they are the means of doing something, they are manners of accessing, as Gadamer claimed, the world. They are not intermediaries between me and the world; they are the way I, as a human—as opposed to a non-human creature—grasp the world, and they can perform that task better or worse.

While we can't aspire to the one true representation of the one real world, we can claim an approximately true representation of the real world, or aspire to it, in our cognitive medium. We know the world is the one and only real world as it systematically affects us and is interpreted through the human perceptual-motor-cognitive apparatus in its historical, cultural modalities. We may not know it the only way it can be known; how would we ever know that? We could never be able to determine the difference between the only ways we can know it and yet some other way; but we can know it as it relates to beings like us and draw conclusions from that. In fact, that's everything, in a sense, that science does.

That there might be other ways to understand the world would only undermine the notion of realism if not only were there other ways, but if those other ways and ours were incommensurable. That is to say, if you could say there are several different ways to understand the world—there's the human way, and then there are some others; how you would know this, I don't know, but imagine you could say there are others—and these different ways are all in contradiction; they're incommensurable, they can't be intertranslated, or if they can be intertranslated they're in conflict. In other words, one view of the world says Galileo's balls will not fall from the Tower of Pisa to the ground but will somehow fall up. But we have no reason to believe that. Even to recognize two vastly different languages as languages, not to mention potentially true languages, true descriptions of the world, presupposes bilingual people, meaning the languages are not incommensurable, as has been shown partly by Davidson and also by MacIntyre.

True representations in different representative media must have a systematic, lawful relation, just as the common sense or brute fact that we have in everyday experience must have a linear relation to the scientific fact, and just as the earlier cognized fact must have a similarly linear relation to the cognized fact subsequent to cognitive progress. In other words, when we move from one understanding of things to another that we decide is more true and more sophisticated, when we learn over time from one moment to another or when we describe something in everyday experience and then look at the scientific analysis of that thing, in all these cases what happens? We have an experience of cognitive progress. It happens to us every day, and it happens to society as a whole. As long as the more advanced notion, the undemanding of the world after cognitive progress, can understand the earlier understanding, can see how it's better and how it captures what the early understanding thought it knew but now sees that it knows more, all this means that we can have a rational notion of what cognitive progress means, and all this implies that we cannot find any such thing as an incommensurable language, or even more strange languages so different from us that they have totally different ways, incompatible ways, of viewing the world and yet are understandable by us. That whole set of problems that some philosophers raise seem very strange and difficult to understand.

At any rate, an account of the relationships between these different understandings of the world—which, again, we do this every day—the child says something about what happened between Janie and Johnny, you saw the same thing, you explain it differently and in a more complicated way, the child cannot understand your explanation but you can understand the child's explanation because yours includes, you might say, the child's explanation as a possibility that you've rejected as not being true. This is rational progress, and it's why, hopefully, adults still get to teach their children. Rational progress, therefore, remains conceivable wherever we can articulate within our new, improved understanding of things—like our newer science, like Einstein's view in special relativity versus Newton's mechanics and his view of space and time—and still articulate the old way of understanding and explain its inadequacy along with the greater adequacy of our new view, that's radical progress; and there's nothing we've seen to say that it can't be done or that it's in doubt.

At any rate, a minimally realist notion of truth, knowledge, and the world, I suggest, is entirely coherent with the adverbial nature of the media of knowing (that is, the judgments, concepts, languages, cultures we bring to experience), perfectly compatible with the denial of presence or privilege (as Heidegger and others have criticized; that is, the claim that we have cognitions that are immediate in their relation to objects, hence irrefragable or indubitable), and it's compatible with the assertion of objective indeterminacy (that not every possible proposition must be either true or false of a real thing, because the latter, like our propositions, vary in their determinateness).

Now that we've talked about rational progress, does philosophy make any, or does it make no progress? We're certainly not on a ladder or a straight line of progress; but neither are we in a circle, spinning around a finite set of intellectual options. It appears to move that we are rather on a spiral, progressing by overlapping cycles. Indeed, philosophy is a famous recycler, after all. In our spiral, resources from the past are constantly put to new uses, which then leave us in a slightly different, in the case of the spiral, the metaphor would mean circularly capturing some of the same resources of the past, but as the spiral goes up it leaves us in a little different position vertically than where we were before. For example, just when everyone in the 20th century thought that Cartesian innate ideas were well lost on the dustbin of history, as some of you may know, the famous linguist Noam Chomsky recycled the notion of innate ideas into his innate linguistic competence in the 1970s; that is, Chomsky said there must be some innate linguistic competence, it can't all be learned. Language can't be learned from nothing, from a tabula rasa. More recently, in the midst of a very sophisticated discussion of neuroscience and the philosophy of mind, neuroscientist Antonio Damasio has recently revived Spinoza's view (of all people) of the relation of mind to body—remember the parallel processes notion—saying that this is a good model to use in the description of contemporary neuroscience.

There are many such examples; and at the same time, to use Popper's term, there certainly is progress in falsification; that is, as philosophy goes on, some views are ruled out, like, I would say, foundationalism. It seems there isn't an eternal circle; there's certainly not a straight line or a ladder; it seems that we have a spiral. We recycle and reuse earlier notions, but we don't, strictly speaking, return to the same positions in the past. In short, over time, we learned some things.

So, now at the end of our long journey from the early 17th century to today, philosophy, along with all our other modes of inquiry, is still in business. In fact, one has to think that the philosopher's job may be more central than ever. For while it's true that over the centuries philosophy has been diminished as more and more fields—first the physical sciences, then the social sciences—have gradually split off from philosophy to pursue their own methods; while that's true, the problem of integrating the knowledge of those fields and of the other fields of everyday life in which we have practical knowledge and practical work, the job of integrating this and seeing them in a common context is greater than ever. The attempt to know the world and ourselves, to know what is true, good, and beautiful, remains a philosophical job; nobody else is taking it on.

The alternative to philosophy would be essentially to stop wondering, to stop asking questions that go beyond the methods and intellectual boundaries of the many contexts of our lives: family life, the sciences, our business, entertainment, our local civic obligations, technology. Each of these spheres, and in each of these spheres, human beings interact and ask questions; but it's only when they step outside that they ask questions about is this sphere good? Is it what it should be? Is it what it ought to be? How am I to understand the relationship between these different parts of my life and our lives?

The choice is either, as Aristotle knew long ago, to accept our unreflective, uncoordinated, often contrary beliefs, or to ask ourselves if they are true and how they hang together. If you ask those questions and try to answer them, you're doing philosophy.

It may be that we're just not built for cognitive rest. Perhaps we never have been, since we ate of the fruit of the tree of knowledge. Human beings are condemned to ask questions beyond and about what they do and what they experience. When we do that, again, we're doing philosophy. So the journey of modern thought is not over; perhaps it's just beginning. I want to thank you for taking this part of the trip with me.

Timeline

1492 .... Christopher Columbus's arrival in the Americas.

1543 .... Nicolaus Copernicus's *On the Revolutions of Celestial Spheres*.

1581 .... Establishment of Dutch Republic (where René Descartes and Baruch Spinoza later wrote).

1632 .... Galileo's *Dialogue Concerning the Two Chief World Systems*.

1641 .... René Descartes' *Meditations on First Philosophy*.

1677 .... Baruch Spinoza's *Ethics*.

1686 .... Gottfried Wilhelm Leibniz's *Discourse on Metaphysics*.

1687 .... Isaac Newton's *Mathematical Principles of Natural Philosophy*.

1689 .... England's Glorious Revolution.

1690 .... John Locke's *An Essay Concerning Human Understanding*.

1710 .... George Berkeley's *Treatise Concerning the Principles of Human Knowledge*.

1739–1740 .... David Hume's *A Treatise of Human Nature*.

1776 .... American Revolution; David Hume's death; Adam Smith's *An Inquiry into the Nature and Causes of the Wealth of Nations*.

1781 .... Immanuel Kant's *Critique of Pure Reason*.

1789 .... French Revolution.

1793–1794 .... The Terror in France.

1794 .... Johann Gottlieb Fichte's *The Science of Knowledge*.

1800 .... Friedrich Wilhelm Joseph von Schelling's *System of Transcendental Idealism*.

1807 .... Georg Wilhelm Friedrich Hegel's *Phenomenology of Spirit* (finished in Jena as Napoleon conquered the city).

1821 .... Napoleon's death.

1831 .... Georg Wilhelm Friedrich Hegel's death.

1843 .... Søren Kierkegaard's *Fear and Trembling* and *Either/Or*; John Stuart Mill's *A System of Logic*.

1844 .... Karl Marx's *Economic and Philosophic Manuscripts of 1844*.

1859 .... Charles Darwin's *On the Origin of Species by Means of Natural Selection*.

1871 .... Otto von Bismarck's unification of Germany.

1877–1878 .... Charles Sanders Peirce's pragmatism essays.

1879 .... Gottlob Frege's *Begriffsschrift* (*Concept Script*).

1900 .... Sigmund Freud's *The Interpretation of Dreams*.

1900–1901 .... Edmund Husserl's *Logical Investigations*.

1905 .... Albert Einstein's theory of special relativity.

1906 .... William James's *Pragmatism*.

1910–1913 .... Bertrand Russell and Alfred North Whitehead's 3-volume *Principia Mathematica*.

1914–1918 .... World War I.

1915 .... Albert Einstein's theory of general relativity.

1916 .... Ferdinand de Saussure's *Course in General Linguistics*.

1921 .... Ludwig Wittgenstein's *Tractatus-Logico Philosophicus*.

1925 .... John Dewey's *Experience and Nature*.

1926–1927 .... Erwin Schrödinger's wave equation; Heisenberg's uncertainty principle.

1927 .... Martin Heidegger's *Being and Time*.

1929 .... Alfred North Whitehead's *Process and Reality: An Essay in Cosmology*.

1931 .... Kurt Gödel's "On Formally Undecidable Propositions of *Principia Mathematica* and Related Systems."

1933–1945 .... Adolf Hitler's chancellorship.

1934	Rudolf Carnap's *The Logical Syntax of Language*.
1939	Adolf Hitler invades Poland.
1940	Fall of Paris.
1941	Japanese attack on Pearl Harbor.
1943	Jean-Paul Sartre's *Being and Nothingness*.
1945	Defeat of Germany and Japan; occupation of central Europe by U.S. and USSR.
1947	Theodor Adorno and Max Horkheimer's *Dialectic of Enlightenment*; Martin Heidegger's *Letter on Humanism*.
1953	Ludwig Wittgenstein's *Philosophical Investigations*.
1960	Hans-Georg Gadamer's *Truth and Method*; Willard Van Orman Quine's *Word and Object*.
1962	Thomas S. Kuhn's *The Structure of Scientific Revolutions*.
1966	Michel Foucault's *The Order of Things*.
1967	Jacques Derrida's *Of Grammatology*, *Speech and Phenomena*, and *Writing and Difference*.
1968	Tet Offensive in Vietnam; assassinations of President Robert F. Kennedy and Martin Luther King Jr.; student revolts in U.S. and Paris; Prague Spring; Cultural Revolution in China.
1974	Donald T. Campbell's "Evolutionary Epistemology."
1979	Jean-François Lyotard's *The Postmodern Condition*; Richard Rorty's *Philosophy and the Mirror of Nature*.
1981	Alasdair MacIntyre's *After Virtue*; Jürgen Habermas's *The Theory of Communicative Action*; Hilary Putnam's *Reason, Truth, and History*.
1989	Fall of Berlin Wall.
1991	Dismantling of USSR.

Glossary

a posteriori: This Latin term literally means following experience, but precisely, knowledge whose justification is dependent on experience.

a priori: This Latin term literally means before experience, but precisely, knowledge whose justification is independent of experience.

aesthetics: The subfield of philosophy that investigates the nature of art and the experience of beauty.

Age of Reason: The 17th-century period of scientific revolution and systematic philosophy that preceded the Enlightenment.

American philosophy: Also known as Americanist philosophy or classical American philosophy, this indigenous American philosophical tradition was practiced from the mid-19th century until the 1930s, when analytic and continental philosophy became dominant in the United States. Its most famous doctrine is pragmatism, and its most famous exponents are Charles Sanders Peirce, George Herbert Mead, William James, John Dewey, George Santayana, and Josiah Royce.

analytic philosophy: Sometimes called Anglo-American philosophy, the predominantly English-language philosophy of the past century stemming from figures such as Gottlob Frege, Bertrand Russell, George Edward Moore, Rudolf Carnap, Ludwig Wittgenstein, and Willard Van Orman Quine that puts a premium on linguistic clarity and the relation between philosophical claims and either logic or science.

analytic proposition: A proposition whose subject logically contains its predicate and hence is true or false by meaning. An example is "All bachelors are unmarried," because "bachelor" means unmarried man. *See also* **synthetic proposition**.

ancient philosophy: Philosophy from the 7th century B.C.E. to the end of the Roman Empire (4th century C.E.).

British emergentism: A school of thought in the 1920s that proposed an alternative to mechanism and vitalism by which complex organization of components of one level (e.g., physical) yield novel, irreducible properties at a higher level (e.g., chemical). Its most prominent exponents were Samuel Alexander, Conwy Lloyd Morgan, and C. D. Broad.

cause: Aristotle held that each thing has four different kinds of causes (conditions without which it would not be): the material cause, or what it is made of (e.g., for an ancient ship, wood); the efficient cause that makes it (the act of building the ship); its formal cause, or structure or form (the blueprint or plan for the ship); and the final cause or purpose of the ship (to sail the ocean). Modern science crucially denied that there are final or formal causes in natural things. David Hume famously criticized causality as "necessary connection."

constructivism: Broadly, an explanation of something through the procedure that produces it; but often in epistemology, the claim that what is known to be real is constructed by the knowing subject(s).

continental philosophy: Philosophies from mainland Europe in the past two centuries, stemming from figures such as Georg Wilhelm Friedrich Hegel, Edmund Husserl, Martin Heidegger, Hans-Georg Gadamer, Jean-Paul Sartre, Theodor Adorno, Maurice Merleau-Ponty, Jacques Derrida, and others, typically nonnaturalistic and hermeneutic in orientation.

critical idealism: Immanuel Kant's name for his version of idealism, which accepts that nonmental things in themselves cause our experience, but our experience is structured a priori by our own cognitive activity. Also sometimes called transcendental idealism.

critical theory: An ambiguous term that in the 20th century was applied to the work of both the German neo-Marxist philosophers of the Frankfurt School and poststructuralist French philosophers.

deism: A religious philosophy modeled on a minimal Christianity, with beliefs in moral rule, the soul, an afterlife, and God, lacking any other theology or ritual practice. Jean-Jacques Rousseau and Immanuel Kant were deists.

deontological ethics: The ethics of duty, which holds that what makes action moral is that the intended act conforms to a rule of moral obligation, regardless of consequences or goals.

direct realism: The claim that in perception, we directly cognize the external object of perception and not merely a representation of it.

dualism: Any theory that claims some subject is composed of two fundamentally different kinds of things (e.g., in metaphysics, that all reality is either mind or matter).

emergence: The claim that some natural systems exhibit properties that are not exhibited by the components of the system. Hence the novel, or emergent, property is irreducible to properties of the components.

empiricism: The epistemological view that all knowledge derives from experience. Empiricism's opposite is **rationalism**.

Enlightenment: The 18th-century western European explosion of secular philosophy, political revolution, and science against "superstition" that bequeathed us the idea that reason, science, and freedom bring progress.

epistemology: The subfield of philosophy that examines the nature and possibility of knowledge and truth.

ethics: The subfield of philosophy that investigates the good life, moral values, and how humans ought to live. Three dominant schools of ethical thought are virtue ethics, deontological ethics, and utilitarianism.

evolutionary epistemology: A theory that tries to account for the nature of human cognition through natural selection, as a result of our biological evolution. The most famous expositors were Donald T. Campbell and Konrad Lorenz.

existentialism: The philosophical movement focused on the analysis of individual existence and the individual's thought and responsibility. Søren Kierkegaard and Friedrich Nietzsche were 19th-century sources of what become existentialism in the 20th century.

explanation: There are many types, categorizations, and theories of explanation in the philosophy of science. One useful recent typology, by William C. Wimsatt, distinguishes three types of explanation: reductive; phenomenological (not related to Husserlian or Hegelian phenomenology); and functional, which explains a system's properties by, respectively, the properties and behavior of its components, its interaction with systems of comparable scale, and its role within an encompassing system.

externalism: In the philosophy of language or mind, the view that meanings supervene or depend on relations of the subject to environment, rather than depending only on intramental processes. Externalism was promoted by Saul Kripke and Hilary Putnam, and its antonym is internalism.

fallibilism: In methodology and epistemology, the notion that all judgments are fallible, there being no significant necessary truths we can discover. It was first formulated by Charles Sanders Peirce.

falsificationism: Karl Popper's theory that inductive inference from observation does not confirm our hypotheses but only disconfirms them. So to accept a theory as true is merely to say it has not yet been falsified.

form: In metaphysics, from Plato and Aristotle, the rule or structure that makes a thing what it is (what it means to be the thing). It organizes a thing's matter and provides a thing's intelligibility.

foundationalism: The attempt to provide an incorrigible, presuppositionless ground for objective or realist knowledge claims. Often claims indubitable, foundational knowledge (e.g., in sense data, innate ideas, or the inner working of Reason itself). René Descartes is explicitly a foundationalist, as are many other modern thinkers.

functionalism: A term used variously inside philosophy and out. In a vague sense, it means understanding something as an operation or activity through what it does, rather than what it is. The most famous use in recent philosophy is to refer to the computational theory of mind, first developed by Hilary Putnam, as a device analogous to a computer. It can also be used for functional explanation generally, explaining a system's behavior by what it accomplishes for an encompassing system. *See also* **explanation**.

hermeneutics: The science of interpretation invented by biblical scholars in the 19th century, hermeneutics in the 20th century became a philosophy by thinkers like Hans-Georg Gadamer that embedded meanings in historical and cultural traditions.

historicism: Generally, the view that some property changes historically; but most famously, the view that norms, like truth or moral goodness, are relative to historical period. Karl Popper famously accused Georg Wilhelm Friedrich Hegel and Karl Marx of historicism.

holism: Generally, the view that the character of individual elements, or their appearances, is dependent on their location in a larger system. In this sense, gestalt psychology and Georg Wilhelm Friedrich Hegel's logic and metaphysics are holistic. In recent analytic philosophy, it more narrowly means Willard Van Orman Quine's view that theories confront experience as a whole, so that disconfirming observations leave it indeterminate as to what part of the theory to replace.

idealism: The metaphysical view that reality is in some important sense mental. Different kinds of idealism press the mentality of the world to differing degrees. Absolute idealism holds that reality is solely mental, that matter does not exist, as George Berkeley held. The more famous German idealists, like Georg Wilhelm Friedrich Hegel, held a more subtle version, taking nature as an expression of spirit. Idealism's opposite is **materialism** or **physicalism** or **naturalism**.

logic: The subfield of philosophy that investigates the rules that make an argument valid. Notice that logical validity is independent of truth: "If all men are cabbages," and "Cahoone is a man," then that "Cahoone is a cabbage" is a valid inference; but because its first premise is false, the argument's conclusion is false. The late 19th century witnessed the creation of the first new logic since Aristotle, and this was crucial to the development of 20th-century philosophy. *See also* **modern logic**.

logicism: The attempt to show that mathematics can entirely be derived from basic logical terms and principles. Bertrand Russell and Alfred North Whitehead's *Principia Mathematica* is the most famous logicist work.

materialism: The metaphysical view that reality is solely composed of matter. Thomas Hobbes and Karl Marx are materialists. Materialism's opposite is **idealism**.

matter: For Aristotle, the physical stuff that individuates a real thing (a substance), particularizing its form.

medieval: The historical period from the fall of the Western Roman Empire (5th century C.E.) through the 15th century C.E.

metaphysics: The subfield of philosophy that investigates the ultimate nature of reality, the composition of all things, and the existence of God. Within metaphysics, the inquiry into being itself is called ontology.

modern: In philosophy, used for the historical period roughly since the start of the 17th century. The late 15th through the 16th centuries are sometimes included under modern but other times distinguished as Renaissance philosophy.

modern logic: Invented primarily by Gottlob Frege (but with independent contributions by Charles Sanders Peirce), a powerful tool for formalizing natural language statements and their proofs. First-order logic (also called first-order predicate calculus) uses variables that range over individuals and includes quantifiers (unlike propositional logic). Second-order logic uses variables and quantifiers that range over sets and properties.

monism: The metaphysical view that only one thing exists; all of reality is a single substance. Baruch Spinoza was a monist.

natural religion: Also known as natural theology or rational theology, the view that the basic tenets of Christianity (or any religion) can be derived through rational argument and/or naturalistic observation, without revelation. William Paley was a famous expositor.

naturalism: Strictly, the view that everything is natural or part of nature, so nothing is supernatural. As such, physicalism and materialism would be versions of naturalism, but the term has often been used more narrowly for views that do not equate the natural with the physical or material (e.g., those of American naturalists like John Dewey and emergentists like Conwy Lloyd Morgan).

naturalistic epistemology: The study of human cognition by natural science, as defined for example by Willard Van Orman Quine, often from the standpoint of evolution. Hence it is sometimes called **evolutionary epistemology**.

pantheism, **panentheism**: Pantheism is the claim that God and the universe are identical. Some philosophers distinguish this from the view that the universe is in God, but God is more than the universe, calling it panentheism. Baruch Spinoza, sometimes called a pantheist, was more strictly a panentheist.

phenomenalism: The epistemological view that we experience not things existing independently of the mind but data internal to our experience, so we cannot know that anything beyond phenomena exists.

phenomenology: This term was used by Georg Wilhelm Friedrich Hegel for his account of the dialectical progression of human experience, by Charles Sanders Peirce for the study of the most general features of experience, but most famously by Edmund Husserl for his philosophical method of studying experience that brackets or ignores all questions of natural existence.

physicalism: The view that reality is physical; this is sometimes used identically with materialism, but properly the physical is a broader category (e.g., vacuums and electromagnetic fields are physical but not material).

positivism: Also known as logical positivism or logical empiricism. The term "positivism" was invented by Auguste Comte in the 19th century to refer to the modern scientific temper of that century but more famously was adopted by the early 20th-century philosophers of the Vienna Circle, like Moritz Schlick, Otto Neurath, and Rudolf Carnap, for philosophical theory that regarded existential or factual questions as exhausted by science, and philosophy's job as logic and the clarification of scientific language.

postmodernism: A family of philosophical, artistic, and social movements that either hold that contemporary advanced societies have abandoned key features of modernity or hold that all presentation of reality (e.g., perception) presumes representation by signs. Most famously defined by Jean-François Lyotard in his *The Postmodern Condition: A Report on Knowledge*.

poststructuralism: The French postmodernist philosophers of the 1960s, like Jacques Derrida and Michel Foucault, are more precisely termed poststructuralists, who apply structuralism reflexively to the theories of the human sciences and philosophy, leading to radical results.

pragmatism: Originally a theory of meaning, it held that the meaning of a term or claim is its role in the guidance of conduct. It is also a theory of truth, although pragmatists differ on its precise formulation: The truth of a claim is its verification, or the satisfactoriness of actions that presume it, or its acceptance by the community of inquirers in the long run. In more global terms, pragmatists accept that meaning and mind arise in the context of social action. Formulated by Charles Sanders Peirce and William James.

process philosophy: Any philosophy that makes all reality and all forms or norms subject to a process of change. Most commonly applied to the work of Alfred North Whitehead but would also fit Henri Bergson and John Dewey, among others.

psychologism: The view of J. S. Mill and others that all meanings of signs, hence logic too, are psychological properties or entities of human organisms. That would mean they are in a sense naturalistic. Both Gottlob Frege and Edmund Husserl, and hence early analytic and continental philosophy, rejected this notion.

qualities: Those properties that belong to a thing independently of its being observed are primary qualities, while those belonging not to it, but only to our experience of it (i.e., those not existing in the object but caused to arise in our minds by its primary qualities) are secondary qualities. John Locke famously expressed this doctrine.

rationalism: The epistemological view, for example, of René Descartes and Immanuel Kant, that not all knowledge is derived from experience, that there is some nonexperiential source of knowledge. Its antonym is **empiricism**.

realism: The view that the something under consideration is real and independent of our activity. It can apply to epistemic or ethical questions. Epistemic realism means the validity of our cognitive judgment is determined by real properties of what is judged. The opposite is antirealism. (Note: Direct realism has a different meaning altogether, though one could be an epistemic realist and a direct realist at the same time.)

reduction, reductionism: In philosophy of science, reduction refers either to explanation of a system's properties as the product of the properties of its components or lower-level entities (explanatory or theoretical reduction) or to the claim that the system is the collection of its parts or lower-level entities (ontological reduction). If reductive explanations are held to be transitive, then this would mean all phenomena are explainable by physics. Some thinkers deny this but maintain ontological reductionism.

relativism: Narrowly, the claim that some property is a relative or relational property. ("Tall" is relational; "human" is not.) In practice, the view that the validity of our judgment is not determined by real properties of what is judged but by the relation of the judgment to the judge or some set of judgments, for example, a theory or culture. It can apply to epistemic or ethical issues.

representationalism: The view, widespread in modern thought, that in perception, that of which we are directly aware is a representation of the external object, not the object itself (e.g., a sense-datum).

Scholasticism: The synthesis of the philosophy of Aristotle and Christian theology that was forged in the 13th century, most famously by Saint Thomas Aquinas, and dominated the universities of central and western Europe from the 14th through the 18th century.

scientific revolution: The development of a new science in the 17th century characterized by a mathematical analysis of motion and matter; the rejection of Aristotle's substantial forms and final causes; and the replacement of the closed Aristotelian-Ptolemaic (geocentric) theory of the universe by the Copernican (heliocentric) system and an open or infinite, centerless universe. Arguably, there have been other scientific revolutions.

skepticism: The epistemological view that what others regard as knowledge is dubitable. There are many versions; only global skepticism doubts that we have any knowledge of real things at all. The ancient Greek Sextus Empiricus (a follower of Pyrrhonism) and the Scotsman David Hume were famous skeptics.

solipsism: The epistemological view that all I experience and know are properties of myself, that all objects of my experience and knowledge are in me.

structuralism: A theoretical approach to the human or social sciences in which the meanings of human actions are derived from networks of signs and/or concepts, for example, in the work of Ferdinand de Saussure and Claude Lévi-Strauss.

substance: The Latinized version of Aristotle's term for what exists in the primary sense, namely, independent physical beings (e.g., you or a chair or the Earth), while other beings are their properties (e.g., your activities, a chair's color, the Earth's roundness). Each substance has its own qualitatively distinct inner form and matter, and their properties, states, and modes as accidents.

synthetic proposition: A proposition whose predicate is not logically contained in the subject and as such can only be made true or false by added information, for example, "There are bachelors on Earth." *See also* **analytic proposition**.

transcendental: A term of art in Immanuel Kant and philosophies related to his, referring to the activity of the mind in shaping experience a priori.

utilitarianism: The ethics of utility, which holds that those acts are good whose consequences maximize social happiness, famously developed by Jeremy Bentham, James Mill, and his son John Stuart Mill.

verificationism: The view, held by some logical positivists (e.g., A. J. Ayer), that the meaning of a claim is the observations that would verify or confirm it.

virtue ethics: The ethics of virtue, which follows Aristotle in focusing on what makes good character, especially which dispositions to behave are morally good (virtues), rather than on rules that determine which action is good or right. This view has returned in recent philosophy, in the work of Alasdair MacIntyre and others.

Biographical Notes

Adorno, Theodor (1903–1969): One of the prominent thinkers of the neo-Marxist Frankfurt Institute for Social Research, which combined the thought of Karl Marx, Georg Wilhelm Friedrich Hegel, and Sigmund Freud. Adorno is the author of *Negative Dialectics* and, with Max Horkheimer, *Dialectic of Enlightenment*.

Alexander, Samuel (1859–1938): An influential English philosopher, one of the British emergentists, and the author of *Space, Time, and Deity*.

Aquinas, Saint Thomas (1224/5–1274): The great integrator of Christianity with Aristotelian philosophy, or Scholasticism, whose writings at first were condemned by the Catholic Church but later became official church doctrine.

Arendt, Hannah (1906–1975): A student of Martin Heidegger, she was one of the great political philosophers of the 20th century. Politically a representative of civic republicanism.

Aristotle (384–322 B.C.E.): A student of Plato, this Athenian philosopher made seminal contributions to almost every field of knowledge. His physics lasted until the 17th century, his biology until Charles Darwin, and his logic until the late 19th century. He was a tutor to Alexander the Great. In the late Middle Ages, he was referred to as The Philosopher.

Bentham, Jeremy (1748–1832): The inventor of utilitarianism, or the ethical doctrine that we should act to maximize general happiness, which he applied to British legal traditions. He hoped thereby to create a scientific criterion for the reform of law.

Bergson, Henri (1859–1941): The French thinker who argued that the mathematical treatment of time was mistaken, as it construed durations as extensionless points. His metaphysics included a fundamental force for creativity in the universe, the élan vital.

Berkeley, George (1685–1753): This Irish empiricist, an Anglican bishop, took empiricism to the extreme of denying the existence of matter, thus becoming an idealist.

Broad, C. D. (Charlie Dunbar; 1887–1971): A member of the British emergentists and the author of *Mind and Its Place in Nature*.

Campbell, Donald T. (1916–1996): A psychologist by training, this American interdisciplinary thinker crossed many fields to become the major exponent of evolutionary epistemology, the view that our cognitive apparatus developed under natural selection.

Camus, Albert (1913–1960): The French existentialist author of *The Stranger*, *The Rebel*, and *The Plague*. After being rejected by the French postwar intellectual establishment because of his political moderation, he received a deserved rehabilitation as a major moral writer in the late 20th century.

Carnap, Rudolf (1891–1970): A Viennese philosopher of logic and science and one of the moving forces behind the logical positivism of the Vienna Circle. His principle of tolerance and incipient pragmatism remained modern as positivism came under attack.

Cassirer, Ernst (1874–1945): A neo-Kantian German polymath whose philosophy ranged from mathematics and physics to the philosophy of culture and the history of all. His most prominent role was as the premier theorist of culture in the 20th century and author of the three-volume *The Philosophy of Symbolic Forms*.

Copernicus, Nicolaus (1473–1543): The astronomer who formulated the modern heliocentric theory of the solar system. Its justification lay less in novel discoveries than in a far simpler mathematics.

Darwin, Charles (1809–1882): The naturalist who invented the modern theory of the evolution of species through natural selection. He is author of *On the Origin of Species by Means of Natural Selection* and *The Descent of Man*, among other works.

Davidson, Donald (1917–2003): An American analytic philosopher who made major contributions to a broad range of issues, including the theory of action, radical translation, metaphor, and the notion of supervenience.

de Beauvoir, Simone (1908–1986): One of the group of French existentialists, she was the author of *The Ethics of Ambiguity*. She also contributed one of the major works of midcentury feminism, *The Second Sex*.

de Saussure, Ferdinand (1857–1913): The Swiss linguist who first applied structuralist principles to language. He had an enormous impact, creating structural linguistics, which eventually led to the work of the famous Prague School.

Derrida, Jacques (1930–2004): A French poststructuralist and the inventor of deconstruction, a radical philosophy of reading philosophical texts as having multiple, indeterminable meanings. He was one of the main instigators of postmodernism in philosophy.

Descartes, René (1596–1650): This French philosopher and mathematician is often considered the father of modern philosophy because he inaugurated the view that all is to be seen from the standpoint of individual consciousness.

Dewey, John (1859–1952): The most prominent of the Americanist philosophers, Dewey made major contributions to philosophy, psychology, and education. He was politically active and associated with progressivism.

Engels, Friedrich (1820–1895): The longtime collaborator of Karl Marx whose father's business supported the two radicals for many years. He also wrote independently of Marx, including the books *Anti-Dühring*; *Socialism: Utopian and Scientific*; and most importantly, *The Origin of the Family, Private Property, and the State*.

Fichte, Johann Gottlieb (1762–1814): A German philosophy professor, Fichte regarded himself as finding the true meaning of Immanuel Kant's work and thereby making a bridge between Kant's critical idealism and German idealism. Fichte was also the author of the *Addresses to the German Nation*, one of the formative works of European nationalism.

Foucault, Michel (1926–1984): Along with Jacques Derrida, he is one of the two most influential poststructuralists and creators of philosophical postmodernism. Unlike Derrida, his work was essentially historical; he sought to portray how the language of the human sciences since the 16th century had constituted modern human being. He was heavily influenced by Friedrich Nietzsche's notions of genealogy and power.

Frege, Gottlob (1848–1925): As the foremost formulator of a non-Aristotelian logic in the late 19th century, Frege made many contributions to both 20th-century logic and analytic philosophy of language. He had a major impact on Bertrand Russell, Ludwig Wittgenstein, and Edmund Husserl.

Freud, Sigmund (1856–1939): The Austrian inventor of psychoanalysis, a psychiatric theory emphasizing unconscious drives and internal mental conflict. His work not only created a new form of psychological theory and treatment but has a continuing impact on cultural and literary analysis.

Gadamer, Hans-Georg (1900–2002): Influenced by Martin Heidegger, Gadamer rehabilitated the 19th-century tradition of biblical interpretation, hermeneutics, as a method of humanistic understanding. His most famous work was *Truth and Method*.

Habermas, Jürgen (b. 1929): The last representative of the Frankfurt School, a former assistant to Theodor Adorno, and the most prominent German social philosopher of the late 20th century. He combined American pragmatism with German thought into a theory of modern democracy. Author of *The Theory of Communicative Action*.

Harding, Sandra (b. 1935): An American philosopher best known for her contributions to feminist epistemology, she argues that modern theory of knowledge and science privileged a masculinist conception of knowledge as objective and based in distance rather than interaction.

Hegel, Georg Wilhelm Friedrich (1770–1831): The most influential philosopher of the 19th century, he constructed an idealist system in which Spirit or God actualizes itself through the course of human history through progressive revelations until the true science of Spirit, the perspective of the Whole, is eventually revealed.

Heidegger, Martin (1889–1976): One of the most influential philosophers of the 20th century, he combined the work of Edmund Husserl's phenomenology with that of Friedrich Nietzsche and Søren Kierkegaard to formulate existential phenomenology. Later, after joining the Nazi Party in 1933 and supporting national socialism throughout the war, he promoted a quasi-mystical philosophy of attentiveness to being.

Hobbes, Thomas (1588–1679): Known more for his great contributions to political philosophy as one of the first modern realists and social-contract theorists, the royalist Hobbes lived in exile in Paris during England's Puritan Revolution, where he was one of the original scientist-philosophers of the mid-17th century.

Horkheimer, Max (1895–1973): A member of the Frankfurt Institute before the Second World War, this philosopher was the author of *A Critique of Instrumental Reason* and a collaborator with Theodor Adorno on *Dialectic of Enlightenment*.

Hume, David (1711–1776): This Scottish philosopher and historian was the greatest skeptic of the modern period. His work created problems, particularly his critique of causality and of inductive reasoning. He played a major role in inspiring Immanuel Kant, and philosophers to the present day struggle to answer his views on induction.

Husserl, Edmund (1859–1938): This German philosopher of arithmetic and logic took a major turn to become the foremost philosopher of experience in the early 20th century. He invented the science of phenomenology as a nonnaturalistic, nonpsychological analysis of the meanings that arise in pure consciousness.

James, William (1842–1910): One of the Americanist philosophers, he made contributions to psychology (his *Principles of Psychology* was a major work of 19th-century scientific psychology) and to the philosophy of religion but is best remembered as the most prominent exponent of pragmatism. Late in his career, he created a pluralist metaphysics called radical empiricism.

Kant, Immanuel (1724–1804): One of the greatest and most influential philosophers of Western history. After a career as a mathematical physicist (he contributed to the formation of the nebular hypothesis), he wrote three major works: *Critique of Pure Reason* as an answer to David Hume's skepticism, *Critique of Practical Reason* to found the ultimate law of morality, and *Critique of Judgment* to form the objective basis of critical aesthetics. He thereby changed the theory of knowledge, ethics, and aesthetics forever and gave German philosophy a new start.

Kierkegaard, Søren Aabye (1813–1855): A religious philosopher who was one of the early influences on existentialism, Kierkegaard wrote a voluminous literature of philosophical reflection under pseudonymous authorship. He is the most intelligible critic of Reason, considering faith to be intrinsically irrational.

Kripke, Saul (b. 1940): An American analytic philosopher who contributed to philosophy of language, logic, and philosophy of mind. Most famously, he rejected Gottlob Frege and Bertrand Russell's canonical theory that names are shorthand for descriptions in favor of a causal or historical theory of reference.

Kuhn, Thomas S. (1922–1996): This American historian of science revolutionized his field by arguing in *The Structure of Scientific Revolutions* that science proceeds discontinuously, through periodic revolutions where one paradigm of fundamental concepts is thrown over for another, raising questions about the rationality of theory choice at those moments.

Leibniz, Gottfried Wilhelm (1646–1716): This early modern German philosopher was a true polymath, student of all sciences and mathematics. He made lasting but piecemeal changes to many areas, but he is best remembered for his unique metaphysics of monads.

Locke, John (1632–1704): The foremost English philosopher of the 17th century, he played a crucial role in both politics and the epistemology of the new science. His *Second Treatise on Government* and *Letter Concerning Toleration* justified England's Glorious Revolution of 1689 and helped to inspire American political thought. His later *Essay Concerning Human Understanding* made the case for an empiricist view of the new science.

Lyotard, Jean-François (1924–1998): This French poststructuralist's work was closest to political and legal theory, and his *The Postmodern Condition: A Report on Knowledge* became the most famous definition of philosophical and social postmodernism in the 1980s.

MacIntyre, Alasdair (b. 1929): This American philosopher was one of the most prominent ethicists of the second half of the 20th century. Early in his career, he participated in the rationality debate with Peter Winch and Ernest Gellner. Late in his career, he formulated a neo-Aristotelian notion of ethics and rationality itself in the books *After Virtue* and *Whose Justice? Which Rationality?*

Marcuse, Herbert (1898–1979): An associate of the Frankfurt Institute of Social Research, he became most famous later in his career as the theorist of the American new left in the 1960s, through his combination of neo-Marxist and Freudian social analysis.

Margolis, Joseph (b. 1924): An American philosopher with the rare ability to work deeply in all three 20th-century traditions: analysis, continental philosophy, and pragmatism. He is the author of many books seeking a pragmatist view of knowledge that accepts relativism but does not undermine a realist interpretation of science.

Marx, Karl (1818–1883): An early left Hegelian, Marx produced the most scientific version of socialism based on Georg Wilhelm Friedrich Hegel's dialectic. His theory eventually became the basis for all forms of Communism in the 20th century, beginning with the Russian Revolution.

Mead, George Herbert (1863–1931): This philosopher and social psychologist was one of the premier classic American philosophers, or pragmatists. A friend of John Dewey's, he derived mind and meaning from the social activity of the human organism, and in particular the human use of gesture.

Merleau-Ponty, Maurice (1908–1961): One of the circle of Second World War existentialists, Merleau-Ponty was perhaps the superior phenomenologist of the group, his works (in particular, *The Phenomenology of Perception*) having remained compelling far longer than those of Jean-Paul Sartre and others.

Mill, John Stuart (1806–1873): The most important English philosopher of the 19th century, he made major contributions to logic—although these became the target for a later generation of logicians—and political and ethical philosophy. His works on utilitarian ethics set the standard for that view, and his analysis of liberty in a republican society remains today the standard view. Mill was also an early advocate for the equality of women.

Moore, George Edward (1873–1958): One of the Cambridge founders of the analytic philosophical tradition, along with Bertrand Russell. His major contributions were, on the one hand, a series of essays showing skepticism and idealism to rest on nonsensical arguments, and on the other, a major work in ethics, *Principia Ethica*, which defended a view of the good as a nonnatural property.

Morgan, Conwy Lloyd (1852–1936): This English psychologist was the moving force behind the British emergentists and the author of *Emergent Evolution*.

Neurath, Otto (1882–1945): One of the Vienna Circle positivists. He is famous for his metaphor that in epistemology and logic we are like seamen trying to fix a ship we are sailing in, since we can only use the knowledge we have while we work on the same.

Newton, Isaac (1643–1727): The greatest scientist of early modern Europe. His discovery that the same laws of motion guide terrestrial objects and planets was the greatest achievement of the scientific revolution.

Nietzsche, Friedrich (1844–1900): The most radical philosophical critic of the Judeo-Christian tradition, and arguably of morality itself. Trained as a student of ancient languages, he identified with pre-Christian ancient values. Chronically ill and fated to become insane at age 45, Nietzsche cut a tragic figure, writing voluminously and brilliantly. He is the author of the phrase "God is dead."

Peirce, Charles Sanders (1839–1914): The inventor of pragmatism. A brilliant philosopher highly familiar with natural science, mathematics, and logic. He remains the source of much of the Americanist tradition of philosophy.

Plato (428/7–348/7 B.C.E.): The author of many dialogues in which Socrates is the main character. Plato is the middle man of the great series of teachers and students that constitutes the center of ancient Greek philosophy: Socrates, Plato, and Aristotle. Unlike his student Aristotle, he believed the intelligible forms of things are eternal and nonsensible, like mathematical objects.

Popper, Karl (1902–1994): An Austrian and then British philosopher of science whose contributions spanned from the logic of induction—where he created falsificationism to answer David Hume—to epistemology to the philosophy of biology to political philosophy (in his book *The Open Society and Its Enemies*). He was one of the most important philosophers of the 20th century.

Prigogine, Ilya (1917–2003): This Belgian chemist and Nobel Prize winner spearheaded work on complex systems in the second half of the 20th century with his focus on far-from-equilibrium dissipative systems.

Putnam, Hilary (b. 1926): A major American analytic philosopher of language and of mind, he was an early proponent of functionalism in the philosophy of mind. His later thought was heavily influenced by pragmatism and the work of J. L. Austin.

Quine, Willard Van Orman (1908–2000): Perhaps the most prominent American philosopher of the 20th century, he began as a student of the positivists but went on to undermine many of their doctrines and endorse ontological relativity.

Rorty, Richard (1931–2007): An analytic philosopher who came to critique the whole genre of analytic and continental philosophy. He was the most famous critic of foundationalism and regarded himself as a radical pragmatist.

Rousseau, Jean-Jacques (1712–1778): The Genevan philosopher who was the chief dissenter of the Enlightenment, denying that advances in the arts and sciences bring moral progress. He famously considered "primitive" man superior and inveighed against both social inequality and concern for social status.

Russell, Bertrand (1872–1970): The most prominent of the early English analytic philosophers, he was a logician, metaphysician, epistemologist, and political philosopher who wrote widely. He was also a famous pacifist and activist.

Sartre, Jean-Paul (1905–1980): The French philosopher who adapted Martin Heidegger's *Being and Time* into French existentialism. A member of the French resistance and a voluminous writer of essays, books, and plays, Sartre was perhaps the most famous philosopher in the world in the two decades after the Second World War.

Schelling, Friedrich Wilhelm Joseph von (1775–1854): The precocious younger friend of Georg Wilhelm Friedrich Hegel who produced the version of German idealism closest to a naturalistic theory.

Schopenhauer, Arthur (1788–1860): Author of a philosophy of pessimism that borrowed from Immanuel Kant the distinction of appearance and things in themselves but made the later will: sheer nonrational striving or power.

Sellars, Roy Wood (1880–1973): An American critical realist philosopher who also produced an evolutionary emergent metaphysics akin to that of the British emergentists. He is also father of the philosopher Wilfred Sellars.

Simon, Herbert A. (1916–2001): An American economist and psychologist who contributed to many fields, most famously concerning information processing in complex physical and social systems.

Smith, Adam (1723–1790): The canonical formulator of free-market capitalism, an economic system left undesigned and uncontrolled, in which the self-interested actions of producers and consumers spontaneously—as if guided by an invisible hand—increase productivity and the general quality of life.

Spencer, Herbert (1820–1903): One of the most prominent of 19th-century English philosophers, he produced a theory of the evolution of all civilization. Spencer was author of the phrase "survival of the fittest."

Spinoza, Baruch (1632–1677): This Jewish Dutch philosopher famously supported the new science and pantheism by arguing that all reality is one substance, which can be called *deus sive nature* (God or Nature).

Spivak, Gayatri Chakravorty (b. 1942): This postcolonial philosopher was born in India and educated there and in the United States. She incorporates feminist, Marxist, and Derridean perspectives to demonstrate how the literature of the colonial European powers constructs and subjugates the subaltern: women, the poor, and the non-Western.

Strauss, Leo (1899–1973): A controversial historian of political philosophy who had a significant impact on political theory and even American politics in the second half of the 20th century.

Voltaire (a.k.a. **François-Marie Arouet**; 1694–1778): The most famous intellectual and man of letters of 18th-century France. He criticized the traditional authorities of royal government and the church and wrote *Candide*.

Weber, Max (1864–1920): He was perhaps the greatest of a long line of German social theorists of the modern age. He authored *The Protestant Ethic and the Spirit of Capitalism*, which found cultural-religious dispositions to lie behind the emergence of capitalist modernity.

West, Cornel (b. 1953): This prominent African American philosopher and minister has worked in many areas of philosophy and as a public philosopher in the Jamesian and Deweyan tradition. As author of *The American Evasion of Philosophy*, he argues for a "prophetic pragmatism" on the basis of the Americanist tradition.

Whitehead, Alfred North (1861–1947): A British mathematician by training, he collaborated with Bertrand Russell to compose the most important work of logic of the 20th century, *Principia Mathematica*, and went on to formulate a unique process metaphysics of reality that incorporated relativity and quantum theory.

Wimsatt, William C. (b. 1941): A philosopher of biology at the University of Chicago, he has done the most sophisticated recent work on emergence and reductive explanation in the context of actual scientific practice.

Wittgenstein, Ludwig (1889–1951): This Austrian was perhaps the most influential philosopher of the 20th century. His early work in logic led to the *Tractatus Logico-Philosophicus*, which influenced the Vienna Circle. After leaving philosophy for many years, he returned to Cambridge to formulate a new philosophy of meaning as used in his *Philosophical Investigations*.

Young, Iris Marion (1949–2006): This American feminist political philosopher was influenced by poststructuralist thought and was the author of many books, including *Justice and the Politics of Difference* and *"Throwing Like a Girl" and Other Essays in Feminist Philosophy and Social Theory*.

Bibliography

Adorno, Theodor, and Max Horkheimer. *Dialectic of Enlightenment*. Translated by John Cumming. New York: Seabury, 1972. Makes the difficult but startling argument that social freedom requires Enlightenment thought, but that the latter by nature leads to Fascism! Leaves us in a very nasty spot.

Arendt, Hannah. *The Human Condition*. Chicago: University of Chicago Press, 1958. A brilliant theory of the relation of labor (work or the creation of artifacts) to political action and critique of modernity (both liberal capitalist and Marxist) for subjugating politics to economics.

Aristotle. *Categories and De Interpretatione*. Translated by J. L. Ackrill. Oxford: Oxford University Press, 1975. The *Categories* are Aristotle's most famous logical work. By defining substance and the other nine categories of all being, it provides an excellent introduction to his *Metaphysics*.

———. *Metaphysics*. Translated by David Bostock. New York: Oxford University Press, 1994. Aristotle's classic account of the nature of substance, potentiality, and actuality. One of the most important works in the Western tradition.

———. *On the Soul*. In *Introduction to Aristotle*, edited by Richard McKeon, translated by J. A. Smith. New York: Random House, 1947. Aristotle's account of psyche, soul, or the life principle and its three levels: vegetative, animal, and human.

———. *Physics*. Translated by Robin Waterfield. New York: Oxford University Press, 1999. Aristotle's account of the physical world, definitive for science until the 17th century.

Barrett, William. *Irrational Man: A Study in Existential Philosophy*. Garden City, NY: Anchor, 1962. A good introduction to existentialism, including chapters on Søren Kierkegaard, Friedrich Nietzsche, Martin Heidegger, and Jean-Paul Sartre.

Baudrillard, Jean. *America.* New York: Verso, 1989. A wild ride through America by the poststructuralist Baudrillard regards the American landscape as a set of symbols of the postmodern hyperreality. A very interesting read for Americans, if not the best way to understand Baudrillard's basic view.

———. *Selected Writings.* Edited by Mark Poster. Stanford, CA: Stanford University Press, 1988. The writings of the maverick postmodernist theorist of media culture and hyperreality.

Berkeley, George. *Three Dialogues between Hylas and Philonous.* LaSalle, IL: Open Court, 1938. Berkeley argues from empiricism to the nonexistence of matter.

Blitz, David. *Emergent Evolution: Qualitative Novelty and the Levels of Reality.* Dordrecht, Netherlands: Kluwer, 1992. A good historical account of British emergentism.

Bordo, Susan. *The Flight to Objectivity: Essays on Cartesianism and Culture.* Albany: State University of New York Press, 1987. A feminist interpretation of René Descartes and the modern masculinist ideal of knowledge.

Brentano, Franz. *Psychology from an Empirical Standpoint.* Translated by A. C. Rancurello, D. B. Terrell, and Linda L. McAlister. New York: Routledge, 1973. Contains the description of intentionality that helped to inform Edmund Husserl's phenomenology.

Burtt, E. A. *The Metaphysical Foundations of Modern Science.* Mineola, NY: Dover, 2003. A useful summary of the metaphysical ideas of key figures of the 17th-century scientific revolution.

Cahoone, Lawrence. *Cultural Revolutions: Reason versus Culture in Philosophy, Politics, and Jihad.* University Park, PA: Penn State University Press, 2005. A philosophical interpretation of the nature of culture and its role in recent epistemology and political philosophy.

———. *The Ends of Philosophy: Pragmatism, Foundationalism, and Postmodernism.* Malden, MA: Blackwell, 2003. A critical comparison of pragmatic and postmodern responses to the end of foundationalism.

———, ed. *From Modernism to Postmodernism: An Anthology.* Malden, MA: Blackwell, 2003. A useful anthology of primary texts from the 17th to 20th centuries, covering mostly philosophy but also related economics, sociology, and art.

Campbell, Donald T. "Evolutionary Epistemology." In *Evolutionary Epistemology, Rationality, and the Sociology of Knowledge*, edited by Gerard Radnitzky and W. W. Bartley III. LaSalle, IL: Open Court, 1987. The most famous essay on evolutionary epistemology, by the man who invented the term.

Carnap, Rudolf. *The Logical Syntax of Language.* Translated by Amethe Smeaton. Chicago: Open Court, 2002. The leading logical positivist's attempt to formulate a theory of linguistic meaning.

Cassirer, Ernst. *The Philosophy of Symbolic Forms.* 3 vols. New Haven, CT: Yale University Press, 1953–1957. Cassirer's magnum opus, the most comprehensive philosophy of culture and its development by a 20th-century philosopher.

Clayton, Philip, and Paul Davies. *The Re-Emergence of Emergence: The Emergentist Hypothesis from Science to Religion.* Oxford: Oxford University Press, 2008. A recounting of the return of the concept of emergence in recent scientific work on complexity and philosophy of mind, and of its potential as a basis in rethinking the relationship of science and religion.

Darwin, Charles. *The Descent of Man.* Princeton, NJ: Princeton University Press, 1981. Darwin's application of his theory of evolution to humans.

———. *On the Origin of Species by Means of Natural Selection.* Oxford: Oxford University Press, 1996. The great work that presented natural selection as the key to the evolution of species.

de Beauvoir, Simone. *The Ethics of Ambiguity*. Translated by Bernard Frechtman. New York: Citadel Press, 1967. The most prominent attempt of a major existentialist at an ethics.

———. *The Second Sex*. Translated by H. M. Parshley. New York: Knopf, 1953. A classic work of second-wave feminism by the existentialist philosopher.

de Saussure, Ferdinand. *Course in General Linguistics.* Translated by Wade Baskin. New York: McGraw-Hill, 1966. De Saussure's structuralist approach to language, which influenced later structuralism and poststructuralism.

Derrida, Jacques. "Differance." In *Speech and Phenomena and Other Essays on Husserl's Theory of Signs*, translated by David B. Allison. Evanston, IL: Northwestern University Press, 1973. One of Derrida's most famous essays, it introduces the notion of differance.

———. *Of Grammatology*. Translated by Gayatri Chakravorty Spivak. Baltimore: Johns Hopkins University Press, 1974. Derrida's account of his view as a new study of writing. The first part is a good introduction to Derrida's theory of writing.

———. "Structure, Sign and Play in the Discourse of the Human Sciences." In *Writing and Difference*, translated by Alan Bass. Chicago: University of Chicago Press, 1978. An important early essay of Derrida's, situating his new view with respect to the methods of the human sciences.

Descartes, René. *Meditations on First Philosophy*. In *The Philosophical Works of Descartes*, vol. 1, translated by Elizabeth Haldane and G. R. T. Ross. Cambridge: Cambridge University Press, 1975. Descartes' most famous short attempt to provide a new non-Scholastic (hence non-Aristotelian) foundation for knowledge and science. *See also* Kenny, *Descartes*.

Descombes, Vincent. *Modern French Philosophy.* Translated by L. Schott-Fox and J. M. Harding. New York: Cambridge University Press, 1980. A good description of post–World War II French philosophy and the developments that led to poststructuralism.

Dewey, John. *Art as Experience.* Vol. 10 of *The Later Works of John Dewey.* Carbondale: Southern Illinois University Press, 2008. Dewey's book on aesthetics is important for understanding that his notion of the practical and instrumental is meant to be combined with a recognition of the intrinsic ends, or consummatory values, in experience.

———. *Experience and Nature.* New York: Dover, 1958. Dewey's naturalistic magnum opus.

———. *Reconstruction in Philosophy.* Boston: Beacon, 1948. A useful statement of Dewey's attempt to understand philosophy itself as a means for the reconstruction of experience.

Fichte, Johann Gottlieb. *The Science of Knowledge.* Translated by Walter Wright. Albany: State University of New York Press, 2005. The best account of Fichte's metaphysics.

———. *The Vocation of Man.* Translated by William Smith. LaSalle, IL: Open Court, 1940. A popular work of Fichte's that shows the moral and social implications of his metaphysics.

Floyd, Juliet, and Sanford Shieh. *Future Pasts: The Analytic Tradition in Twentieth-Century Philosophy.* Oxford: Oxford University Press, 2001. A nice collection of reflections on the history of analytic philosophy.

Foucault, Michel. "Truth and Power." In *The Foucault Reader*, edited by Paul Rabinow. New York: Pantheon, 1984. The essay is Foucault's Nietzschean reading of truth as itself an effect of the will to power. The reader is a very useful collection of Foucault's work.

Frege, Gottlob. *The Frege Reader.* Edited by Michael Beaney. Malden, MA: Wiley-Blackwell, 1997. Highlights of this collection include "On Sense and Reference," "Function and Concept," "On Concept and Object," and selections from *Begriffsschrift* and *The Foundations of Arithmetic*.

Freud, Sigmund. *Civilization and Its Discontents*. Translated by James Strachey. New York: W. W. Norton, 1962. Freud's late speculative work arguing that the progress of civilization inevitably leads to an increase in the sense of guilt, and hence unhappiness.

Gadamer, Hans-Georg. *Truth and Method*. Translated by Joel Weinsheimer and Donald G. Marshall. New York: Continuum, 1994. The most prominent expression of 20th-century hermeneutics in the human sciences.

Gay, Peter. *The Enlightenment: An Interpretation*. 2 vols. New York: Knopf, 1966–1969. An accessible intellectual history of the 18th century.

Habermas, Jürgen. *The Theory of Communicative Action*. Translated by Thomas McCarthy. 2 vols. Boston: Beacon Press, 1984, 1987. Habermas's brilliant magnum opus provides his unique theory of modernity, combining epistemology and social theory.

Harding, Sandra. *The Science Question in Feminism*. Ithaca, NY: Cornell University Press, 1986. One of the major statements of feminist epistemology.

Hegel, Georg Wilhelm Friedrich. *Phenomenology of Spirit*. Translated by A. V. Miller. Oxford: Oxford University Press, 1977. Hegel's most beautiful work is actually an introduction to his three-volume *Encyclopedia*. It presents the development of the forms of human spirit throughout history.

Heidegger, Martin. *Being and Time*. Translated by Joan Stambaugh. Albany: State University of New York Press, 1996. The newest translation of Heidegger's most important work, one of the two most influential philosophy books of the 20th century.

———. *Martin Heidegger: Basic Writings*. Edited by David Farrell Krell. New York: Harper and Row, 1977. The best collection of Heidegger's later writings, it also includes the introductions to *Being and Time*.

Hume, David. *An Enquiry Concerning Human Understanding*. New York: Liberal Arts, 1955. Hume's skeptical epistemology, published separately a few years after his *Treatise of Human Nature*.

———. *A Treatise of Human Nature*. Oxford: Oxford University Press, 1975. Hume's great early work, presenting both his epistemological skepticism and his ethics. See especially the conclusion to book 1.

Husserl, Edmund. *Cartesian Meditations*. Translated by Dorian Cairns. The Hague: Nijhoff, 1977. Another of Husserl's introductions to phenomenology, this one specifically relates his theory to René Descartes. Also, the final meditation is Husserl's attempt to show that phenomenology can account for intersubjectivity, or sociality.

———. *The Crisis of the European Sciences and Transcendental Phenomenology.* Translated by David Carr. Evanston, IL: Northwestern University Press, 1970. Husserl's historical introduction to phenomenology, written late in his career, was influenced by Martin Heidegger and the rise of existentialism.

———. *Ideas Pertaining to a Pure Phenomenology and to a Phenomenological Philosophy*. Translated by Fred Kersten. 2 vols. Dordrecht, Netherlands: Kluwer, 1998. Husserl's first book-length introduction to transcendental phenomenology. *See also* Kohák, *Idea and Experience*.

James, William. *Pragmatism*. Indianapolis, IN: Hackett, 1981. The classic statement of James's version of pragmatism.

Kant, Immanuel. *Critique of Pure Reason*. Translated by Paul Guyer and Allen W. Wood. New York: Cambridge University Press, 1998. The great epistemological work of Kant, who changed philosophy forever with his Copernican revolution.

———. *Prolegomena to Any Future Metaphysics*. Translated by James Ellington. Indianapolis, IN: Hackett, 2002. This is Kant's shorter popularization of the argument of his *Critique of Pure Reason*. A perfectly good presentation of his critical philosophy, it presents the *Critique*'s main doctrines in novel formulations that are worth reading for their own sake.

———. *Religion within the Limits of Reason Alone*. Translated by Theodore M. Greene and Hoyt H. Hudson. New York: Harper, 1960. An expression of Kant's deism, understood as natural, or rational, religion: religion not based on revelation.

Kenny, Anthony. *Descartes: A Study of his Philosophy*. New York: Random House, 1968. A good secondary work on René Descartes.

———. *The Legacy of Wittgenstein*. Oxford: Basil Blackwell, 1984. A good secondary work on Ludwig Wittgenstein.

Kierkegaard, Søren. *Fear and Trembling: A Dialectical Lyric*. Translated by Walter Lowrie. Princeton, NJ: Princeton University Press, 1941. Kierkegaard's defense of religion as antirational and nonethical, rooted in his analysis of the biblical tale of Abraham and Isaac.

———. *The Point of View for My Work as an Author: A Report to History and Related Writings*. Translated by Walter Lowrie. New York: Harper, 1962. Kierkegaard's explanation of his use of pseudonyms in his other works.

Kohák, Erazim. *Idea and Experience: Edmund Husserl's Project of Phenomenology in Ideas I*. Chicago: University of Chicago Press, 1978. A good introduction to Husserlian phenomenology.

Koyré, Alexandre. *From the Closed World to the Infinite Universe*. Baltimore: Johns Hopkins University Press, 1968. A nice historical work on the change from the medieval to the modern view of the universe.

Kuhn, Thomas S. *The Structure of Scientific Revolutions.* Chicago: University of Chicago Press, 1962. Kuhn's bombshell, one of the most influential books of the second half of the 20th century, which argued that science advances through revolutions where one paradigm is replaced by another.

Leibniz, Gottfried Wilhelm. *Discourse on Metaphysics, Correspondence with Arnauld, and Monadology.* LaSalle, IL: Open Court, 1945. Leibniz's neo-Aristotelian metaphysics of atomic substances, or monads. Read the *Monadology* last.

Lévi-Strauss, Claude. *The Raw and the Cooked.* Translated by John and Doreen Weightman. Chicago: University of Chicago Press, 1983. A prominent example of Claude Lévi-Strauss's structuralist approach to anthropology.

Locke, John. *Essay Concerning Human Understanding.* New York: Routledge, 2000. The most comprehensive statement of early modern empiricism by the most important English philosopher of the 17th century.

Lorenz, Konrad. "Kant's Doctrine of the A Priori in the Light of Contemporary Biology." In *Konrad Lorenz: The Man and His Ideas*, edited by Richard I. Evans, 129–217. New York: Harcourt Brace Jovanovich, 1975. A wonderful statement of evolutionary epistemology as a response to Immanuel Kant's theory of knowledge.

Lyotard, Jean-François. *The Postmodern Condition: A Report on Knowledge.* Translated by Geoff Bennington and Briam Massumi. Minneapolis: Minnesota University Press, 1984. The most famous and best statement of the postmodern as the condition of post–World War II Western society.

MacIntyre, Alasdair. *After Virtue.* Notre Dame, IN: University of Notre Dame Press, 1984. MacIntyre's critique of modernity's deontological, existential, and utilitarian approaches to ethics, in favor of the Aristotelian virtue ethics approach.

———. *Whose Justice? Which Rationality?* Notre Dame, IN: University of Notre Dame Press, 1988. MacIntyre's argument that rationality itself must be embedded in historical traditions.

Marcuse, Herbert. *One-Dimensional Man.* Boston: Beacon Press, 1955. A prominent statement of the late Frankfurt School, combining the ideas of Sigmund Freud and Karl Marx to critique late capitalist society.

Margolis, Joseph. *Pragmatism without Foundations: Reconciling Realism and Relativism.* New York: Basil Blackwell, 1986. A difficult but important attempt to retain realism while accepting relativism, all on a pragmatic basis.

Marx, Karl, with Friedrich Engels. *Economic and Philosophic Manuscripts of 1844.* In *The Marx-Engels Reader*, edited by Robert Tucker. New York: Norton, 1972. The early, or "Western" Marx, primarily concerned with the alienation of the individual.

———. *Manifesto of the Communist Party.* In Tucker, *The Marx-Engels Reader.* Section 2 of this political pamphlet contains Marx's best description of modernity.

———. Preface to *A Contribution to the Critique of Political Economy.* In Tucker, *The Marx-Engels Reader.* This contains the best short summary of Marx's entire theory.

Merleau-Ponty, Maurice. *The Phenomenology of Perception.* Translated by Colin Smith. New York: Humanities Press, 1962. A classic post-Husserlian theory of human experience. Merleau-Ponty is arguably the most phenomenologically astute and interesting of the existential phenomenologists.

Mill, John Stuart. *On Liberty.* Indianapolis, IN: Hackett, 1978. The most famous statement of the proper limits on group interference in the liberty of the individual ever written.

———. *A System of Logic.* London: Routledge and Kegan Paul, 1974. The view of logic and inquiry that was most influential for the second half of the 19th century, and against which Fregean analytic philosophy and Husserlian phenomenology rebelled.

———. *Utilitarianism*. Indianapolis, IN: Hackett, 1979. The classic definition of Mill's version of the moral theory of utilitarianism.

Monk, Ray. *Wittgenstein: The Duty of Genius*. New York: Free Press, 1990. An excellent biography of Ludwig Wittgenstein, also a good introduction to his philosophy.

Moore, George Edward. "A Defence of Common Sense." In *G. E. Moore: Selected Writings*, edited by Thomas Baldwin. New York: Routledge, 1993. Another classic Moore essay against skepticism and idealism.

———. "Proof of an External World." In *G. E. Moore: Selected Writings*, edited by Thomas Baldwin. New York: Routledge, 1993. Moore's attack on idealism and skepticism, which Ludwig Wittgenstein responded to in *On Certainty*.

Murphy, John P. *Pragmatism: From Peirce to Davidson*. Boulder, CO: Westview Press 1990. A good, short summary of pragmatism in both the classical American thinkers and among key analytic philosophers through the 20th century.

Nietzsche, Friedrich. *Beyond Good and Evil*. Translated by Walter Kaufmann. New York: Random House, 1966. All in all, this is perhaps the most representative of Nietzsche's mature aphoristic works, covering all the major topics in his philosophy.

———. *The Gay Science*. Translated by Walter Kaufmann. New York: Random House, 1974. This aphoristic work is particularly important in expressing the death of God, the eternal return, and Nietzsche's conclusion that a joyful response to them is possible.

———. *On the Genealogy of Morals*. Translated by Francis Golffing. Garden City, NY: Anchor Books, 1956. The best expression of Nietzsche's critique of Judeo-Christian morality, in three essays, not aphorisms.

Passmore, John. *A Hundred Years of Philosophy*. Harmondsworth, UK: Penguin Books, 1968. Probably the best history of philosophy—mostly

Anglo-American, with some European thinkers—from the mid-19th century through about 1950.

Peirce, Charles Sanders. "How to Make Our Ideas Clear." In *Philosophical Writings of Peirce*, edited by Justus Buchler. Mineola, NY: Dover, 1955. Peirce's first published definition of pragmatism, although he doesn't use the word.

Pinkard, Terry. *Hegel: A Biography.* New York: Cambridge University Press, 2000. A good biography by a major contemporary Hegel scholar.

Popper, Karl. *Conjectures and Refutations: The Growth of Scientific Knowledge.* New York: Basic Books, 1962. A good presentation of the views of Popper, one of the most important philosophers of science of the 20th century.

———. "Natural Selection and the Emergence of Mind." In *Evolutionary Epistemology, Rationality, and the Sociology of Knowledge*, edited by G. Radnitzky and W. W. Bartley III. LaSalle, IL: Open Court. 1987. This essay is Popper's contribution to evolutionary epistemology.

Prigogine, Ilya, and Isabelle Stengers. *Order out of Chaos: Man's New Dialogue with Nature.* New York: Bantam, 1984. The famous expression of the new concern for complexity in late 20th-century physical and chemical science, by the Nobel Prize winner Priogogine.

Putnam, Hilary. *Reason, Truth, and History.* Cambridge: Cambridge University Press, 1981. An excellent summary of Putnam's early- to midcareer views, in which he seeks a pragmatic realism.

Quine, Willard Van Orman. *Ontological Relativity and Other Essays.* New York: Columbia University Press, 1969. A good collection of some of Quine's most important essays, especially on natural kinds, ontological relativity, and naturalistic epistemology.

———. "Two Dogmas of Empiricism." In *From a Logical Point of View: Nine Logico-Philosophical Essays*. Cambridge, MA: Harvard University Press, 1980. In one of the most influential papers of the 20th century, Quine undermines two of the pillars of logical positivism.

———. *Word and Object*. Cambridge, MA: MIT Press, 1964. Quine's famous systematic expression of his behaviorism; chapter 2 presents the indeterminacy of translation thesis (about "gavagai").

Randall, John Herman. *The Career of Philosophy*. 3 vols. New York: Columbia University Press, 1965. This is a wonderful history of philosophy since the Renaissance, emphasizing philosophy's relation to history and culture, not just philosophical doctrines.

Rorty, Richard. *Consequences of Pragmatism: Essays, 1972–1980*. Minneapolis: University of Minnesota Press, 1982. This is a good introduction to Rorty's mature views in relation to pragmatism.

———. *The Linguistic Turn: Recent Essays in Philosophical Method*. Chicago: University of Chicago Press, 1967. This is a nice anthology of Rorty's analytic philosophy, before his postmodern turn.

———. *Objectivity, Relativism, and Truth*. Cambridge: Cambridge University Press, 1991. Helps to refine some of the ideas of Rorty's *Philosophy and the Mirror of Nature.*

———. *Philosophy and the Mirror of Nature*. Princeton, NJ: Princeton University Press, 1979. Perhaps the most influential philosophy book in English of the late 20th century, in which Rorty first expresses the views that made him famous.

Rousseau, Jean-Jacques. *The First and Second Discourses*. Translated by Judith Masters. New York: St. Martin's Press, 1969. Rousseau's criticisms of the modern age, for which he was heavily criticized by other Enlightenment figures.

———. *On the Social Contract, with Geneva Manuscript and Political Economy*. Translated by Judith Masters. New York: St. Martin's Press, 1978. Rousseau's social contract theory of politics.

Russell, Bertrand. *A Critical Exposition of the Philosophy of Leibniz, with an Appendix of Leading Passages*. Ithaca, NY: Cornell University Press, 2009. Russell's remarkably good examination of Gottfried Wilhelm Leibniz. This also shows that Leibniz is the one 17th-century metaphysician that had special relevance to early analytic philosophy.

———. "Descriptions." In *Twentieth-Century Philosophy: The Analytic Tradition*, edited by Morris Weitz. New York: Free Press, 1966. This is one version of Russell's famous theory of descriptions, prominent in 20th-century analytic philosophy until it was attacked by Saul Kripke.

———. "A Free Man's Worship." In *Mysticism and Logic*. Mineola, NY: Dover, 2004. This is Russell's famous atheist essay.

———. *The Philosophy of Logical Atomism*. LaSalle, IL: Open Court, 1985. Russell's most comprehensive positivist philosophical statement.

Sartre, Jean-Paul. *Being and Nothingness*. Translated by Hazel E. Barnes. New York: Washington Square, 1993. Sartre's central metaphysical statement on being-for-itself, or consciousness, and being-in-itself.

———. "Existentialism as a Humanism." In Cahoone, *From Modernism to Postmodernism*. The classic lecture introducing Sartrean existentialism to a popular audience, delivered in Paris during the German occupation.

Schelling, Friedrich Wilhelm Joseph von. *Philosophical Inquiries into the Nature of Human Freedom*. Translated by James Gutmann. LaSalle, IL: Open Court, 1936. Schelling's provocative statement on freedom, the problem of evil, the Absolute, and creation.

Schopenhauer, Arthur. *The World as Will and Representation.* Translated by E. F. J. Payne. New York: Dover, 1969. Schopenhauer's major work substitutes will for things in themselves, in effect making a historical bridge between his predecessor Immanuel Kant and his successor Friedrich Nietzsche.

Sherburne, Donald. *A Key to Whitehead's "Process and Reality."* New York: Macmillan, 1966. This is an excellent introduction to the difficult Alfred North Whitehead book. Keep the glossary at your elbow while reading *Process and Reality*.

Simon, Herbert A. "The Architecture of Complex Systems." *Proceedings of the American Philosophical Society* 162 (1962): 467–482. Simon's argument that natural selection, or trial-and-error processes, can only have achieved the complex forms that exist if it operated on hierarchically arranged systems. So naturally evolved systems must be hierarchically organized.

Smith, Adam. *An Inquiry into the Nature and Causes of the Wealth of Nations.* Indianapolis, IN: Liberty Fund, 1982. This classic statement on the new market economy by the great Scottish Enlightenment philosopher is one of the most influential works of the 18th century.

Spinoza, Baruch. *Ethics.* New York: Penguin Books, 1996. This is Spinoza's greatest work, arguing from the fact that all reality is one substance and its attributes, to strict determinism, to the implications for the ethical life. *See also* Wolfson, *The Philosophy of Spinoza.*

Spivak, Gayatri Chakravarty. "Can the Subaltern Speak?" in Cahoone, *From Modernism to Postmodernism.* Spivak's famous expression of postcolonial philosophy, related to postmodernism and poststructuralism.

———. *In Other Worlds: Essays in Cultural Politics.* New York: Methuen, 1987. This book provides a broader range of Spivak's work.

Strauss, Leo. *Natural Right and History*. Chicago: University of Chicago Press, 1999. This work is Strauss's critique of modern political philosophy.

Weber, Max. *The Protestant Ethic and the Spirit of Capitalism.* Translated by Talcott Parsons. Mineola, NY: Dover, 2003. Weber's most famous work argues that the inner-worldly asceticism of Protestantism (versus Catholicism) played a central role in forming the modern capitalist world.

———. "Science as a Vocation" In *From Max Weber: Essays in Sociology*, translated by H. H. Gerth and C. Wright Mills. New York: Oxford University Press, 1946. This classic work of philosophical sociology, on the distinctiveness of the modern age, is a must-read.

Weitz, Morris. *Twentieth-Century Philosophy: The Analytic Tradition.* New York: Free Press, 1966. A good collection of essays in early- to mid-20th-century analytic philosophy.

West, Cornel. *The American Evasion of Philosophy*. Madison: University of Wisconsin Press, 1989. This work expresses West's broader view of "prophetic pragmatism," using the American pragmatic tradition for social change.

———. "A Genealogy of Modern Racism." In Cahoone, *From Modernism to Postmodernism*. This essay is an example of the application of poststructuralist methods to the problem of race.

Whitehead, Alfred North. *Process and Reality: An Essay in Cosmology*. New York: Free Press, 1969. This is Whitehead's magnum opus on metaphysics and cosmology. *See also* Sherburne, *A Key to Whitehead's "Process and Reality."*

———. *Science and the Modern World.* New York: Mentor Press, 1925. A more accessible work than *Process and Reality*.

Whitehead, Alfred North, and Bertrand Russell. *Principia Mathematica*. 3 vols. Cambridge: Cambridge University Press, 1950. The famous logicist attempt to derive mathematics from logic is one of the most influential works of the 20th century.

Wimsatt, William C. *Re-Engineering Philosophy for Limited Beings: Piecewise Approximations to Reality*. Cambridge, MA: Harvard University Press, 2007. An excellent interdisciplinary postpositivist philosophy of science arguing that reductive explanation and emergence are compatible.

Wittgenstein, Ludwig. *On Certainty*. Translated by Denis Paul and G. E. M. Anscombe. New York: Harper and Row, 1972. Wittgenstein's last work, it shares the viewpoint of his *Philosophical Investigations* but is trained on the philosophical quest for certainty. *See also* Monk, *Wittgenstein* and Kenny, *The Legacy of Wittgenstein*.

———. *Philosophical Investigations*. Translated by G. E. M. Anscombe. New York: Macmillan, 1953. In what is perhaps the most influential philosophical work of the 20th century, Wittgenstein forms a new philosophy of language games. *See also* Monk, *Wittgenstein* and Kenny, *The Legacy of Wittgenstein*.

———. *Tractatus-Logico Philosophicus*. Translated by D. F. Pears and B. F. McGuiness. London: Routledge and Kegan Paul, 1981. Wittgenstein's early work on logic and knowledge that was greatly admired by the positivists. The famous ending endorses a kind of mysticism. *See also* Monk, *Wittgenstein* and Kenny, *The Legacy of Wittgenstein*.

Wolfson, Harry Austryn. *The Philosophy of Spinoza: Unfolding the Latent Processes of His Reasoning*. Cambridge, MA: Harvard University Press, 1934. This is a famous secondary work on Baruch Spinoza.

Young, Iris Marion. *Justice and the Politics of Difference*. Princeton, NJ: Princeton University Press, 1990. This work is a fine example of feminist politics inspired partly by poststructuralism or postmodernism.

Notes